Do It Now!

D1403135

Break the Procrastination Habit

REVISED EDITION

Dr. William J. Knaus

John Wiley & Sons, Inc.
New York · Chichester · Weinheim · Brisbane · Singapore · Toronto

Library of Congress Cataloging-in-Publication Data

Knaus, William J.
    Do it now! : break the procrastination habit / William J. Knaus. —
Rev. ed.
      p. cm.
    Includes index.
    ISBN 0-471-17399-1 (pbk. : alk. paper)
    1. Procrastination.   I. Title.
    BF637.P76K53   1997
    155.2'32—dc21   97-15790

10 9 8

Contents

PART THREE   Strategies for Overcoming Procrastination

12 Procrastination Styles: A Fresh Look at an Old Problem   143

13 Your Imagination Can Help You Get It Done   161

Foreword

Procrastination adversely affects many lives. But we currently have many effective methods to change devastating procrastination patterns. Dr. Bill Knaus has been actively developing such methods for years. His major work has come to fruition in this timely book, which holds great promise of help for even the most inveterate procrastinator.

Fortunately, we have many ways to examine procrastination and to counter this time-thief practice. The awareness-action approach advanced in Dr. Knaus's book shows how to identify the underlying dynamics of the procrastination habit, and how to take action to overcome this drain on time and life.

Now, those who seriously wish to rid themselves of procrastination have a tested pathway to gain command over their time rather than be controlled by the procrastination habit. To discover more, read the pages within. I'll use no more time so that you can quickly begin.

—L. RENE GAIENNIE, PH.D.
Senior Vice President, Singer Company (ret.)
Fellow, American Psychological Association

Foreword to the Revised Edition

This is an excellent book for people who want an organized, well-coordinated program to help themselves kick an age-old problem habit. This revised edition of *Do It Now!* takes the reader from the top to the bottom and from the inside out and back again in the area of procrastination. This complete text is well grounded in the reasons why people put things off and in how to stop procrastinating and start living.

Another compelling feature of this book is what it is not. It is not another quick-fix pitch like so many others that flood the popular psychology self-help book market. This book elegantly tells the reasons behind the strategies for overcoming this all-too-common and troublesome human tendency. It shows how to stop stalling and get done what needs to be done. For the tougher minded among us, Dr. Knaus's methods can be assessed for their impact and outcome. This is a rare and helpful advantage that the reader can put to good use.

—Dr. John W. Edgerly
Director, University of North Carolina Counseling Center

Preface

In 1972, Dr. Janet Wolfe of the Albert Ellis Institute asked me to come up with a popular new workshop topic. This was a challenging assignment. Then the idea came to me in a flash: why not do a workshop on procrastination?

I had good reason to think this topic had universal appeal. As I looked around, I saw signs of procrastination everywhere. Many of my friends, business associates, and psychotherapy clients repeatedly complained about putting things off. I even had to admit to myself that I procrastinated on handling administrative detail, sending out my bills, and writing.

When the main hall filled, we dealt with the workshop overflow by assigning people to various rooms with closed-circuit televisions. We scheduled additional workshops that same weekend to satisfy everyone who wanted to participate in the original program. Since that date, tens of thousands of people have attended workshops and programs on how to stop procrastinating. Hundreds of thousands have read my books. Indeed, the workshop at the Albert Ellis Institute continues, under different leaders, and draws many who are tired of procrastinating and want to do more with their time.

When I wrote the original edition of this book, I found no other self-help books on procrastination, other than a book I initiated and wrote with Albert Ellis. Even that first procrastination book first came out privately. At the time, publishers did not believe that there was a market for the subject.

As with many new ideas, there was resistance to the idea of a book on procrastination until the idea worked its way into the mainstream. Undaunted, I wrote *Do It Now: How to Stop Procrastinating*. I was determined to make these ideas available to the millions who anguish because of procrastination. *Do It Now* hit the bookstore shelves in 1979 and continued selling. A market for the book clearly existed that went beyond my expectations.

Since I originated this work on procrastination, there has been a flood of books and articles on the topic. I've even read articles on pigeon procrastination and about how the human brain procrastinates in making choices on where and when to shift a gaze.

I am pleased with the rising tide of interest in procrastination. I am delighted that so many procrastinators can now take advantage of the tested strategies that have come about in the past twenty-five years since my original workshop on this topic. Moreover, our reasons for optimism now grow in leaps and bounds as the pool of information on procrastination continues to grow.

Acknowledgments

I want to thank Drs. Nancy Knaus of the Monson Developmental Center, George Elias of Assumption College, and Jack Shannon of Seton Hall University for their review and comments for this revised edition. I also thank my editor, Chris Jackson, for his helpful contributions and guidance through the evolution and production of this book and to the others at John Wiley & Sons who generously supported the growth of this work. As always, I take final responsibility for what is written herein.

Introduction

Come with me as we journey into the inner world of procrastination. On this trek, we'll look into the primary types, causes, and complications of procrastination. We'll explore hidden places within the mind that can distort perception and trigger procrastination. And we'll look at many ways to get over, under, around, or directly through the procrastination barriers in our lives.

This awareness-and-action book espouses the position so well expressed by the philosopher Immanuel Kant, who said, "Experience without theory is blind, but theory without experience is a mere intellectual play." I designed the revised *Do It Now!* to help you: (1) develop an awareness of the foundation of your procrastination problem and (2) identify workable action solutions to overcoming procrastination.

The famous author Henry David Thoreau once said that for every thousand persons hacking at the branches of evil, only one person chops at its roots. Unfortunately, most people who procrastinate often chop at their individual acts of procrastination rather than attack the roots of the problem. I designed *Do It Now!* to get you right to the heart of this enigmatic nemesis.

PROCRASTINATION ON THE RISE

The electronic, information, and social revolutions have reshaped our world. Because of extraordinary technological and social changes, we have unique challenges that hold opportunities for those who will press forward. Knowing how to take charge of your time and life is more important today than ever before.

Inventive people in this era have given us great electronic tools for operating efficiently and effectively by making it simpler to get to information, communicate, schedule, create, and produce more with greater speed and better quality.

Of course, each yin has its yang and each opportunity has a downside. Living in rapidly changing times, growing numbers of people procrastinate when they feel confused and do not know what else to

1

do. They respond to the changes around them with unsteadiness and lack of purpose. For this reason, growing numbers of people flounder and fall by the wayside in these volatile and competitive times.

Society is changing in some ways that trigger and reflect procrastination. The persistent emphasis on quick fix solutions to complex human problems continues to create a surrealistic view of life. Technological changes occurring with blinding speed have caused many to look to the future warily, believing that they can never learn enough or compete well enough to succeed. These conditions, and more, have sent many running confused to their burrows, stunned by the challenges of our times.

The implications are clear. The future looks bleak for those who are unprepared to deal with ambiguity and to manage new challenges. Depression, irresponsibility, and procrastination are some destructive outcomes accompanying this gloomy perspective for those who are the casualties of this age.

Although procrastination is a pronounced symptom of our times, and although it is tempting to blame changing conditions for surges in procrastination, external changes do not cause procrastination. They merely set the stage—sometimes in powerful ways—for this outcome. We remain the major architects of our destinies. We choose what goes into our autobiographies.

AWARENESS AND ACTION

The conditions that rocket procrastination are serious and complex. Nevertheless, the remedies and solutions for people who want to take charge of their lives are quite potent. Because of our knowledge of procrastination—its causes and solutions—no person willing to work at making changes needs to remain permanently in a procrastination rut.

There are good solutions for overcoming procrastination that we can organize around an awareness-and-action problem-solving framework. Without problem awareness, you won't get far in changing your life for the better. Without directed, purposeful, and constructive action, awareness stays in the realm of joyful revelation. Put these two parts together, and practically anybody can defuse procrastination and use their time to better their lives.

The cognitive revolution in psychology originated with psychologist Albert Ellis's pioneering effort to develop rational emotive behavior therapy (REBT). The stalwarts of this revolution emphasized ways to change self-defeating thinking, develop emotional resources, engage in productive problem-solving activities, and maintain a sense of adaptability. *Do It Now!* grows out of this tradition as well as my personal practice with thousands of people who call themselves procrastinators.

WHAT IS PROCRASTINATION?

Although procrastination is needlessly putting off, postponing, or delaying a timely, relevant, priority activity, there are many types and causes for procrastination. There also are other complications. What makes up a timely, relevant, priority activity can vary. For example, in deciding between competing priorities of equal weighting, what is the priority? If you can get a minor task done swiftly now, or face greater complications later, does this minor task then rise to a priority level and temporarily supplant your more pressing goals? At what point does putting off activities such as taking a shower or doing the dishes become a form of procrastination? If you are only a *little*, but still routinely, late on much of what you do, have you gone over the line? When you go over a deadline to avoid discomfort, have you entered the realm of procrastination? Do isolated procrastination acts eventually grow into a procrastination pattern? Do self-reports of procrastination prove accurate or do some people overestimate or underestimate the effects procrastination has on their lives? If you obsess away your day, feel immobilized, struggle to get going yet fall behind, is this procrastination a symptom of something else?

The procrastination process is personal. It varies from person to person. The same person can show considerable variability in procrastination as well as personal initiative. What you might procrastinate at one time you might get done quickly at another time. In a way, some forms of procrastination are like a mixed headache that includes migraine, stress, sinus, and depressive features. What works for a stress headache won't work for a migraine. Aspirin does not touch depression. The sinus condition may require another treatment. In a similar way, procrastination is far more complex than the dictionary definition makes it appear.

Because of normal human variability and procrastination complications, one formula for change will not fit all. We have different thinking and emotional styles, so some approaches work better for some than others. Also, different times and situations can require different strategies. Therefore, use the methods I outlined in this book selectively and actively. Avoid spreading yourself too thin. Tackling too much at once is another way of procrastinating. But do something!

As you embark on your journey to reduce needless delay and to obtain greater satisfaction with living, I won't wish you luck. Instead, I wish you the will to persevere and to experience the good sweat of accomplishment. In this process I wish you more than desire to beat procrastination; I wish you the courage to try.

PART ONE

The Pitfalls
of Procrastination

What They Are and How
to Recognize Them

Stop Fiddling and Start Doing

In the Old Testament we find: "To every thing there is a season and a time for every purpose under the heaven; a time to be born and a time to die; a time to plant and a time to pluck up what has been planted." In other words, life finds structure through time.

We intertwine our concepts of self and time. When we view ourselves as using time wisely, we feel confident and capable. When we use time ineffectually, we feel lost. When we procrastinate, we feel hurried and stressed because we are afraid that we are wasting our lives, yet we continue to avoid doing what we know we would best do. This is the fundamental *procrastination paradox:* when we try to buy time by procrastinating, we condemn ourselves to running out of time. We attempt to catch up, only to let down our guard and renew the cycle. This procrastination paradox can undermine our brightest hopes for the kind of future we'd like to create for ourselves.

THE PROCRASTINATION DECISION

If you are like practically every other human being on this planet, you do many things well and on time. Yet you sometimes find yourself needlessly putting off, postponing, delaying, or avoiding timely and relevant activities. This is the procrastination decision.

Procrastination is a universal bane of life. People put things off until tomorrow, and when tomorrow comes, they put them off until the next tomorrow. They subscribe to a system of unrealistic thinking where they fiddle away the present in a futile hope for a better tomorrow. Since this fantasy rarely translates into action, few of the activities that get put off get done in a timely fashion; some just don't get done.

At the extreme, the classic procrastinator's ploy, to needlessly delay until another day or time, has many potentially unpleasant personal consequences. People afflicted with procrastination often create elaborate excuses to cover their delays, or even make jokes about their own procrastination. But a pattern of procrastination often leads to a sense of helplessness, feelings of being overwhelmed, and a lack of a sense of accomplishment. That's why procrastination is no joke.

There is scarcely a person who doesn't put some things off and, at some level, realize that he or she is engaging in a form of procrastinating. Even the most efficient, organized, and decisive person will occasionally procrastinate. But whether you're an occasional or chronic procrastinator, you have good reason to feel encouraged. Procrastination is a learned behavior—I don't know of any procrastination *gene!* What we learn we can unlearn. But, as with the common cold, there is no final cure. Nevertheless, it is my intention to help raise your consciousness about procrastination and to point to ways to improve your *getting it done percentage* and to feel better about yourself and your accomplishments. It doesn't take much to produce this outcome. A slight positive shift in direction toward greater personal effectiveness can help reduce the procrastination burden.

WHAT PEOPLE PUT OFF

Most people who procrastinate know they are procrastinating. They may not always fully understand the mechanisms behind it, or the extent, but the fact of their procrastination is no mystery.

I have taken many surveys of what people put off and found considerable variation in specific acts and general patterns of procrastination. Procrastination ranges from relatively benign acts of letting dishes pile high in the sink to serious forms of habitually frittering away time and potential. At the extreme, we also find people who indulge their paralyzing fears, needlessly stick with dead-end jobs, or feel preoccupied and overwhelmed with a pileup of many uncompleted projects while other urgent details of life sit idly.

Some procrastination delays are predictable. Thousands of post offices have April fifteenth parties for people who file their taxes at the eleventh hour. The last-minute Christmas rush is legend. Libraries count on collecting overdue fines to help pay expenses. Garages, closets, and drawers warehouse the results of unfulfilled promises. Physicians pull their hair out when patients put off necessary health care.

The procrastination list is long. College applications gather dust. You show up late because you didn't get started on time. You go into a frenzied rush at the eleventh hour to prepare for an important meeting. You lose opportunities because of inaction. You may also procrastinate on meeting health goals, building cordial social relations, or overcoming a tendency to take on more tasks than you can realistically manage. You may doubt yourself, fear failure, and avoid situations that threaten your self-image.

Procrastination frequently takes the form of "let George do it." Here we assume someone else will take responsibility to do what is right. We see this form of procrastination in many avenues of life but especially in areas of civic responsibility where people put off doing their homework to keep public officials accountable for their spending and public actions. This is a subtle but serious form of procrastination, for tyranny thrives on others' procrastination as much as it does on fear and weakness.

Some procrastinators experience confrontation anxiety and avoid competitive situations where the outcome is uncertain. You may habitually avoid what you think is a hassle. When you are in a procrastinating state of mind, your wishes to become more assertive, find a new job, kick a problem habit, or develop more self-confidence stay in the realm of fantasy.

This process of delay exists in different degrees and at different levels of intensity—from inconvenient to immobilizing. At the level of *inconvenience,* you indulge your procrastination avoidance and escapist interests but not to the point that you seriously disadvantage yourself. At the *troublesome* level, you cause yourself some damage, but normally you can repair or excuse it. At the level of *immobilization,* your life centers on avoiding and escaping many important responsibilities. You often feel immobilized and unable to act. You repeatedly procrastinate even when you wish to do otherwise. Your procrastination is chronic.

You might correctly conclude from this analysis that while specific acts and patterns of procrastination vary among individuals, they are as common as summer mosquitoes. And all forms of procrastination, from the inconvenient to the immobilizing, are frustrating, self-abusive, obstacles to effective functioning.

THE CHECK IS IN THE MAIL

Procrastinators have a knack for using credible-sounding excuses to justify their inaction, and when they temporarily avoid responsibility, this reinforces their procrastination behavior. Procrastinators often craft these creative explanations in order to avoid social sanctions. Commonly, the procrastinator's goal is to maintain a "good public image." It doesn't matter that the excuse is paper thin, as long as other people pretend to accept the explanation.

This avoidance effort often works well enough to reinforce excuse making because most people who hear procrastination excuses are too polite, or don't have the interest or evidence to confront the procrastinator. Also, people generally prefer to give procrastinators another chance before confronting the situation.

Let's look at some classic excuses by schoolchildren, college students, people who show up late for meetings, professionals, trades people, and substance abusers. By examining these procrastination excuses, you may never see them in the same light again.

Children and young adolescents who put off doing their homework have many ways to kick up dust to sidetrack their teachers: the dog ate my homework. I left my work on the bus. I had basketball practice and too many chores to do. I had a headache. I was sick. My family is poor and I had to work last night to buy food. I forgot.

College students can come up with some quite exotic excuses, including "aliens abducted me." One student, after eight years of undergraduate school, was into his final course. At the end of the semester he came to me to explain why he had not done his assignments and had skipped the examinations: "I know you write books on procrastination so I knew you'd understand why I didn't get the work done."

My favorite procrastination excuse came from a student whom I had for three different courses. In the first course, he said his grandmother died and he had to attend her funeral. That's why he didn't show for the final examination. He said it was his mom's mother, and he volunteered, "I was very close to her." The following year he also failed to show for the final. He told me that his grandmother had died. I asked him which side of the family. He said it was from his mother's side. He had no explanation for how she had died two years in a row. A year later he gave the same excuse. You guessed it. The same grandmother. He procrastinated on coming up with a new excuse.

People whose procrastination causes them to show up late or miss meetings often come up with some interesting reasons to explain their lateness. Here are a few: I had a flat tire. I lost my way. I got caught in traffic. The subway train broke down. I ran out of gas. We had a family emergency. The alarm didn't go off. The battery in my watch died. The smoke alarm went off and I had to deal with the fire department.

How do professionals explain away their procrastination? There was not enough information. I had to do more research. I had to reprioritize. We had inventory problems. Gee, I thought you would have received the report by now. I sent it by FedEx last week.

Blame it on the computer. The electronic age has given us a new list of excuses. The system crashed. A virus ruined the files. Someone input the wrong information. Your information wasn't in the computer. These new excuse-making opportunities have the advantage of blaming an inanimate source for some needless delays. It's a *procrastination paradox* that an efficiency tool gets the blame for inefficiency.

In the trades, people who don't show up to give estimates may later call to say that they were overwhelmed with work, ill, or had to go out of town and conclude with, "Can we reschedule?" Other excuses include: The loader broke. We didn't get the parts. I had to fire the person working on your project for lateness. It will be ready any day now. Other projects took longer than expected. My assistant did not get back from vacation yet. The supplier misplaced the paperwork.

Substance abusers use excuses to justify their addiction and to evade reality in a way that serves to delay, postpone, or put off kicking a serious and destructive habit. Among alcohol abusers and dependents, for example, we hear such preposterous ideas as: "I need to drink because it helps my arthritis"; "I think better after a few drinks"; "My boss is a tyrant, that's why I drink"; and "The latest research shows that drinking prevents heart attacks. If one drink is good, a six-pack must be better."

LIFE CYCLES OF PROCRASTINATION

As a species, we humans have a built-in drive for mastery over our environment. Procrastination represents a partial breakdown in the drive for mastery that can occur at practically any age and stage of life.

Why does procrastination occur at various stages in our lives?

Childhood

The procrastination habit can start in childhood for different reasons, including:

➤ Children with learning problems may develop an aversion for frustrating learning tasks, and they generalize this to practically any frustrating activity.

➤ We hear the five-year-old say the familiar "I don't want to." Parental inconsistency in responding leads such children to conclude that they can sometimes avoid responsibilities, so why not test the limits consistently?

➤ Television commercials about toys, cartoons, and children's action stories create a phony reality, and the child comes to develop a sense of disappointment when things in life do not come so easily. Such outcomes lead to inaction through more television—or video game—escapist activities.

➤ Some unstructured and poorly organized families model ways to act inefficiently and ineffectively . Children learn from observing and imitating their primary models.

➤ Some people grew up in extremely authoritarian environments where their parents demanded unquestioned compliance and obedience. Later in life some put things off because they do not trust their judgment.

➤ School self-esteem programs that say whatever children do is equally wonderful help foment an illusion that will not be fulfilled later in life. Some self-esteem programs tempt the more capable to work at a slower pace because there is no special reward for competence. The slower students can later run into difficulty dealing with disappointment when reality later teaches a different lesson.

Many exceptions exist. Some children grow up under conditions where procrastination is the norm, yet they rarely procrastinate in their adult lives. Depending on the situation, childhood conditions may or may not contribute to patterns of adult procrastination.

Adolescence

You can find the seeds for procrastination in your adolescent years. Fears about an uncertain future combined with developmental changes, feelings of awkwardness, moodiness, and fear of embarrassment can leave many feeling confused. Such conditions of mind fertilize the seeds of procrastination. This also is a period of separating from the family and of forming alliances with peer groups. Though this has advantages, it also has a downside. If the peer group downgrades efficiency, few subgroup members will march out of step.

Early Adulthood

Procrastination can erupt in early adulthood. Ninety percent of college students procrastinate in notable ways. Twenty-five percent of college students have serious procrastination habits. Some of these individuals find difficulty managing themselves efficiently in self-structuring circumstances where there are many appealing distractions. New responsibilities can also evoke resistance in those used to a less responsible lifestyle.

Some people develop perfectionist symptoms in graduate schools that overemphasize learning details and precisely following a set discipline. A too inflexible curriculum can stimulate perfectionism when the training methods funnel people down ever narrowing pathways where they come to believe there is only one right way to think. This acquired perfectionism can hinder experimenting with new ideas and blunt efforts at invention. That is a serious form of procrastination.

Later Adulthood

When you make a poor career choice, you may find yourself resisting the job functions and eventually putting some of them off. Since people who enjoy a specific career track have overlapping interests, you may be in conflict with coworkers in your field, as opposed to following a career track consistent with your interests, temperament, style, and abilities. Career track conditions that are inconsistent with your interest patterns, temperament, and the preferred job functions you wish to do provide a fertile field for job burnout.

Retirement is supposed to be an age when you can do more of the recreational things that you did not have time to do before. Trips, hobbies, second careers—all are possible. Take these opportunities too casually—as though there was always a later time to begin—and life passes too quickly to start.

You might flounder in retirement because you put off figuring how to structure your time around worthwhile projects. At that stage, vaguely planning to go fishing or saying you expect to travel when you retire supports procrastination. A lack of specifics correlates with procrastination.

Interestingly, many people don't recognize that procrastination can occur at different levels within an important area of their lives. The manager who feels overwhelmed and works long hours often procrastinates on delegation. This delegation issue may be a symptom and a problem. At a deeper level, this person may procrastinate on planning, organizing, and monitoring the efforts of others. At a still deeper level, the person may feel unworthy, project this doubt on others, and then compulsively take responsibility for practically everything to avoid facing this problem. At a different level, the person may procrastinate on finding a career better suited to his or her interest, temperament, and personal style.

THE DO IT NOW! METHOD

Breaking procrastination patterns takes knowledge, purposefulness, will, and effort. Since there is no final cure, you also will constantly have to work to keep your procrastination in check. If you intend to get more personal value out of your time and life, you would better face this fact sooner rather than later. Those who refuse to face this reality will get practically nowhere in overcoming their procrastination.

Fortunately, much of the work in overcoming procrastination involves a journey in self-discovery. During this journey you develop your resources and resourcefulness. During this adventure, you stimulate your ability to stay on top of the challenges that you face. You create opportunities and take advantage of opportunities that come about through serendipity.

You won't find a regimented time-management formula within these pages. That makes life too sterile and colorless. It is also unrealistic. So we won't examine time through a microscopic lens to see how to squeeze value from every second. We humans have limitations to our cognitive and physical capacities, and so we cannot act like perpetual motion machines. Instead, we'll use the *Do It Now! Method: doing reasonable things, in a reasonable way, within a reasonable time.*

Trying to do reasonable things in a reasonable way within a reasonable time raises the question of what is reasonable? Reasonable means your actions are bound by common sense, and they are rational because they are neither excessive nor extreme relative to the conditions that challenge you. However, circumstances do vary and the timing and pacing of what you do can prove unpredictable and demanding. For instance, you can have multiple responsibilities and limited time to meet these responsibilities and thus have to "burn the midnight oil." Pressured efforts are, therefore, reasonable under demanding circumstances. Paying your bills on the twentieth of the month may prove reasonable when this action allows you to avoid last-minute snafus. Allowing yourself downtime and recreational time is reasonable when the activities you use to fill those times yield a sense of balance and control over your time and your life.

When facing a real challenge, where time is important, many people who normally procrastinate rise to the occasion, often acting with alacrity and effectiveness. In a sense, the competency drive returns from hidden places in the mind, often with surprising strength. The Do It Now! Method will help you produce this response with greater regularity, allowing you to overcome procrastination in every reasonable situation—from paying your bills on time to taking on new and rewarding challenges in your personal and professional life. Getting on top of the stuff you put off can pay dividends. You'll have more stress-free time for yourself. You'll get ahead of the game. But millions who want to stop procrastinating and improve the quality of their lives still don't know how to change their patterns of behavior, so they procrastinate in overcoming procrastination. Fortunately, there are ways of significantly overcoming procrastination. That's what this book is about.

2

Mapping Your Procrastination Territory

In This Chapter

➤ The procrastination inventory
➤ Inventory instructions
➤ Interpreting the inventory

The world looks different from different vantage points, yet remains the same. Most people who struggle unsuccessfully with their procrastination problems limit themselves in one of three ways: (1) they don't have a good handle on what is going on, (2) they try to solve the wrong problem, or (3) they try to permanently eliminate their problems by making demanding declarations such as, "You should do better." This type of demand often makes as much sense as cutting off a toe to cure a headache. Yet millions of people take this wrong approach to solving their problems. They make the wrong diagnosis for what is going on, then wonder why they are not getting anywhere.

I designed the following test to help you to become a master procrastination detective, put your procrastination into focus, and identify potential opportunities for change.

THE PROCRASTINATION INVENTORY

The *procrastination inventory* is an informative, and fun, way to look at your procrastination acts and patterns. Although this is not a standardized test, the exercise can help you develop a clearer perspective on your procrastination. You can use the inventory:

➤ To identify general trouble spots warranting your attention.

➤ To identify specific incidents in which procrastination is likely to erupt.

➤ To assess the degree to which procrastination and problems related to procrastination pervade your life.

➤ To provide data you can refer to and use in the many exercises suggested throughout this book.

➤ To use for pre- and post-program comparisons so that you can assess your progress.

INVENTORY INSTRUCTIONS

Each entry in the inventory begins with a simple statement about procrastination. Cite examples from your life that *support* or *refute* each statement in the inventory. These can be activities that you are currently putting off or ones that you have felt plagued by and that continue to represent prime procrastination problem areas.

After you finish listing examples, circle the letter that comes closest to describing your frequency of procrastination for that item. For this exercise, **R** = rarely, **O** = occasionally; **F** = frequently; **V** = very frequently.

The following sample item shows you how to fill out the inventory:

➤Sample

1. I am late finishing routine tasks.

Examples:

Reports started near the deadline and sometimes turned in late. Regularly pay bills after the due date. Ask for extensions on taxes. Inspection sticker for automobile two months late. Return library books on time.

Rating: R   O   Ⓕ   V

THE INVENTORY

1. I normally begin and complete important projects at the eleventh hour or later.
   Examples:

   Rating: **R** **O** **F** **V**

2. I put off scheduling myself for routine medical and dental evaluations.
   Examples:

   Rating: **R** **O** **F** **V**

3. I join the last-minute rush when I buy holiday presents.
   Examples:

   Rating: **R** **O** **F** **V**

4. I pay my bills late.
   Examples:

   Rating: **R** **O** **F** **V**

5. I switch over to more comfortable activities when faced with an uncomfortable priority or when I feel pressured to do something of significant importance.
   Examples:

   Rating: **R** **O** **F** **V**

6. I fall behind in my correspondence.
   Examples:

   Rating: **R** **O** **F** **V**

7. I can't stand inconveniences.
   Examples:

   Rating: **R** **O** **F** **V**

8. I feel helpless about stopping procrastination.
   Examples:

   Rating: **R** **O** **F** **V**

9. I greatly delay, or fail to return, phone calls.
   Examples:

   Rating: **R** **O** **F** **V**

10. I do things that needlessly slow others down.
    Examples:

    Rating: **R** **O** **F** **V**

11. I feel disorganized and inefficient.
    Examples:

    Rating: **R** **O** **F** **V**

12. I show up late for appointments.
    Examples:

    Rating: **R** **O** **F** **V**

13. I repeat patterns I want to change.
    Examples:

    Rating: **R** **O** **F** **V**

14. I withhold expressing what I feel.
    Examples:

    Rating: **R** **O** **F** **V**

15. I collect materials to use on a project and then delay doing the project.
    Examples:

    Rating: **R** **O** **F** **V**

16. I avoid situations where I believe I won't be very successful.
    Examples:

    Rating: **R** **O** **F** **V**

17. I dwell upon injustices.
    Examples:

    Rating: **R** **O** **F** **V**

18. I drink, eat, or smoke more than I should.
Examples:

Rating: **R O F V**

19. I repeatedly replay arguments in my head.
Examples:

Rating: **R O F V**

20. I daydream of accomplishing great feats.
Examples:

Rating: **R O F V**

21. I tell myself that tomorrow I'll begin.
Examples:

Rating: **R O F V**

22. I indulge my desire to avoid doing anything that is an inconvenience or a hassle.
Examples:

Rating: **R O F V**

23. I worry that other people do not like me.
Examples:

Rating: **R O F V**

24. I won't deprive myself, and thus I'll indulge in that extra dessert or snack.
Examples:

Rating: **R O F V**

25. I avoid conflict.
Examples:

Rating: **R O F V**

26. I get so angry with myself that I can't control my feelings.
Examples:

Rating: **R O F V**

27. I make promises to myself, or others, that I put off keeping.
Examples:

Rating: **R O F V**

28. I feel bored.
Examples:

Rating: **R O F V**

29. I lack drive or energy.
Examples:

Rating: **R O F V**

30. I feel as though there is just one crisis after another in my life.
Examples:

Rating: **R O F V**

31. I complete written reports (homework) late.
Examples:

Rating: **R O F V**

32. People who procrastinate should be punished.
Examples:

Rating: **R O F V**

33. I lose track of time and fall behind.
Examples:

Rating: **R O F V**

34. I put off exercising.
Examples:

Rating: **R O F V**

35. I wait too long and lose opportunities.
Examples:

Rating: **R O F V**

36. I avoid my chores.
Examples:

Rating: **R O F V**

37. I fall behind on administrative detail (keeping records, filing materials, getting rid of paperwork).
    Examples:

    Rating: **R O F V**

38. I don't attempt to keep up with developments in my career area.
    Examples:

    Rating: **R O F V**

39. I come up with ploys to excuse my procrastination.
    Examples:

    Rating: **R O F V**

40. I store too much "stuff" in my drawers, closets, attic, basement, or garage.
    Examples:

    Rating: **R O F V**

41. I don't trust my judgment.
    Examples:

    Rating: **R O F V**

42. I try so hard to maintain control that I lose control.
    Examples:

    Rating: **R O F V**

43. I think I should be doing a better job in following through with my responsibilities.
    Examples:

    Rating: **R O F V**

44. When I'm afraid I'll fail, I back away.
    Examples:

    Rating: **R O F V**

45. My life feels incomplete.
    Examples:

    Rating: **R O F V**

46. When I feel angered I act against others' wishes.
    Examples:

    Rating: **R O F V**

47. I put securing comfort above personal effectiveness.
    Examples:

    Rating: **R O F V**

48. I create preconditions for doing important "have to" activities, then I put off achieving the precondition.
    Examples:

    Rating: **R O F V**

49. I make good plans but then don't follow through.
    Examples:

    Rating: **R O F V**

50. I feel uncommitted.
    Examples:

    Rating: **R O F V**

51. I have few rewards in life.
    Examples:

    Rating: **R O F V**

52. I believe I am drifting through life without much structure.
    Examples:

    Rating: **R O F V**

53. I need to feel inspired or motivated to begin and complete a difficult or unpleasant task.
    Examples:

    Rating: **R O F V**

54. I feel guilty for the things I haven't done.
    Examples:

    Rating: **R O F V**

55. I don't plan.
    Examples:

    Rating: **R O F V**

56. I think I'm a loser.
    Examples:
    Rating: **R   O   F   V**

57. Procrastination comes naturally.
    Examples:
    Rating: **R   O   F   V**

58. I feel self-conscious among
strangers.
    Examples:
    Rating: **R   O   F   V**

59. I usually have something that I
put off that leaves me with a nagging feeling of incompleteness.
    Examples:
    Rating: **R   O   F   V**

60. I make vacation (trip) reserva-
tions just before the time to leave.
    Examples:
    Rating: **R   O   F   V**

INTERPRETING THE INVENTORY

You can score your inventory to obtain both a general procrastination rating and special scores for different procrastination subcategories. To obtain a general score, assign one point to every Rare item, two to Occasionally, three to Frequently, and four to Very Frequently. Then total your score.

> ➤ If you score a total of 60 to 100 points, you see yourself as an efficiency superstar, perhaps in a class by yourself.
> ➤ Between 101 and 120, you are likely to have some procrastination trouble spots, but otherwise you are doing quite well. With some exceptions, your procrastination is mainly within the inconvenience zone.
> ➤ A score between 121 and 180 brings you increasingly into the trouble zone. Your procrastination is a distinct bother, but you can normally explain it away or repair the damage. In different areas you'll have a mix of inconveniencing, troublesome, and immobilizing procrastination areas.
> ➤ Beyond 180, your procrastination can prove immobilizing, and you are likely to have a hard-core, chronic procrastination problem to deal with.

You can also break the inventory down into major categories of maintenance, developmental, and health procrastination.

> ➤ A total rating of 20 or above on the following inventory items suggests a maintenance procrastination pattern: 3, 4, 6, 9, 11, 31, 36, 37, 40, 60.

➤ A total score of above 54 on items 13, 14, 16, 17, 18, 19, 22, 23, 25, 26, 28, 29, 30, 32, 35, 38, 41, 42, 44, 45, 46, 49, 50, 51, 52, 54, 58 suggests a developmental procrastination pattern.

➤ A total score above 16 on items 2, 17, 18, 19, 24, 26, 29, 34 means that your procrastination is likely to affect your long-term health interests negatively.

Chapter 3, on the major procrastination traps, will teach you what each of these procrastination categories is. Part 3, on strategies for overcoming procrastination, will show you Do It Now! solutions that you can apply to each category.

This inventory surveys some areas that you may not have associated with procrastination but that may, in fact, be the root causes of your problem.

➤ If you scored over 33 on items 8, 11, 13, 14, 16, 23, 41, 44, 54, 56, 58, you may have a problem with self-doubts. Time spent in self-doubting often robs time from involvement in self-fulfilling activities. You should pay special attention to chapter 10, Approval Seeking and Putting It Off.

➤ A total score of 36 on the following items brings you into the discomfort-dodging zone: 7, 10, 11, 20, 22, 24, 25, 26, 28, 30, 34, 36, 37, 42, 46, 47, 50, 52. This suggests that you are inclined to avoid challenging yourself, magnify inconvenience, and give up too easily. Many of your goals are probably vague. You are likely to have difficulty tolerating the unpleasant elements that lie on the pathway to your goals, and have difficulties following through. Check out chapter 11, Discomfort Dodging and Procrastination.

➤ You emphasize diversions over action if you have a total score above 18 on the following items: 5, 15, 20, 21, 33, 39, 46, 48, 53. Beyond a score of 18, carefully examine chapter 5 to help you move beyond your diversionary ploys. Also, pay special attention to the discussion in chapter 3 about self-worth.

POSTSCRIPT

Whether you make a beeline toward getting things done or procrastinate you will find a gap to traverse. You are, for example, at point A and you want to get to point C. To get from A to C you have to go through B first. In the procrastinator's gap, the B contains such obstacles as self-defeating beliefs, doubts, discomfort dodging urges, and

Do It Now!

Using Your Inventory

The completed inventory can also help you prioritize your tasks. Go back to the inventory and identify the statements that you marked **F** or **V**. For each of those statements, go to the example section and make a list of the significant items. When you're finished, you will have a list of tasks that you are currently procrastinating on doing. Rank them in order of priority. Now you can begin attacking the items on your list. As you whittle down the highest priority activities, the secondary ones will rise to take their place. You whittle them down, as well. As you eliminate the items on the list, you will take steps to develop a more confident, effective, self-accepting you.

excuses that divert you from doing relevant things in a timely way. The gap also includes your positive motivations, common sense, and ability to traverse the obstacles. You can call upon these positive abilities at any time to help yourself bypass the procrastination barriers and beeline it to point C, where you finish what you set out to accomplish. The procrastination inventory helps identify what to look for in the gap that sidetracks you from reaching your destination. However, the best way to traverse the gap is to start and to keep your sights on your destination.

Knowing where we procrastinate and where we act effectively can give us a reasoned perspective of where we can put our efforts to change and where we can maintain and build what is already working well. Your procrastination inventory results can help you develop awareness of your procrastination problems, keep these matters in perspective, and provide ideas that prepare you for change.

3

Procrastination Traps

The barriers we create grow as we shrink before them. Not all procrastination is alike. The more you know about the different ways you procrastinate, the more opportunities you create for yourself to get off the well-worn procrastination path.

We usually see and identify our most obvious procrastination acts. But sometimes the pattern is not so readily seen. And just as you can't explain color unless you can see color, unless you can see the patterns of procrastination in your life, you're doomed to continually repeat them.

Acts of procrastination fall into recognizable groupings. As you read about these groupings, some of the described procrastination experiences will probably sound familiar and make you say, "That sounds like me." When you have a recognizable procrastination pattern that is shared by hundreds of millions of people throughout the world, throughout the ages, you know that hundreds of millions have struggled and still struggle to free themselves from the same procrastination traps you wrestle with today. And if you can recognize and define your own self-defeating procrastination pattern, you can surely find many proven ways to alter the future for the better by taking steps to reduce or eliminate the behavior. Perhaps you'll invent a few good ways of your own.

Before we can understand the common procrastination patterns, we'll need to look at the difference between procrastination and laziness. Then we'll explore common procrastination patterns, low-grade procrastination, and hindrance procrastination.

PROCRASTINATION AND LAZINESS

While people who feel lazy often procrastinate, laziness and procrastination are often different. Laziness is an apathy for activity. Procrastination, on the other hand, is an active state of avoidance that often involves creating elaborate excuses for putting things off.

Procrastination is far more complex that simple laziness. Most procrastinators have ambitions and desire accomplishments. They are also normally highly motivated to invent reasons for not getting things done. But most feel agitated as a result of their procrastination.

Because of the different forms procrastination takes, and the causes, motivations, diversionary tactics, and escapist activities associated with the decision to delay needlessly, procrastination is normally different from a symptom of laziness.

Complacency

Complacency overlaps with but differs from laziness. Complacent people don't try because they don't think that they have to make a special effort. They are frequently self-satisfied.

Complacency can link to indifference, but it also can follow overconfidence. That is why great sports teams sometimes lose to teams with lesser talent.

Complacency can sneak up on you when you feel self-satisfied with your current position and abilities. Because you believe you can handle what you need to do, you don't feel any inner or external pressure to get started. In this state of mind, you are oblivious to the troubles headed toward you. When procrastination catches up, you feel chagrined about not doing what you believed you could have easily done.

COMMON PROCRASTINATION PATTERNS

We can look at procrastination activities as isolated acts. However, these acts normally fall into the patterns of maintenance, developmental, and health procrastination.

Do It Now!

Complacency

The answer to complacency is challenge. Identify problems and challenge yourself to meet the test. Look for opportunities to stretch your resources. Pick meaningful activities that are within reach but not yet grasped. By exercising initiative, you can break the chain of complacency and help end your procrastination patterns.

Maintenance Procrastination

Maintenance procrastination includes putting off activities necessary to your day-to-day life. This covers such things as holiday shopping, washing dishes, mowing the lawn, getting regular medical and dental checkups, changing the oil in your car, keeping your keys in the same place, planning a trip, paying bills on time, making appointments, or discarding materials that are no longer useful such as old clothing, magazines, furniture, and so forth.

People who delay in self-maintenance areas often report feeling anxious and overwhelmed because they feel that their lives are clutterd. They feel a strong sense of disorderliness. At the extreme, some let their personal hygiene decline and harm their social and intimate relationships. A sense of anxiety can lead to maintenance procrastination, but maintenance procrastination then also promotes further anxiety.

Developmental Procrastination

People who avoid self-development activities will normally describe themselves as depressed, anxious, immobilized, or in a rut. Developmental procrastination involves needless delays in:

➤ Dealing with troublesome personal problems (e.g., passivity, dependency, agoraphobia, overeating, smoking, perfectionism, shyness, aggressiveness, anxiety, or inattentiveness)

➤ Taking advantage of leisure activities that add pleasure to life and create a sense of balance (e.g., developing an attractive hobby or pastime, absorbing oneself in a vital interest, traveling, creating, building, cultivating—any worthwhile activity that is therapeutic, fulfilling, constructive, or pleasurable)

➤ Improving career opportunities (e.g., improving work skills and seeking challenging opportunities)

➤ Developing qualities to improve the depth and quality of significant interpersonal relationships (e.g., building trust, active listening, sharing, expressing feelings, and so forth)

➤ Building on aesthetic, spiritual, and educational interests (e.g., nature, art, religion, reason, or knowledge)

➤ Learning and taking advantage of the tools of the electronic and information revolutions.

Developmental procrastination can happen for a number of reasons. You could have a poor sense of timing or mistakenly assume that you can accomplish more than you can within the time that you have available. But there are three primary causes for developmental procrastination:

1. The perfectionist work ethic taken to the extreme
2. Boredom
3. Cloaked maintenance procrastination

The perfectionist work ethic in the extreme. Some very active people take on too many projects with tight deadlines. They fall behind on priority developmental activities because they overload themselves with projects and commitments.

What about the saying "When you have something to do, give it to a busy person"? This is a good idea when the busy person works very efficiently and can throw off details the way beavers build dams. However, some workaholics appear very busy, but the work is *busywork*. They might take on multiple responsibilities, but don't count on their timeliness or the quality of their output. For example, as part of my job as a management consultant, I once looked at a pile of projects in a "busy" person's in basket. Some documents dealt with projects that were five years overdue, with appended memoranda explaining the delays. What we had was a paper shuffle.

What if you believe in the perfectionist work ethic and have inner conflicts over taking some "downtime"? Although a work ethic has advantages and some people truly prefer doing their work to other activities, being a hard taskmaster has its own downside.

Taken to an extreme, the perfectionist work ethic of perpetually keeping your nose to the grindstone is an ideal that often falls far short of reality. When you live every moment based on the belief that you are not working hard enough, or progressing fast enough, you may have lost sight of self-development possibilities, including enriching your life with a broad range of experiences, knowledge, and pleasures.

Boredom. Some people experience more than their share of dull, monotonous, repetitious, and tedious tasks. Because many are often in chronic states of boredom, they paradoxically put off trying new or potentially exciting activities that they could look forward to doing. Often lacking a sense of direction and time, weeks pass before they consider responding to what has already happened. This is a classic form of *development procrastination.*

The Beatles in their song "Eleanor Rigby" used a dreary tune to describe Rigby as she waited by the door with nothing to do until the grim reaper arrived. So it is with the bored procrastinator who waits, complains about "nothing to do," and waits again.

The bored person procrastinates on developing entertaining interests and skills. Although boredom is common during adolescence, beyond that point, the pattern becomes increasingly likely to result in ennui, a depression born of boredom and a resultant sense of inertia.

The cloaking device. Developmental procrastination can sometimes interact with maintenance procrastination. In one of my procrastination workshops a participant, Carol, complained about putting off finding a new, larger apartment.

When I asked her why she wanted a larger apartment, she said, "Why, of course, to store my *New York Times* newspapers. I'm running out of space."

Carol stored the *Times* because she wanted to read the editorial page so that when she went to a party, she would sound well informed. However, she put off reading the editorial page. She stocked the papers, telling herself that she would someday get around to reading the editorials. She also refused to attend parties because "What if someone brought up last month's editorial and I had not read the paper? I'd feel like a fool."

The group switched their approach and helped Carol to look at her perfectionistic need to look *all-knowing* to avoid disapproval.

The group was incredulous that Carol had outgrown a two-bedroom apartment because of her newspaper collection. Because Carol lived nearby, she invited the group to see for themselves.

It was true. Carol had papers piled to the ceiling. The group quickly convinced her that she had better work on her perfectionism. They showed her that the newspapers were a distraction, that her "collection" caused her to feel physically crowded, and that she would be far better off without her *New York Times* collection.

The group helped Carol start her cleaning projects. Within a week she had a clean apartment. She no longer had a "need" to live in a larger apartment. Her real problems were uncloaked.

Carol had a classic case of maintenance procrastination. In her case, maintenance and developmental procrastination overlapped. These two procrastination forms often do coexist. The person who puts off completing a college application for fear of rejection may misplace the application because of procrastinating on filing paperwork. The person who puts off kicking a smoking habit may let cigarette butts go stale in ashtrays around the house or apartment.

Health Procrastination

Health care procrastination involves putting off regular or necessary physical, dental, or mental health care examinations. Most important, this includes putting off preventive activities that could reduce the necessity for care later. Many women, for example, put off giving themselves breast self-examinations or having mammograms.

At the extreme end of health care procrastination, we find some people who put off getting a medical check after feeling serious chest pains. Some people lose teeth because they put off going to the dentist until it is too late. Others procrastinate on ridding themselves of debilitating anxiety, perfectionism, alcohol abuse, depression, hostility, and other unnecessary and unwanted cognitive, emotional, or behavioral problems. Many in this health care avoidance group will say "I'll get around to it" or "It's not serious" or "It will go away on its own." When such denial blends with procrastination it can be health threatening.

There is no law that says that adults have to take care of their health. The decision is discretionary. Nevertheless, any decision to procrastinate on assuring good physical and mental health deserves scrutiny. To avoid self-care by indulging fear, threat, or hassle avoidance, for example, is clearly irrational.

LOW-GRADE PROCRASTINATION

There is tremendous variation in what people find important: family, work, relationships, hobbies, learning, exploring, and self-development are all possibilities. But sometimes these important parts of life lose ground to low-grade forms of procrastination. Low-grade procrastination includes collecting significant amounts of clutter in your closets and drawers, running out of certain foods because you haven't shopped for weeks, sending out holiday cards late, waiting until the last minute to get your automobile inspected, putting off returning

➤ **Do It Now!**

Health Care Procrastination

If you have long thought making prudent healthy lifestyle changes can benefit you more than disadvantage you but have continually put it off or failed to follow through, put your health care procrastination sharply in perspective by making a list of the pros and the cons for your physical or mental health development. Use the following outline to start.

	Health Care Pros	*Health Care Cons*
1.	_____	_____
2.	_____	_____
3.	_____	_____
4.	_____	_____

By considering the repercussions of health care avoidance, you can gain a stronger motivation to take care of your health needs in a timely fashion.

phone calls, or avoiding following up on productive ideas that initially excited you. In short, low-grade procrastination is a lot of little things that add up to a real inconvenience.

In a sense, many procrastinators lose sight of the *principle of the cumulative effect*. Here you repeat a combination of minor but different acts of procrastination. The tasks accumulate. This causes a low-grade stress that spreads to influence important areas of your life.

Not all separate acts of procrastination have a pervasive and pernicious effect. You might put off completing your taxes until April 15, but past experience tells you that you will get it done before the deadline, so you don't experience any significant strain. However, when you are aware of what you're not doing and experience the tax deadline as "hanging over your head," then you have a low-grade procrastination tension.

Low-grade procrastination has an interesting twist. Some people do a reasonably good job sticking to their major priorities but eschew support activities (mailing letters, getting supplies, sending out bills) because they define them as (1) not important enough to get to right now, (2) too time-consuming, and (3) unpleasant. However, when you neglect activities that support your priorities, you are likely to suffer from a sense of disorganization and have fewer priority accomplishments. This pattern can significantly contribute to a sense of emotional malaise, mild stress, and chronic irritability.

The low-grade acts of procrastination are likely to be the toughest form of procrastination to overcome. Although you may occasionally experience acute stress with this low-grade pattern, it rarely rises to an extreme such that you feel immobilized, out of control, and helpless. You can live with them in much the same way that you can learn to live with a hangnail. Yet over a lifetime, the low-grade tension that often accompanies these acts cumulatively adds up to years of inefficiency and irritability.

Those who identify their low-grade procrastination pattern and make a consistent and diligent effort to stay out of this procrastination rut normally feel less strain. They have more energy to deal with their priorities and rightly view themselves as making progress.

HINDRANCE PROCRASTINATION

If someone asked you what personal freedom means to you, would you say, "Doing whatever pleases me"? If so, then what is the difference between this definition of freedom and self-indulgence?

Hindrance procrastination is an act of self-indulgence that has some unpleasant long-term personal consequences. As social creatures, much of what we do, or don't do, also touches the lives of other people. We don't live in a vacuum. So your procrastination can impact the lives of others. In hindrance procrastination, you impede the interests of others. Sometimes this is intentional, sometimes it is unintentional. Thus, when we become absorbed in our own avoidance efforts, we may lose sight of how we can needlessly delay other people's interests. Self-sabotaging hindrance ploys can wreak havoc on friendship, love, and career relationships.

There are four primary forms that hindrance procrastination takes: Hostility, rebellion, indifference, and lateness.

Hostility

Many members of this group gain a false sense of power and control through their delaying tactics. They accomplish this by dawdling, obstructing, lagging in their commitments, backing out of agreements, or by aggressively asserting power. However, most members of this group put off what they find aversive, and their personality issues are secondary to this aversion avoidance process.

Rebellion

A classic group of procrastinators falls into the rebel trap. Here the procrastination actions mask anxiety, unhappiness, helplessness, insecurity, or hostility. Stalling, delaying, obstructing, and dawdling actions that are a part of this pattern reflect resentments that often translate into substandard performances.

Michael is a quintessential rebel. He has a history that supports his present procrastination. He thinks that his parents overly controlled him as a child, his teachers made too many demands on him, and his coaches were forever telling him what to do. Still battling the ghosts from his past, he decides that it's payback time. At work he puts off delivering his reports until the latest possible time, arrives late for meetings, and tries to beat the system in whatever way he thinks he can get away with doing. At home, he throws his clothing everywhere to show his wife she can't force him to be tidy.

Rather than make active assertions against the "demands" of "society," the rebel actively procrastinates against these impositions and presents the attitude "You can't make me."

On the other hand, a passive rebel may agree to any assignment, project, or activity but resent the agreement and then put off the imposition. The passive rebel says yes and means no. This form of procrastination then serves as an oppositional or nonassertive way of saying no. Where resentment turns to procrastination, such reactions can result in a counterreaction. Some call these "rebel" procrastinators to task for their feigned "forgetfulness," procrastination, and other delaying tactics. At that point, the cycle begins anew.

Few passive rebel procrastinators consciously plot and scheme and tell themselves, "Gee, I'm afraid to turn people down because I believe they will overpower or dislike me if I do. So I will agree to the task. Then I will put it off, or mess up the job. That will teach them to force me into doing what I don't want to do." However, these are the ideas that lead to the procrastination process.

Indifference

Some people adroitly avoid penalties for putting things off. They believe that putting things off is a perfectly acceptable practice if what you put off gets forgotten or eventually done. They are normally indifferent to the impact their procrastinating behavior has on other people. Some don't care.

The *regal syndrome* is a variation of this procrastination form. Unless the activities please them, regals won't do them. Instead, the regal expects others to serve. Used to standing at the focal point, the regal attracts attention through a refusing and pouting form of procrastination.

Lateness

Although all forms of procrastination involve delays, *lateness* is perhaps the most classic form of hindrance, where you show up late for meetings, appointments, dinner parties, weddings, the movies, and so forth. People with lateness procrastination patterns follow a set of delay rules where they:

➤ Underestimate the amount of time required to prepare for the event they plan to attend.

➤ Start their preparation efforts right about the time they need to leave, thus making it impossible to arrive on time.

➤ Make sure that they answer the phone if it rings as they are about to go out the door, which adds to the delay.

➤ Misplace their car keys, coat, shoes, or other accoutrements that relate to the event.

➤ Count on the event starting later than usual.

➤ Scurry about looking for directions or stop en route to ask directions.

➤ Look hurried, breathless, and hassled when they arrive.

➤ Dip into their procrastination excuse-making bag to pull out an enticing-sounding reason for their delay.

➤ Swear that they'll do better next time, but when next time comes, feel rushed and end up delayed.

Lateness procrastination can have other complications. If you experience a mild social anxiety, or feel uncomfortable about visiting new places, you might coddle this discomfort by delaying your departure until the last possible moment. Your lateness procrastination can come about at different times for other motives. This process can also involve hindrance procrastination on some occasions, and self-doubts at other times. Lateness procrastination can truly be enigmatic.

People who fall into this lateness procrastination rut are normally reasonable people. But why would reasonable people maintain a habit that they see will promote needless distress and possible social censure? Part of the answer lies in *hope substituting for reason*. They often hope that the future will differ from the past and forget the philosopher George Santayana's dictum that "those who cannot remember the past are condemned to repeat it."

Lateness procrastination continues for different reasons. Some don't want to admit that they don't control their time very well, and that is why hope substitutes for reason. Others habitually lose track of time and then remember too late that they have an event to attend. Details take time to tackle, and many underestimate the time required to get things done. It may take longer than you think to reach a destination. For example, you are going to drive to your destination. You don't take into account the time it will take to get to your automobile. There may be unexpected traffic tie-ups and delays. You may not find a parking space. If you are taking public transportation, your bus, train, or subway may be late. The list of possible impediments goes on and on.

The solution to lateness procrastination partially hinges on making better time estimations and then acting upon those estimations. This change process includes:

> ➤ Taking actual time measures for preparatory activities. If you are a man and shave, brush your teeth, and get dressed before you leave, how much time does it take to accomplish these results? If you are a woman who showers, washes her hair, dresses, and puts on makeup before she leaves, how much time does this take? Each person may discover that he or she underestimates the time needed to finish these tasks. Thereafter, allow time to complete this preparatory work with enough latitude so you don't pressure yourself to rush.
> ➤ Calculate the time used to locate items required for the trip. This exercise may quickly suggest the value of keeping common items in familiar locations so you know where to look.
> ➤ Avoid doing discretionary tasks as you are in the process of leaving. For some, this is the time to do dishes, tidy the laundry, put the lawnmower into the garage, and so forth. These tasks will not disappear and so can be done at a later time.

These activities can help you improve your ability to get and stay organized so that you can get to places on time.

POSTSCRIPT

The Roman Emperor Marcus Aurelius (A.D. 121–180) had a useful insight on procrastination: "Do the things external which fall upon you distract you? Give yourself time to learn something new and good, and cease to be whirled around. But then, you must also avoid being carried about the other way. For those too are triflers who have wearied

Do It Now!

Hindrance Procrastination

If your procrastination activity can negatively affect the health, welfare, finances, and reasonable peace of mind of other people, *concentrate on doing the "right thing" and get it done on time!* Deal with your self-absorptions, hostility, rebelliousness, or regalness by taking a more mature path: accept your responsibilities and carry through.

If someone you dislike, or don't find credible, makes demands on you, but you find completing the activity on time is very much in your interest, separate the other person's personality from your personal advantage. For example, if you are overweight and can profit from losing weight, and another overweight person suggests that you drop fifteen pounds, what's the advantage in rebelling against the idea? Disregard the source and concentrate on doing what's most advantageous for you.

themselves in life by their activity, and yet have no object to which to direct every moment, and, in a word, all their thoughts." The procrastination that Marcus Aurelius recognized nearly two thousand years ago we see in the same and different ways today.

The activities we put off are not all alike. Putting a task aside when we can gain greater advantage elsewhere may be a rational decision. Defeating a developmental procrastination problem may involve some steps that differ from defusing a maintenance, health, low-grade, or hindrance pattern.

You can often consciously apply the skills you develop overcoming one form of procrastination to other areas. Sooner or later, you can shift from a pattern of avoidance to one where you work to advance your enlightened self-interests.

4

The Seeds of Procrastination

In This Chapter

➤ Procrastination as a habit
➤ Procrastination as a symptom of a larger problem
➤ Procrastination as a defense

The causes of procrastination are as numerous as the different types of seeds that germinate into the weeds that grow in a garden. Some people hate hassles or inconvenience and put practically any complication on the back burner. Others delay because they fret and wring their hands, fearing they will make a mistake or do the "wrong thing." Although there are a broad range of procrastination motives, almost all of them fit into one of three different categories:

1. Problem habits
2. Symptoms
3. Defenses

Knowing how these three psychological motives work, and work together, will help you to get directly to the core of your procrastination practices. Let's start with procrastination as a problem habit.

A PROBLEM HABIT

A habit is an automatic way of behaving that receives little conscious recognition. It is only when we make ourselves aware of our habits that we can begin to understand how they contribute to, or diminish, our lives. For example, you might tie your left shoe before your right and never notice it, unless someone calls it to your attention. But imagine if you did have to think about tying your shoes, or how to suds yourself in the shower, or any of the other myriad mundane tasks we perform automatically every morning. You'd be mentally exhausted before you even got to the door. So it's clear that some habits are positive and useful; they make us use our time and energy more efficiently. But we are also susceptible to falling into habits that actually interfere with our ability to efficiently conduct our daily lives. Procrastination is one of these "problem habits."

Procrastination is a problem habit when we routinely and impulsively put off tasks that we consider unpleasant, difficult, threatening, or uncomfortable. People will rarely put off what they want to do or "have to do." But they are quick to put off what they find unpleasant, frustrating, onerous, or threatening. When we conclude that a job is difficult or discomforting, a predictable series of ideas, feelings, and reactions is set into motion that result in avoidance and procrastination.

But when procrastination becomes a problem habit, it begins to include even common and mundane tasks. Writing and mailing a letter, paying bills, washing dishes, and returning a phone call are normally not difficult. But we can make them seem difficult by habitual anticipations of discomfort or by making them seem onerous.

When trapped in habitual procrastination patterns of thought and avoidance activities, you may wonder, "Why do I keep putting myself through this emotional wringer?" But like a sleepwalker in a trance, you keep going through the same procrastination motions. But there are ways of breaking the procrastination habit.

Like most problem habits, procrastination is rooted in your thoughts, muscles, and emotional chemistry. This is one reason why changing a procrastination pattern can prove so challenging. But you can overcome your procrastination problem habit by:

- ➤ Stopping the chain of thoughts that lead to procrastination by challenging irrational ideas;
- ➤ Resisting procrastination feelings by commanding your muscles to engage in necessary activities;
- ➤ Improving your body's chemistry by looking at tasks as challenges rather than as threats. The "challenge mentality" correlates with positive changes in your body and better cardiac output, which can help you to think more clearly as you take on necessary projects.

But the first step to overcoming this problem habit is awareness. When executing a procrastination habit, you normally act the same way without stepping back to see what you are doing. That is one of the reasons why procrastination is resistant to change. When you don't take the time to understand your procrastination habit, chances are that you won't make much progress. But you increase your chances for change when you identify the procrastination habit patterns you follow.

The Procrastinator's Maze

The procrastination process is similar to a conditioned response. We link an undesired, unpleasant, or uncomfortable task to "avoidance" or define it as a "waste" of time because we want to do something different. We set up a chain of associations. We blindly move from link to link in the chain scarcely aware of what we are doing.

To see the conditioned linkage between words and actions, just think of the word *task*. Do you feel a sense of resistance welling within you? What do you associate with the word *task*?

Although different people have different associations, you may think of a task as a chore, duty, job, or onerous responsibility, and you will feel a sense of resistance in your mind, muscles, and emotions. Under these conditions, you might notice that it takes an extra mental and physical effort to override the feelings of task resistance. Even if you don't flinch at the word *task,* you may still feel resistance toward specific activities that you view as onerous, threatening, or inconvenient.

Few of us relish using our time to finish chores or to do things we find unpleasant, and so we will often feel tempted to put these activities off until another day or time. When we repeatedly indulge an impulse to delay common everyday tasks, we can generalize this pattern to other parts of our life. Thus, procrastination can reach beyond the mechanical tasks of life that we don't like to do and come to involve the avoidance of normally pleasurable activities because of some preliminary hassle. At other times, we may absorb ourselves in the mundane to avoid higher-level challenges. When we lose ourselves in mundane details, we simultaneously sidetrack ourselves from finding ways to do such developmental activities as expressing our feelings, advancing our interests, and overcoming onerous problem patterns such as procrastination. Truly, the procrastinator's maze has many twists and dead-end pathways.

The Procrastination Gamble

There is more to this habit-conditioning process. Procrastination has some short-term benefits that reinforce this avoidance habit. One is a sense of relief that you have gotten yourself temporarily off the hook. Although such benefits are unpredictable and illusory, they can prove very influential.

There are other ways that you may seem to be rewarded for procrastinating. You may accidentally get some new information that simplifies the task. You get off the hook when someone else finishes the project for you, relieving you of task tension. You get considerable attention from others who encourage you to get things done. You view yourself as a clever fellow because you get away with your procrastination. In this sense, the con is like a gamble.

When you get two or three of these "rewards," they can reinforce a procrastination habit. According to conditioning theory, when you feel tense, resistant, or uncomfortable about doing something, then avoid the task and experience relief, you are likely to repeat the behavior that brought relief. Most people prefer immediate gratification to delayed gratification.

On the other hand, if you feel a rush of excitement that you might win the *procrastination gamble,* you might procrastinate again because you calculate that the odds will be better the next time. Getting these benefits for procrastinating can help make your procrastination more resistant to change.

Habits of Mind, Behavior, and Consumption

Problem procrastination can become even more debilitating when it combines with other tenacious problem habits, such as self-defeating habits of mind, behavior, and consumption.

Mind. Habits of the mind are invisible. Yet we see their marks everywhere. Procrastinators who habitually demand effortless success exhibit a habit of the mind. The well-known idea that "tomorrow is better" also represents a habit of mind. Habits of mind also include unrealistic fears of rejection, or well-rehearsed expectations that all people should adhere to your rules.

Some procrastinator's habits of mind include time-thief ideas such as, "I don't want to," "This is too hard," "I'll do it later." Unless you are aware of these habitual inner dialogues, you are likely to think more like a stewer than a doer.

Behavior. Problem behavior habits include nail biting, gambling, and, of course, procrastination. As you will see more of in chapter 5, procrastinators often substitute irrelevant behaviors that sidetrack them from unpleasant tasks. These substitute, or escapist, activities give them a false but temporary sense of accomplishment.

Consumption. Habits of consumption include substance abuse, such as drinking too much, overeating, or smoking. People who fall into this trap use rationalizations ranging from "I'll take care of my problem tomorrow" to "I'm not causing anybody any harm" to "I'll do what I want." In this sense, consumption habits and procrastination share a common core. Both activities involve making paper-thin excuses to explain away what the procrastinator doesn't want to face today.

Breaking the Habit

It normally takes time and a determined effort to kick a problem habit and sustain the advantage. For those who want a shortcut, there is the Gordian knot solution. According to an ancient myth, whoever unraveled the Gordian knot would rule the world. The ancient Macedonian king Alexander looked at the knot, examined its complexities, then drew his sword and cut it. You can apply the same Gordian knot principle: reverse your procrastination problem habit by simply doing the things that need to be done now.

If the Gordian knot solution seems too uncertain, there are other ways to break the problem habit. Our common sense and reasoning ability are our best hopes for kicking problem habits of the mind, of behavior, and of consumption. Through our reasoning ability, we can develop an awareness of what happens when we go through the problem habit process and we can teach ourselves to stop ourselves from carrying it through to its conclusion. We can train ourselves to dampen the habit fuse and avoid the discharge.

An alternative habit-breaking strategy involves developing an "easy attitude" toward the problem habit. When confronted with an urge to engage in your procrastination habit, allow yourself to experience the discomfort of not fulfilling the habit command without grimacing and tensing. This easy attitude allows you to experience the habit or avoidance urges, study them, and then do something else to get past them. The something else is to start the procrastinated activity at its logical beginning and let the feelings of resistance have a "life of their own" until they fade away.

A PROBLEM SYMPTOM

Procrastination can be a symptom of closely related problems: low frustration tolerance, discomfort dodging, and self-doubt "downing."

Low Frustration Tolerance

People with low frustration tolerance tend to overreact to circumstances that hinder or block their goals. They tend to be "sensation sensitive," living in fear of discomfort and intolerant of their own bad feelings. They often overfocus on their tensions and magnify them. They fear feelings of fear and discomfort and impulsively try to throw these feelings off through diversions or any other means of avoidance. Procrastination is a common by-product of this tension avoidance process.

People with low frustration tolerance act like *comfort junkies,* who demand that they get what they want without a hassle. For some members of this large group, life seems unbearably tough. Minor inconveniences rapidly become crises as members of this club preoccupy themselves with the injustice of being inconvenienced and how bad they feel.

To avoid hassles, this low frustration tolerance crowd procrastinates on developing perspective, self-control, and understanding. They feel strongly tempted to delay what they don't feel like doing. Their impulsive or avoidance acts often result in spoiling what they do, once they get around to doing it.

Discomfort Dodging

We *discomfort dodge* when we avoid any unpleasant but important activity because we want to avoid hassles. Like the snake phobic, who has an exaggerated fear of being bitten by a snake and thus never enters the woods, discomfort dodgers engage in faulty, misguided thinking.

People who procrastinate tend to be finely attuned to sensations of comfort and discomfort. They will do anything to avoid an anticipated source of discomfort. For example, some people on a warm day at the seashore resist jumping in the water and going swimming. They exaggerate in their minds the momentary discomfort of feeling cold before their bodies adjust to the temperature change. Yet once in the water, the same people are inclined to remark to themselves, "The water isn't really as cold as I thought; in fact, the water is quite pleasant." So it seems that often the resistance is found in the process of stewing before the doing.

In discomfort dodging the goal is to avoid feeling bad, uncomfortable, anxious, or inconvenienced. In a sense, people with an aversion to discomfort often inconvenience themselves by magnifying the meaning and significance of the uncomfortable activities. That makes the put-off activities seem more weighty and difficult than they are.

Discomfort dodging can intensify to the point that we avoid enjoyable activities when we associate some minor hassles with them. For example, you may think roller-skating is enjoyable but find the steps involved beforehand (dressing, putting the skates on) too much of a hassle, and thus a reason not to go.

We see this pattern of discomfort dodging in areas that require a lifestyle change. For example, recent information on the benefits of exercise, low-fat diets, and avoiding being overweight have challenged many who want to take advantage of this information, yet they put off making these important lifestyle changes because of the anticipated discomfort of changing their habits.

Procrastination is more than an inconvenience when it comes to health issues. The process can have a life-limiting effect. Yet we hear the familiar "I know this is good for me, and I will probably do something about it eventually."

There is something that people with this procrastinating mind-set want more than they want improved health. That something is to avoid the discomforts and restrictions that normally accompany a lifestyle change. However, restriction, responsibility, and persistence form the only safe path out of the procrastination jungle.

When you practice discomfort dodging, the tendency to continue practicing it gets stronger. This practice can culminate in an outcome where you put off small inconveniences, such as writing a letter of recommendation for a colleague, because of the minimal discomfort involved.

The subtle danger of discomfort dodging is that you tend to put small inconveniences aside—and then those small inconveniences grow into larger hassles. In this cycle we may remember to do them several times, then continue to put them off again, and finally complete them far too late, if at all!

Do It Now!

Discomfort Dodging

Stop fiddling with ideas about how difficult or unpleasant a task is and start doing something constructive to dispense with it. Commit to doing at least one "frustrating" activity each day that you would normally postpone.

Self-Doubt "Downing"

Albert Bandura's self-efficacy theory states that people who believe that they can exercise control over their lives will normally organize, coordinate, and regulate their activities around this belief. In other words, believing that you are effective and decisive will help you to act effectively and decisively. On the other hand, people who believe that they are generally ineffectual, or ineffectual at a specific task, are more inclined to procrastinate. A combination of low self-efficacy and anxiety can jointly contribute to expectations of failure, which results in a downward spiral of paralyzing procrastination.

Self-efficacy, personal confidence, and productivity are tightly linked. People who get reasonable things done in a reasonable way, within a reasonable time, normally view themselves as more able and effective. People who suffer from self-doubts usually live up to their poor expectations for themselves. At the extreme, self-doubters preoccupy themselves with their faults. When depressed, they very often seek confirmation of their negative views and may feel worse when reinforced or praised for their better actions.

A pattern of doubting one's abilities can lead to second-guessing, hesitations, self-doubt "downing," a sense of worthlessness, procrastination, and more self-doubts. So if a person doubts his ability to make friends, he can "down" himself for this presumed "defect," put off trying to make friends, and then "down" himself for having few friends. This self-handicapping series of actions represents a challenging set of barriers to overcome.

CONTINGENCY WORTH

As a practical matter, what we do is an extension of what we think and feel; our actions are really a partial representation of who we are. People who are used to just "getting by" have different aspirations from those who strive for excellence. They follow a pathway of mediocrity as though it were their inevitable lot in life. However, when we feel chronically unhappy and disturbed about ourselves, procrastination can be a symptom of our psychological self-portraits. Part of this results from tying our sense of worth to our performance.

People in achievement-oriented cultures normally place a high value on performance. In such an environment, people with unique skills and abilities in sports, business, the trades, professions, and so forth normally command high financial rewards and recognition for their accomplishments. Nevertheless, the rewards we receive for our accomplishments and what we perceive as our personal worth are different. You don't have to tie your entire personal worth to transitory, ever-changing rewards. Rewards and recognition may pass judgment on your performances, but they do not judge your *self*.

People who fall into the contingency worth trap (*contingent* means "dependent upon") think their worth and some of their select performances are the same. Because of this one-way style of thinking, they place themselves on a seesaw. Do well, and you are up. Do poorly, and you are down. With this mind-set, their sense of worth bounces between extremes.

SELF-CONCEPT DISTURBANCES

When you feel a sense of worthlessness, you are likely to have a self-concept disturbance. Self-concept disturbance is indicated when you persistently doubt yourself, second-guess yourself, hesitate, make half-hearted efforts, repeat yourself, fret about anticipated mistakes, over-compensate for a false sense of inadequacy, and avoid, escape, and evade action.

When you fall into this extreme contingency worth trap, you will likely suffer from performance anxiety and procrastinate. That typically happens when you place too much pressure on yourself to prove yourself and too little pressure on improving yourself. Under these conditions, you may believe that all failure is fatal. Within this procrastination paradox, you want to prove yourself but put off the sort of improving that might do the proving.

In this contingent state of mind, rather than risk exposing a fallibility, you'll reflexively put things off, particularly self-development activities that you can start at any time. You may even feel uneasy, uncomfortable, and hesitant to experiment with, say, a new computer software program when nobody is around because you hate feeling unsure and making mistakes. Entrenched in a pattern of self-doubts, you put a chill on learning new skills and deprive yourself of benefiting from this learning. In short, self-doubts often lead to self-doubt "downing." If you are uncertain of a stellar performance, you may "down" yourself in anticipation of not being good enough.

With this negative self-view and emotional tension, you are primed to act in a self-defeating way. You'll avoid beneficial opportunities because you don't think you deserve to succeed. With this mind-set, you consistently operate well below your potential or do something and snatch defeat from the hands of victory.

In a self-concept disturbance state of mind, doing well does not fit with your sense of identity. So you don't do well. Yet you don't just fear failure, you dread failure. Then, in a self-defeating tactic, you struggle to keep your self-concept frozen in time by concentrating on maintaining the status quo. Although you may still have dreams, you frustrate them through procrastination.

As self-observant creatures who can think and create, we can entertain many different ideas about ourselves. Thus we don't have to stick with a self-concept disturbance. Other views are possible.

Self-Concepts in Context

Our self-concept is stable but does change in different contexts. The normally tolerant, capable, confident, and dynamic trial lawyer may feel so insecure about herself when it comes to intimate relationships that she acts immaturely. A professional athlete concentrates on perfecting his athletic skills and allows little time for other activities. Although he becomes renowned in his sport he falls short on social skills.

In life we play many roles: child, friend, lover, parent, inventor, hobbyist, worker, manager, healer, and so forth. In each role our self-concept may vary. Procrastination occurs in some contexts more so than in others. Some settings may normally be free of procrastination. You can gain some insight into procrastination—and also into your self-concept—when you look at situations where you have a positive self-view and don't procrastinate and where you have a negative self-view and do procrastinate. What is the difference in the situations? What is the difference in your thinking about the situations?

The Synthesis

I have discussed discomfort dodging and self-doubt independently, but in reality they act in concert. Both self-doubt and discomfort dodging are usually the result of self-defeating attitudes.

When you believe that some activities are too onerous, inconvenient, or threatening to do right away, you'll organize, coordinate, and regulate your life around these avoidance beliefs. Under these conditions, you won't need a psychologist to tell you that you are going to feel self-rejecting or unhappy with yourself when you act according to your procrastination beliefs.

When people procrastinate for reasons of comfort or self-doubt, they normally substitute one activity for another, decide later is better, or avoid the issue altogether. When you make comfort your priority, this reflects a false need for freedom from hassles or from unpleasant emotional sensations. When comfort priorities reign, the person acts like an *ergophobe* (one who fears effort).

When we make our egos our main priority, we seek to protect that ego by striving for universal approval, perfection, and control. Procrastination then comes when we avoid activities that could potentially tarnish this fragile self-image. When you routinely see yourself backing away from challenges and shortchanging yourself on accomplishments and confidence, you fertilize the seeds of inferiority, and discomfort seems less tolerable.

These connected attitudes, like twin dragons of the spirit, plague the mind and block energies. When these two attitudes rule together, they retard advancement.

Self-doubt is an uncomfortable feeling. When it occurs in a person who wishes to dodge discomfort it becomes a signal of an inability to control one's thoughts and feelings. This in turn leads to more uncomfortable feelings of inadequacy. While you are in this reciprocal self-doubt and discomfort dodging cycle, the norm is stewing rather than doing. But fortunately, self-doubting and discomfort dodging attitudes are changeable habits of mind. These problematic attitudes are subject to the laws of learning. We learn these self-defeating procrastination-creating attitudes, and we can counter them by taking advantage of opportunities to do what you might normally put off.

OVERCOMING LOW FRUSTRATION TOLERANCE AND SELF-DOUBTS

Developing and sustaining a getting-it-done pattern can displace procrastination. You can accomplish this outcome by allowing yourself to:

1. Plan for attaining what you desire and follow the plan
2. Work to destroy the problem at its source (self-doubt and discomfort dodging)
3. Apply logical and objective evaluations
4. Actively engage projects you normally put off

Furthermore, since there is a strong interrelationship among self-doubt, discomfort dodging, and procrastination, changes in one can lead to changes in the other two.

Stress inoculation is a method where you subject yourself to increasing degrees of frustration to develop a tolerance for necessary tension. Start building frustration tolerance now by starting an activity that you normally would find frustrating. Tune into your inner voice of frustration. What does this voice say? What is valid? What is not? This brief analysis can give you some important insights into your "stop power," or how you put on the breaks in the face of frustration rather than starting to accelerate.

You can attack self-doubt "downing" by striving to develop your primary competencies. This striving for competency represents an extension of the self. Here the difference between contingent worth and self-development is the difference between proving your worth and improving your capabilities.

Striving for excellence usually has benefits. By striving to better use your potential, you can learn more about your positive qualities. While this process does not assure that you will develop an accepting self-concept, you are more likely to experience a growing sense of confidence in your abilities as a person who can produce measurable results. Consider the alternative: you withdraw and procrastinate and let you capabilities lie idle. What does that do for your self-concept?

PROCRASTINATION AS A DEFENSE

What do the following terms have in common: laxity, idleness, slackness, undisciplined, laissez faire, shirking, dodger, malingerer, couldn't-care-less attitude, and self-indulgence. They are all words and terms pejoratively applied to people who habitually delay. When the terms are applied to people, as opposed to their actions, they become over-generalizations, false characterizations, and are normally unwarranted. Perhaps character generalizations explain why people who procrastinate get defensive and develop excuse making to an art form. However, when procrastination results from a fear of failure, or is a disguise for a phobia or a symptom of self-doubt, it is hardly simply a case of slacking off.

Procrastination can be a defense against fear of failure, inadequacy, a sense of loss of control, or other unpleasant psychological malady. It also can occur because of negative beliefs about the onerous consequences of succeeding at a task. This is sometimes known as fear of success.

People behave defensively when they feel vulnerable, threatened, and sensitized. Defenses serve to protect "egos" from unpleasant awareness. So if you make your worth contingent on living according to your *ego ideal,* and the ideal is a real stretch for any reasonable human being, then you might dodge make-believe threats to your image by backing off from meeting timely challenges.

An outcome of the defensive procrastination ploy is that you can always tell yourself that if you tried, you might have done better. Now there is some hope for the future.

When you fear failure, you might put your mind to work to find ways to play it safe. Here you might think that major challenges might be better put off until another day or time—perhaps when you are better prepared or where you have a guarantee for success.

Some of us fear success. Fear of success is a defense in the following four ways:

1. When one fears being unable to keep up the pace
2. When success seems like too much of a strain, people with this outlook may doubt their ability to continue and see themselves fading and failing
3. When you don't think you deserve to succeed, which usually means that you'll find a way to sabotage your progress

4. When "success" is inconsistent with your sense of identity, doing better than you expect of yourself can threaten that identity

In short, fear of success is usually fear of the consequences of success.

▶ # Do It Now!

Fear of Failure

When you put your ego on the line, you may find many reasons to procrastinate to avoid failure. However, you can break this pattern. By looking at activities as experiments that improve your knowledge and ability to take on future tasks, you could use the feedback from your failures to build your resources and resiliency. This outlook essentially eliminates failure from your life. Now you've redefined your actions as a series of experiments. Here there are no failures, only learning what works, what doesn't work, and where you can improve.

Defusing Defensiveness

Procrastination is a paradoxical defense. With this *procrastination paradox* defensive ploy, you avoid doing the very things that would normally help you to develop confidence in your ability to get things done. Perhaps the primary question is what's at stake when you act defensively?

When you become defensive because you don't believe you are adequate to meet a reasonable challenge, then you might wisely try to figure out what "not being adequate" means. Does it mean that you lack practice? Does it mean that you would operate better in a league that is more consistent with your abilities? (Not everyone can play—or would want to play—in the major leagues in baseball, for example.) Do you believe that you are a substandard human being? Each of these premises has implications for understanding procrastination as a defense.

If you lack practice, how do you stop yourself from practicing? If you are expecting too much from yourself, you may scale up your efforts as you scale down false expectations. If you believe you are a substandard human being, perhaps you would best take this up with a cognitive behavior therapist who could help you defuse what you will soon enough discover is a spurious self-view.

How do you overcome a fear of success? Listen to what you tell yourself about success—the real inner message. Are you telling yourself you don't deserve to win, that you should let the other people have a chance, that you don't have the stuff to sustain a gain? Pin the idea down. Clarify it. Figure out why this line of thought is self-defeating. Then get skeptical about this false logic. Keep applying a reasoned skepticism until you can no longer find a reason to believe the unreasonable.

POSTSCRIPT

Chances are you habitually do something you'd like to stop. For example, do you want to quit worrying, smoking, gambling, drinking too much, or building up credit card debt?

Whatever our procrastination history, whatever the causes of procrastination, the ultimate solution remains the same. You overcome procrastination by what you do. You don't necessarily have to feel motivated. You can focus your mind on the problem and order your muscles into action to get it done.

It is easy to understand why you may decide to change and yet continue to fall short of your goals. Although the Do It Now! solution is simple, we may find ourselves tangled in a broad spectrum of conflicting procrastination motives. We may lose sight of our goal. We may fall into the trap of substituting one form of procrastination for another.

When you suffer from procrastination as a habit, symptom, and defense it can be tough to get rid of. But when you forcefully face each of these interacting conditions, constructive actions to shrink the procrastination behemoth in one way can simultaneously cause positive changes by creating refreshing new habits, frustration tolerance, and a positive self-concept.

Through your willingness to go forward and face new challenges, you can do much to unravel the procrastination paradoxes and overcome them. So what starts as a complex collection of weeds contains the seeds for new growth.

Diversionary Ploys

Those who were blind knew not of the elephant they touched. In folklore, the wheedler is the cajoler, conniver, bamboozler, flatterer, tempter, teaser, and deceiver. Sometimes the wheedler shifts from these roles and applies an arbitrary and coercively commanding pressure that demands obedience. We all have such a wheedler within us who is skilled in the art of deceiving. This wily part of us is sometimes so skillful in self-deception that the credibility of the con is seldom questioned.

Well-practiced procrastination diversionary routines, or self-cons, are clever distractions that create a temporary but false sense of well-being. It is almost as if we have a wheedler within that hypnotizes our minds and orchestrates our procrastination. The wheedler within is at its best when we render decisions that, in easing the burden of self-doubt, help us to dodge what we believe is uncomfortable. One such wheedler-inspired decision is to procrastinate.

THE WHEEDLER'S TACTICS

Of course, the person who decides to procrastinate rarely applies that label to the decision before the fact. Instead, the wheedler's voice guides us into putting off making an uncomfortable phone call or completing a report by gliding us into some substitute activity like eating a piece of cake. It also inspires the decision that later is a better time to

The wheedler

begin. The wily wheedler willfully supplies the seductive idea that delaying is a good thing until feelings of comfort and readiness prevail. Thus a sly decision that sounds like an action step is really done to avoid acting. The conscious or unconscious cagey decision to divert from the less comfortable priority to a substitute activity just serves to reinforce the procrastination habit.

Wily wheedler ways perpetuate procrastination. The sooner you recognize your procrastination diversions, and honestly and skillfully deal with them, the quicker you will start getting more done. To help you in this effort, I shall describe three major diversionary styles: action, mental, and emotional. I'll also suggest some ways to get beyond these crafty ploys.

ACTION DIVERSIONS

A person feels anxious about writing a report and finds chain-smoking, overeating, sleeping, playing solitaire, doing push-ups—almost anything but the report more rewarding. These action diversions, or "addictivities," are symptoms: the person detours from a priority to engage in more comfortable substitute behaviors. In a way, addictivities reflect an addiction to comfort.

When feeling discomfort at the prospect of squaring up against a "have to" activity that could stimulate uncomfortable self-doubts, some people take to these addictivities like a professional swimmer takes to water.

Computer Addictivities

People continue to find interesting new addictivities. For example, by the mid-1990s Internet use has become very common. Now we find tens of millions of people "surfing the net." Some use this medium to gather information and to communicate. However, I have met many "surfers" who get absorbed in the Internet to avoid facing many challenges of their daily lives—some spend fifty or more hours weekly in "chat rooms" and in other Internet diversions. In a sense, it is ironic that a device built to save time is a diversion for some to waste time.

Some spend too much of their time playing with computers, and this fascination leads to family problems and other interpersonal difficulties when these folk become unavailable to attend to activities of daily living. They become computer casualties. So although we have new ways to distract ourselves, the result is the same: people who procrastinate manage to find diversions; some diversions lead to further procrastination.

Home Office Addictivities

The burgeoning of the "home office" has created great opportunities for those who want to work on their own. But with this opportunity comes many challenges and, naturally, opportunities for procrastination. Here we find many frittering away their hours in diversionary pursuits such as hanging around the refrigerator and eating, spending hours on the phone, watching television, or mulling about doing things randomly. Some go shopping for supplies whenever they feel bored. To relieve the burdens of the day, chats with neighbors claim many casualties.

This process of artful dodging mimics many elements of the creative process. In both processes we become absorbed in and committed to the activity. But though two people who spend many hours working may appear similar, one may be a workaholic, artfully dodging discomfort by engaging in busywork and routinely running hard to catch up, while the other is a creatively involved artist, teacher, or businessperson.

Television and Escapism

Most human beings profit from recreational time, and television viewing is one way to relax. However, television viewing beomes an escapist activity when you routinely substitute channel surfing for priority activities.

If you watch television an average of 3 hours a day, this adds up to 21 hours a week or 65,520 hours over 60 years. Assuming you are awake 16 hours a day, this translates into 11.2 years of waking hours dedicated to television viewing. Imagine what you could do with these hours if you used them for developmental activities.

Of course, we're not designed to be perpetual motion machines. Therefore, I suspect that few television viewers would use all 65,520 hours for self-development work—we do require some downtime. Nevertheless, when you use television as an escapist activity, you might entertain this question: What am I trying to escape? The specific answer to this question is as important as the realization that you are using television viewing as a substitute for more important activity.

Pseudoconflicts

Procrastination is complicated by pseudoconflicts that divert you from resolving a real conflict. One such conflict is the "Should I or shouldn't I?" debate. This is an addictivity in the sense that you preoccupy yourself with a self-induced conflict instead of getting on with productive activities.

Here's how pseudoconflicts can come into play: you become anxious worrying about a perceived problem, such as your popularity. You convince yourself that no one likes you. You feel tense. Then you develop an urge to eat all the cake in the refrigerator to snuff out the tension. Next the diversionary conflict erupts: "Should I or should I not eat the cake?" The "to eat or not to eat" conflict escalates the anxiety. When you believe that your anxiety will continue if you don't eat the cake, you decide to resolve the conflict by eating the cake.

Thus, rather than taking on the root cause of your anxiety—your concern over your popularity—you distract yourself with a meaningless pseudoconflict over the cake. The real problem is put off and forgotten until it reappears later still unresolved.

Overcoming Addictivities

If you are aware of the ways you divert yourself, you can start to change this pattern now! Start by listing your suspected addictivities (reading, smoking, cleaning, talking on the phone). Identify the goals from which these addictivities divert you. Note *when* you are likely to employ diversions (e.g., "When I anticipate going to a social affair"). Now, use the onset of the diversion as a *signal* to deal with situations you feel normally tempted to derail with an addictivity. Try these techniques:

> ➤ Keep your eye on the original problem (in our example: popularity) and try to identify precisely what is bothering you. Determine if the problem is largely real or imaginary; work at solving the real problem.
> ➤ Disrupt "Should I or shouldn't I?" delaying conflicts by internally screaming STOP! each time you get into one of these phony conflicts. Here is where a diversion can pay off. The STOP! distracts you from the pseudoconflict. You can then abandon the pseudoconflict and concentrate on the real problem.
> ➤ Bear with the discomfort by contracting with yourself that you won't eat the cake (make the phone call, place a bet on the horses, argue with your spouse) for at least fifteen minutes. In that time the desire to pursue the action diversion normally fades.
> ➤ Watch for seductive wheedler reasoning in which you give yourself appetizing reasons for engaging in the addictivity: "What is the harm?"; "It will feel good"; "Why deprive myself?"; "You deserve to have some pleasure." Tune into the subterfuge behind these seductive ideas, challenge the wheedler, work that crafty character into a corner, and make *it* hold up the white flag.
> ➤ Make up a series of questions like the following to ask yourself whenever you start to con yourself into the addictivity: (1) What makes it so important for me to have to _____ (addictivity) right this minute? (2) Why do I need to feel good by _____ing? (addictivity). (3) What other forms of pleasure can I have right now that will help me over time? (4) If I deserve to have some pleasure, why do I need the displeasure of the after-

math of _____? (addictivity). You can write these questions on a three-by-five card, in a message on your computer, or tape-record them and play them back during an addictivity crisis.

➤ Use a paradoxical technique to exaggerate your situation. The technique involves purposefully carrying on an exchange with yourself like this: "You poor soul. You really can't handle discomfort. You really have a good reason to doubt yourself because in truth you really are helpless to fight your urges. These urges are too big and strong for you to ignore—give in to them and keep on giving in to them. Feel good for the moment. Your living in the moment is all that matters now. Don't look to the next moment." This technique can help you build a healthy opposition to the addictivity and is not a means of putting yourself down.

➤ # Do It Now!

Addictivities

You also can contain your addictivities through your powers of concentration. For example, habits are instantly broken when doing so is important enough. Suppose you traveled to a country whose inhabitants drive on the left side of the road. If you decide to drive, you quickly adapt to the left side. You have the capacity to break habits and can put that capacity to use even when your immediate survival is not at stake. Try using these powers to curb your addictivities.

Short-Circuit the Switchover Technique

The night before an important biology examination, we find our procrastinating heroine busily consumed in reading her text in English grammar and going over her mistakes on the last examination. Unfortunately, she still has much material to study to pass the biology exam. Here the student is engaging in what I call a *switchover technique.*

Switchover occurs when you shift from an urgent but difficult task to an important but lower-priority task. Although a common procrastination ploy, you can turn diversion to advantage. Switchover can be helpful if you agree to spend only five minutes on the diversionary activity and then to use the momentum built up during that five minutes to switch back to the priority task.

MENTAL DIVERSIONS

Imagination can be a great source of new ideas, but it can also be a mental vehicle for ducking the unpleasant. Clever creatures that we are, we sometimes use imagination for diversion. We can dodge problems through our intellectual processes, sometimes creating complex ways to think ourselves out of acting productively. These habits of the mind involve wheedler thinking.

People have many irrational reasons to procrastinate. No matter the area of procrastination, many procrastinators generally create a false optimism, believing that their problems will be easier to contend with in the future. Unfortunately, this "better future" concept disguises the reality that procrastination patterns will not magically disappear someday in the future. Because of this unrealistic thinking, the procrastination pattern thwarts both present and future happiness.

We have a marvelous ability to create mental myths. Through this imaginative capacity, we can entertain one another around campfires by telling tales of frightening monsters that exist only in the world of the mind. Through imagination we create these illusions that seem real but are not that way at all!

We are equally adept at creating procrastination myths that gain credibility because they sound so sincere and real at the time that we may feel a glow of confidence that what we put off will really get done. However, like any illusion, we judge its worth by its results. Such procrastination lingers over our heads like the Sword of Damocles hanging by a hair.

Our procrastinating thinking patterns are schemas around which we interpret experience; they describe how we organize our experience. These schemas, or mental patterns, shape and constrain perception, provide understanding, and explain and guide our responses.

A schema asserts influence over *experience*. People with strong tendencies for procrastination thinking, for example, have schemas that draw on memories that produce visceral reactions when they first perceive an unwanted activity. These procrastination schemas, or memory traces, come to the foreground whenever we face an uncomfortable activity that we want to postpone. The four major *mental diversions* that supply the tune for these hesitation waltzes are the *mañana trap,* the *contingency mañana, catch-22,* and *backward* traps.

The Mañana Trap

Have you heard the story of the person who announced that he would straighten out his files in his next life after reincarnation? That's the extreme end of the mañana ploy, or the art of putting off until tomorrow what you can do today.

People wheedle themselves into procrastinating by convincing themselves that they will get the uncomfortable task done tomorrow or sometime soon. When tomorrow comes, they tell themselves the same nonsense again.

Mañana is a powerful self-deception. The ploy enables a person to:

➤ Avoid admitting he or she is procrastinating
➤ Avoid looking at the roots of the problem
➤ Maintain a good image
➤ Feel hopeful

Several false assumptions undergird the mañana idea:

➤ "There is nothing wrong with delay if I get to it at another day or time."
➤ "I'll begin later when I'm rested."
➤ "Perhaps later this will come easier."

Students are great adherents to this principle, particularly those who decide to put off their homework until after the party or after supper.

Mañana comes in many forms. John wants to get in shape so that he can make a good appearance at the beach. The thought of exercising and losing twenty pounds doesn't appeal as much as the result of "looking good." Our wannabe he-man decides to start later. Once he tells himself later is better, he now feels better because he has plenty of lag time before he starts. He thinks, "No need to rush into these things."

John starts his program late in the fall. He soon quits. He rationalizes by saying, "It is too late in the season for developing physical fitness to make a difference. I'll start again in the spring."

The mañana principle has tricky layers. One of these subploys includes the element of waiting for the "moment of inspiration."

A person who believes he can work only when inspired, temporarily eases tension by assuming work will be easier later because it will be done with inspiration. Unfortunately, "moments of inspiration" are rare and typically fizzle after a brief flourish of activity.

Mañana and Murphy's Law. Psychologists Arnold A. and Clifford N. Lazarus in their book, *The Sixty Second Shrink: 101 Strategies for Staying Sane in a Crazy World*, point out that most procrastination ideas are task-interfering thoughts. Mañana ideas are classic examples of such task-interfering thoughts. They thrust today's activities into the future where they become susceptible to Murphy's Law.

In 1949, military captain Edward Murphy observed that if something can go wrong, it often will go wrong. Murphy believed that if there are more than two ways of doing something, and one way will lead to catastrophe, someone will do it wrong. Moreover, random events, rare occurrences, and unexpected snafus can combine to gobble the time it takes to get something done as well as ruin a result.

The eleventh-hour rush, which so often follows a mañana procrastination decision, strengthens the validity of Murphy's Law. You decide you will let some ideas "simmer" before you write your report. The eleventh hour arrives. In a frenzied dash, you begin to work using your computer as a word processor. You have your report partially done and accidentally hit a wrong key combination. You receive this error message: "You have performed an illegal function. Your data will be lost." Unfortunately, in your haste to complete the report, you didn't save the material. Now you have to start from scratch.

In the wee hours of the morning, as you sit red-eyed over an empty pot of coffee, you finish the report. You hit your print control. You get another message on your screen. You are low on ink. You execute the print command and keep your fingers crossed. Relieved, you see the first page print dark. Unfortunately, your fourth through fifth pages fade and you can't read the remaining twelve pages. You have no replacement ink cartridges. At 4:00 A.M., you have no hope of rousing a store owner out of sleep so you can buy a cartridge. The size of your disk is 3.5 inches, but the computers at your office use the ancient 5.25-inch floppy variety, so you can't print your work when you arrive at the office. At 8:00 A.M., you are scheduled to present your report to your company's steering committee. Murphy's Law strikes again.

The existence of Murphy's Law argues for giving yourself ample slack time to get important things done. Completing reports a week in advance of schedule gives you the opportunity to avoid negative, randomly occurring eleventh-hour pitfalls.

The Contingency Mañana Trap

You have a burning desire to write the great American novel and make a fortune from the movie rights. To assure that you have the right writing tools, you decide to enroll in a Ph.D. program in English. You feel convinced that this is an important and necessary step on the way to your goal. Next you put off filing your graduate school application because you want to do more research to find the best graduate English program. Welcome to the world of contingency mañana.

The contingency mañana ploy operates when a person makes completing an emotionally important project dependent upon completing a less important one first. Thus the procrastinator gives unimportant, irrelevant, but deceptively credible preliminary activities priority over the main activity. Now there are *two* things to procrastinate about—the substitute activity and the relevant activity.

The contingency mañana principle is an important component of many procrastination problems. It is a subtle but powerful delaying tactic. The following examples illustrate how the principle works.

George procrastinated about establishing new friendships. First he excused himself by claiming that it wouldn't pay to try until he moved into a new apartment. After all, until then he wouldn't have a comfortable room in which to entertain his guests. When he moved into a new apartment (after six months' delay), he decided he had to furnish it lavishly before he could have visitors. After all, he couldn't have any prospective friends think he lived in barren surroundings. When George bought furniture, he discovered that he didn't have attractive curtains, so he then deluded himself into believing that he had to have the "right" curtains to entertain properly. He searched two months for the "right" curtains and then ordered curtains that wouldn't be delivered for six to eight weeks.

George points with pride to his preparatory accomplishments. He found a new apartment, moved in, bought new furniture, and ordered curtains. But by setting up his contingencies in this way, he delayed reaching out to potential friends.

George sets up contingencies to cover his fears. He believes he can't establish friendships until he reorganizes his apartment. Secretly, he fears that he won't make friends even if his apartment looked like a *House Beautiful* picture. Nevertheless, he repeatedly detours his efforts away from directly dealing with his basic fear of rejection.

The contingency mañana appears in other forms. Lou won't ask Suzie to marry him until he's "ready" (saved money, straightened out his head). "Somehow" he spends more than he earns and excuses himself from starting therapy because of the lack of financial resources.

Judy won't start her weight-loss program until she's sure that she has obtained and read all the scientific literature on that subject. She tells us she wants to make sure that she does it the right way. Then she avoids the library work because she thinks she needs to take a course on how to do a scientific literature review. Then she procrastinates on learning to do the research.

What do the mañana and contingency mañana ploys have in common? The decision to do today's unwanted activity in the future. Both excuses sound appealing but lead to ongoing delays in completing the activity. Nevertheless, the mañana or contingency mañana decision may cause us temporarily to feel better because we anticipate that we will take action sometime. We've made a decision. The sow's ear again has become a silk purse.

The Catch-22 Trap

The catch-22 diversion is similar to the contingency mañana principle. In each case there is a condition that we must meet before a primary project can be directly and actively dealt with. However, with the contingency mañana principle there is at least a theoretical chance to succeed. But with the catch-22 ploy there is no chance. If you hold to this view, you're finished before you start.

In Joseph Heller's novel *Catch-22*, the character Yossarian wanted to get out of the army. The only way to get out was to be adjudged crazy. If he claimed he was crazy, the authorities wouldn't discharge him because it is normal to appear crazy under wartime conditions. On the other hand, if he didn't do anything, they wouldn't notice him at all. In short, there was no way out. This is catch-22.

Wayne fell into the catch-22 trap. He decided that he had to look like a male model to have a charming mate, but that mate would also have to look like a willowy model. Since Wayne doesn't look that good and probably never will (even with plastic surgery), he concludes that he can't find romance.

Wayne could only accept a beautiful woman as a mate. However, since he was fat, bald, and fifty, he thought no beautiful, willowy woman would want him. Once when a beautiful woman seemed interested in him, he sabotaged the relationship because "she had to have bad taste to show interest in me."

Sally joined Wayne in the catch-22 club. She believed that she could not get a promotion unless she had an M.B.A. degree. She also believed that she did not have a high enough IQ to get the degree. Although she had never had an IQ test and graduated with a 3.6 average in college, she convinced herself that she was doomed to stay in her current customer service role forever. Because she convinced herself that nobody would promote her, she avoided initiative and appeared to management like a person "well suited for her current position."

Wayne and Sally created self-fulfilling prophecies. They did not get what they wanted because they foreclosed on themselves from the start. The power of catch-22 is that you can't win even when you can win.

Caught in the catch-22 mind-set, the players often view themselves as victims of impossible circumstances. While this view frequently brings on gloomy and depressed moods, the excuse makes it easier to assume the role of a self-declared martyr because one so nobly faces impossible "odds."

The Backward Trap

Some of us look back into our past in a way that takes time from today. People caught in the *backward trap* go on psychological expeditions into their past in the hope of finding mental artifacts in their history to explain their current problems. Sometimes these archaeological pursuits cause their own form of procrastination problems. Many of these self-initiated journeys lead to dead ends, as they take time and effort from what you can do today.

The backward ploy binds us to the past. We often procrastinate on current activities while stuck in a historical abyss. While dwelling on our past, we neglect our present and sabotage our future. Thus people who look for what went wrong in their past often think of negative experiences over which they either had no conrol or can't remedy today. Rather than find answers in the past, they normally find new sources for distress.

Many such *seekers* see their lives as a series of mistakes and deprivations. They blame themselves for events that often they were not able to control. Then they feel hopeless because they cannot change what was. I have yet to find anybody who has managed to work him- or herself out of the rut through this method.

June habitually ruminated about her past. She thought about the negative experiences she had with her parents. She recalled feeling humiliated by them. She blamed herself for her parents' bickering and for her mother's bout with alcoholism. She lamented that she should have been able to stop the family conflicts and to protect her younger brothers from learning about their father's affair with his secretary.

June felt hopeless because of the oppressive thoughts she had about her past. June still rummaged through the labyrinth of her mind to "discover truth" and to sort out what had brought her to this point in her life. "Perhaps," she thought, "I could free myself and get on with my life." Yet the harder she tried to find the "truth" in her past, the further behind she fell on daily maintenance activities and the more often she felt overwhelmed.

Although having insight into the relationship between key historical events and your contemporary problems can have value, mulling over past hurts does not change the past. The past is done, gone, kaput!

What happened, happened. Whether it should not have gone that way or whether other events should have transpired is irrelevant.

Don't get me wrong. The past is relevant. Our cumulative experiences assert powerful influences on how we think and feel and what we do today. However, our memories can be quite selective and fallible. As suggestible creatures we have a remarkable capacity to magnify, embellish, and exclude information from our mental vision. We often don't question some more negative generalizations in our thinking. And while our selective perceptions, recollections, and images can be very influential for shaping our current outlook, when we make the past a present absorption, we take time and energy from what we have and can do today.

Although you probably can recall many negative past events, you have the option of reframing the events from more than one balanced and reasoned perspective. When you reframe, you look at the picture from different angles. Through this reframing process you might conclude, "If nothing else, I'm alive and have choices!" That's clearly a desired perspective.

What happened to June? At my suggestion she talked with her brothers, who, as it turned out, had quite a different view of their parents. June's brothers thought that their childhood was good about 90 percent of the time. True, they reported rough spots in their parents' relationship, but their parents normally resolved their problems. As to their mother's alcohol abuse, this lasted about eighteen months, and she has not had a drink since. There was no evidence that their father had an affair. June assumed this because her father acted friendly toward his secretary.

Her brothers reminded her that except during the eighteen-month period when their mother acutely abused alcohol, both parents normally attended their kids' school activities. Both showed considerable affection to all their children.

June came away from that discussion with her brothers with a different point of view. She started to tackle her own career and family problems that she had been putting off. Within a few months after those revelations, June showed solid progress in dealing with her maintenance and development procrastination challenges.

We normally pay a price for past misdeeds. Our histories will have many disappointments, frustrations, untoward events, and favorable events, joys, and satisfactions. What we mainly have control over is what we now do and how we plan and prepare for the future. The past is a guide, but our voice of reason also guides and can keep us focused on doing what we can do.

Recognizing and Dealing with Mental Diversions

Try the following breakaway ideas to escape from the mental diversion traps:

1. Write down three activities you currently put off that you strongly would like to complete.

   _____ .

   _____ .

   _____ .

2. List what you tell yourself that causes you to delay. Listen to your inner wheedler voice. Do you hear yourself saying any of the following?: "I'll get to it tomorrow." "Not right now." "I'll do this after I do something else first." "Later." "I'll never succeed."

   _____ .

   _____ .

   _____ .

3. List the advantages of doing it now. For example, pretend you have a crystal ball. What advantages do you see in your future if you progress in overcoming the procrastinated activities you listed?

   _____ .

   _____ .

   _____ .

As you write out this counterprocrastination process, your choices should come into a sharper focus. The wheedler voice, for example, often has less influence when detected.

Once you have exposed your wheedler habit of mind, try to change the pattern by establishing an objective for each put-off activity. As an example, let's take "I want to weigh 150 pounds and maintain my weight at that level." Then:

➤ Determine what you will do to meet that objective. For example, identify the number of daily calories needed to maintain weight at 150 pounds.

➤ Over each weekly period, do not exceed the daily number of calories required to maintain your weight at 150 pounds.

➤ Counter mental diversions by verbalizing aloud to yourself: "What seems tough to start today will probably be just as tough tomorrow." "I certainly can begin the first step, so I must have the ability to follow with the second step." "Even if I have the ability to complete the program before I start, I can learn to develop my skills as I go."

➤ Recognize that creating a self-loathing outlook, because you used mental diversions before, is a distraction that turns a real silk purse (recognizing your problem) into a sow's ear.

➤ If you can invent mental diversions, you have creative powers you can channel for purposeful ends. See if you can't *imagine* a way to convert mental diversions into a creative productive process.

➤ When you hear your wheedler voice, change the voice to the voice of a rival or a person you would normally prefer to avoid. This immediately casts the wheedler in a different light. The wheedler con is not likely to sound so seductive when conveyed through the voice of a rival.

EMOTIONAL DIVERSIONS

A classic procrastination ploy is to wait to feel emotionally ready before acting. This is the contingency mañana ploy with an emotional twist.

People procrastinate because they get too deeply involved in avoiding and escaping challenges. They attempt these escapes by immersion in various dysfunctional feel-good solutions. Immobilizing emotional diversions can result from psychological inhibitions to participate in new ventures. They are an attempt to insulate oneself from a tendency that is too readily triggered to believe that facing a conflict will feel too uncomfortable.

Emotional diversions also overlap with addictivities. People who think they need to feel good sometimes resort to the use of addictive substances. These escapist pursuits include getting stoned to melt the pangs of psychic pain and produce temporary euphoria; drinking alcohol to get a high, to lose inhibitions, or to forget; taking amphetamines to speed up and stimulate; popping Valium or Xanax to calm and tranquilize.

People who feel depressed often believe they don't have the energy to act; or they think, why bother, whatever I do will be futile. Yet activity is often among the best remedies for depression.

Another emotional crutch is to get rid of bad feelings (anxiety, depression) by trying to force those feelings out of awareness. Singing or repeating rhymes to oneself is one way of blocking feelings, and this method sometimes temporarily works. But attempts to will bad feelings away typically result in the procrastinator being more deeply enveloped by the unwanted feelings. It is this strict focus on getting rid of the feelings that signals an emotional diversion. The person becomes more entangled with unpleasant thoughts about the feelings, desperately ruminates on how to get rid of the feelings, neglecting the real problem.

What unites these different emotional diversionary tactics? It is the motivation to escape the unpleasant and to procrastinate in taking on your real problems. In the end, all such feel-good methods fail because they don't solve real problems.

The Escapist Sequence

Emotional diversions flow along different pathways. One process involves the following sequence: a person first experiences a negative feeling (anxiety), becomes increasingly aware of it, and then decides to get rid of the anxiety to feel good. This desire leads to attempts to force the feeling to go away. But the feeling doesn't disappear. Perhaps the anxiety is an emotional signal that a problem exists that requires attention. Trying to squelch the feeling doesn't get rid of its trigger. Perhaps thinking about the feeling and trying to force it out of awareness only fuels it. In any event, the more effort expended trying to eliminate the feeling, the more the feeling persists.

This process can erupt without much warning. The person fears feeling bad and is sensitive to slight, negative emotional changes, and a downturn in the emotional barometer escalates the escapist process to panic proportions with a triggering anticipation such as "Oh, no, here it [the feeling of anxiety] comes again!" Now it becomes even more important to stop the flow of feelings. When that happens, the unwanted feeling burgeons.

A frenzied effort to force the rapidly escalating anxiety out of awareness, rather than on solving the problems or correcting the irrational thoughts that may have evoked this sensation, leads to *double troubles* when you not only suffer the original anxiety but also now anguish over the anxiety itself. This immobilizing anxiety causes you to procrastinate in finding and fixing the real problem.

The flip side of this emotional diversion is becoming enraptured with a positive feeling by getting carried away with good feelings. Upon receiving a compliment, you might glow and preen to a state of ecstatic excitement. Once aware of this great glow, you may try to sustain it, and this has a paradoxical effect. The good feeling slips. In this case, you procrastinate because you become obsessed with restoring the good feelings, rather than meeting your next challenge.

Dealing with Emotional Diversions

Engulfing yourself in unpleasant feelings often is a result of seeking answers to the wrong questions. By asking yourself, "How am I going to feel less tense . . . how am I going to feel happy?" you could be seeking a magical way to manufacture a good feeling or could be asking yourself a rhetorical question that has this answer: there is no way out. These feel-good questions are incomplete when the answers don't address what to do to *get it done.* Thus the question is misleading and counterproductive. For example, John wondered how he was going to feel less tense when he attended a business conference to present facts on a computer program his company had developed. One solution might be to learn relaxation techniques or to pop tranquilizers. Either solution might help reduce tension. But since John was attending the conference to make a presentation, the relevant question was "How can I make my talk effective? What strategies can I employ to make my points clear?" When John asked relevant questions, he healthfully passed over the contingency questions and dealt directly with the problem. As a by-product of his working to solve the problem, he overcame his tension.

The following steps may help you to accomplish similar goals:

➤ Review instances in which you become entangled in negative feelings.
➤ Note what you are attempting to accomplish in such circumstances.
➤ Jot down the external problems that you are trying to contend with. Ask questions concerning how you can accomplish such objectives (rather than become absorbed in a hapless pursuit of trying to feel better).
➤ When you begin to feel flooded with anxiety (depression), give up your struggle to control your feelings. Instead, engage in activity directed at contending with the problem. So rather than rid yourself of the anxiety directly, try shifting your attention to acting purposefully to resolve the problem.
➤ If you become enveloped in excitement, it is just as important to frame a question concerning why you are overresponding. Exaggerated feelings of elation are profoundly pleasant while they

last but can prove disorganizing. To maintain a state of objectivity about the sources of these excited feelings critically examine the stimulating condition, your thinking about the condition, and the outcome of this surge of good feeling.

POSTSCRIPT

Procrastination is a choice. Putting things off represents a decision. The reasons for the decision are likely to be interesting, informative, and yield some answers. However, whatever the form and causes of procrastination, the output is behavioral: you do something to get the short-term benefit of avoiding something productive that you feel uncomfortable doing.

We are myth-making creatures with great capabilities of inventing fictions to explain reality. We do this every day, and often we are unaware of what we are doing. Fictions weaken our action decisions and strengthen avoidance decisions.

The various ways we have to sanitize our procrastination habit are how we also make up science fiction stories. Through personal art and guile we conjure up some stories that are very convincing. At least, we often fool ourselves with our own creations.

Procrastination pushes activities into the future when they may or may not get finished. The procrastination solution is sometimes a subtle renunciation of the "self." For example when you promise yourself you'll do something tomorrow, and when tomorrow comes, you put it off again, what does this say about the value you place in the promises that you make to yourself?

Allowing the wheedler side of our personality to run the show puts limits on our ability to do many things we needlessly delay. Beating this wheedler involves recognizing the wheedler and refusing to accept wheedler excuses, activities, or emotional entanglements. Instead, you forthrightly face your procrastination, stand on your integrity, and get it done.

6

Patterns of Change

In This Chapter

➤ The five steps to change: Awareness, Action, Accommodation, Acceptance, and Actualization

Along the paths of life we find many branches and opportunities to change. Change and development are processes, not events. Eventually developmental efforts lead to the question "What has happened that is different?" The following five stages of change and a final section on "flies in the ointment" map a path to change.

Let's look at a five-stage awareness and action process to learn Do It Now! skills. You can use this structure to guide yourself through the labyrinths of the mind, past the time barriers of procrastination, and beyond that to a life of mastery. The five steps to change are *awareness, action, accommodation, acceptance,* and *actualization.*

AWARENESS

How do you know when you need to stop doing one thing and start doing something else?

Awareness is a conscious recognition and understanding of the significant things that are happening within and around you. For example, once you are clear that your procrastination does you much more harm than good, you have reached a state of awareness where you have a choice to act now, later, or never in squaring off against this thief of time.

It normally takes time, space, and increasing mental and action skills to break from a procrastination pattern. You might make this happen *sooner than later* by developing your understanding of the stages that people follow when they go from routinely procrastinating to improving and progressing in getting things done and having more fun.

Awareness is not an all-or-nothing affair. This process exists at different levels of consciousness from oblivion to enlightened understanding.

Oblivion

Most of us don't pay much attention to our cognitive processes. We know they are there. We know that we sometimes think too much, don't think enough, or are too forgetful about what we don't want to remember. We also can come up with good ideas to solve problems and can apply knowledge and experience. However, we often leave our thoughts unquestioned.

In a state of oblivion, we don't pay attention to what we believe or tell ourselves. We react. So when procrastination is a habit, we pay more attention to avoiding and excusing than to the cues, thoughts, and muscular reactivity that trigger procrastination. We might be inclined to blame other folk, circumstances, our histories—practically anything but our attitudes of mind underlying the procrastination we perpetuate. Yet what we need to know to develop a map of this habit territory is often very close to the surface of conscious awareness. We just don't pay enough attention.

Without awareness, we have no basis for self-initiated change. True, you can find external agents and conditions that can reshape your procrastination activities. An employer tells you to get a report in on time "or else." You want to keep your job, so you override your procrastination voices and habit pattern to save your job. You are a recruit in the military. You keep your area policed and tend to your maintenance functions to avoid unpleasant consequences.

But except in highly regimented and structured environments, where there is tight follow-up, we are normally the ones who structure our time to cause the results we seek to produce. This is normally the case in self-developmental activities where we seek to improve ourselves through getting better and more effective at what we do. But unless we have an awareness of why we put off such activities, we are likely to exist in a state of oblivion.

The Twilight Zone

In the *twilight zone* of awareness you begin to make the first connections between what is going on within you and the events around you. In this stage you may experience a nagging sense of discomfort. This can be a positive signal. Discomfort is informative.

When you first enter the twilight zone of awareness, you can come up with thousands of rationalizations and excuses to explain away what you do not want to see or believe. These rationalizations include: (1) perhaps circumstances will change on their own, or (2) you need to go on a psychological expedition into your past to find the answers to set yourself free. These diversionary pursuits are like psychoscopes (looking outwardly through a distorted inner "lens") that keep reality out of focus.

Enlightened Self-Awareness

Twilight turns to light when you make the connection between your more serious procrastination actions and their consequences. Once you see the procrastination problem for what it is, you have the choice of doing something to fix it. If you don't see how you are motivating yourself to procrastinate, and you don't think to develop actions to overcome procrastination, how are you to change this self-defeating pattern?

You are entering an *advanced stage* of awareness when you begin to make connections between your thoughts, feelings, and actions. Now you can better establish an optimistic direction where you don't yield to your procrastination urges. You are on the threshold of *enlightened* awareness.

Enlightened self-awareness engages our capacity to know, to discover, to invent, to prevent, or to cope in ways that generally bend our interests to reality. This level of awareness enables you to feel a connection between your constructive beliefs and what you do.

How do you develop an enlightened awareness? In our waking hours, we are constantly observing, acting, and processing information. Throughout life we receive responses from the results of our beliefs and actions. We also receive reactions from others. The art is to discriminate between truth and deception. We also learn from reading books and booklets that give information about change. Some ideas that we read may strike a welcome chord.

We can develop enlightened awareness in other ways. Critical events can occur that consume attention. You may experience a job loss, a broken relationship, a failing grade, or learn that you are at coronary risk. Through the medium of such critical experiences, you may force yourself to deal with your psychology to bring your inner world back into balance.

Positive critical events are also catalysts for invention and change. However, opportunities and challenges slip by when we deceive ourselves by thinking that later there will be another opportunity. This "tomorrow" mind-set can make it seem as if the hourglass will forever turn and that the grains of sand that flow through time will remain endlessly in motion.

The Procrastination Log

The procrastination log is a simple awareness-development strategy to keep track of what is going on when you procrastinate. This log is a useful platform for recognizing procrastination patterns and trends, and it can provide information to help you develop plans and actions for making change.

Organize your journal entries by putting each procrastination situation on a separate page. Following this procedure you are better able to compare similarities and differences among procrastination events. By following five or more different procrastination situations, you'll develop concrete data to formulate an action plan.

After about six weeks of recording your procrastinations—sometimes sooner—you can often see patterns and trends that can help you define the general process you follow when you procrastinate. However, some readers will find that once they decide to keep a log, they have fewer acts of procrastination to record because the log reminds them to stop procrastinating, and so they procrastinate less.

In devising their procrastination log, some people prefer a "freewheeling" approach. They record their thoughts, feelings, and observations in each separate procrastination category and make new entries in their journal as events unfold. This gives them a running tally of the process they put themselves through as they procrastinate.

The procrastination log can follow a highly structured approach where you: (1) list the activity you put off; (2) define whether it falls into maintenance or developmental procrastination or into another procrastination category; (3) record your initial thoughts and feelings about the postponed activity; (4) identify diversionary tactic(s); (5) assess the impact of the procrastination decision (Who does it affect and how?); (6) estimate the short-term and long-term benefits and disadvantages. You can add other categories to a structured journal, including procrastination motivations such as discomfort dodging, self-doubt, or habit. You can build in a subsection for recording general observations and another for your insights.

There is currently no compelling evidence to say which procrastination log structure is generally more effective for what type of procrastination style. Thus, you may find that an unstructured approach, where you make a running tally and blend different acts of procrastination together in your log, is as helpful as any other journal approach.

You may want to experiment with your procrastination log. If you prefer a freewheeling style, try a structured approach. If you prefer a highly structured approach, try a running tally approach. Sometimes these intentional changes can enable you to step outside of your normal way of perceiving to gain a slightly different perspective on what is happening when you procrastinate.

ACTION

Awareness and action interact. Awareness is an "inner" action when it represents a change of thought and heart. Awareness also blends into *action*. However, you formally enter the action phase of change by taking concrete, measurable steps in your behavior to help achieve your goals. Here you translate your constructive beliefs into movement.

In this action phase, you may discover that your original analysis was on the mark because the results you produce are consistent with your original judgment. However, the results of what you do also may differ from what you anticipated. Now you have information from your actions that you can use to modify your plan, and this feeds back to your sense of awareness.

Awareness is critical to overcoming procrastination but action is more so. Analogously, awareness about how to drive an automobile is different from driving. Reading ten books on how to drive an automobile will not make you an expert driver if you have not driven before or have limited experience. You can, however, get from a book ideas about where to put the key, how to steer your car, how to make right turns, and other aspects of driving. You can, in other words, plan or prepare to drive successfully, but you can develop on-the-road driving skills only by setting driving as your goal and then by practicing driving.

Setting Achievable Goals

Self-improvement normally begins with goal setting. Effective goal setting requires time and effort to plan and follow through.

Goal setting also involves looking closely at what you want to accomplish. Will overcoming a specific procrastination pattern help you improve the quality of your life, reduce unnecessary strain, help you achieve important long-term objectives, or aid you in building self-confidence? If your goals promise those results, then you have incentives for overcoming that particular procrastination pattern. Other incentives may include getting a burden off your back, the good feeling that comes with living in a clutter-free environment, or doing the self you will be in the future a favor by eliminating a dysfunctional procrastination habit.

General goals include managing frustrations, improving interpersonal skills, building self-acceptance, getting and staying organized, or coping effectively with self-sabotaging irrational thinking patterns.

Once you've established a general goal, break it down into measurable specifics (not getting specific with yourself is a way of procrastinating). For example, the planned steps to a goal, such as improving your personal effectiveness, can include: (1) talking to three close friends or relatives about where you can most improve; (2) talk to yourself about where you want to stop procrastinating and list in writing these specific target changes; (3) in a simulated circumstance (you rehearse with a friend or "coach") practice promising new ways of acting effectively; (4) practice your newly developing skills in real-life conditions; (5) record your results and make adjustments based on concrete responses. A general goal broken down into specific steps that you organize in sequence gives you an action plan.

Action Planning

The following Seven Step Self-Management process includes a sequence of organized steps for overcoming maintenance, developmental, hindrance, low-grade, and other types of procrastination.

1. *Identify* problem procrastination patterns. The procrastination log and procrastination inventory help provide information on the patterns.
2. *Analyze* your current motivations to continue procrastinating, the cues or conditions that stimulate procrastination thinking and activities, and the resources you have available to promote purposeful changes.
3. *Develop* a mission statement to provide direction and incentive for change. The mission statement incorporates the idea that you do something to accomplish something. For example, pay all bills when they arrive to avoid falling behind on payments, causing you to feel rushed and have a poor credit rating.
4. *Plan* strategies that include ways to engineer changes through developing your personal resources for "getting it done." This is your master design for change.
5. *Organize* your resources by establishing priorities, setting *reasonable* schedules, deciding what you can delegate, structuring your day to get small items out of the way quickly before they become big burdens later, and so forth. The organization supports the plan.
6. *Implement* the plan by following your organizing structures. You follow your plan by directing and controlling your activities with firmness and flexibility to achieve the desired result.
7. *Evaluate* by measuring the ongoing outcomes of your plan. Here you note factors such as fatigue, better-than-expected progress, barriers you had not originally anticipated, or an inner resistance

to the plan that was not there at the time of conception. You use this information as a basis for looping back through the steps of identifying, analyzing, developing, planning, organizing, and implementing a new evaluation.

The self-management cycle of change is an ongoing process. Conditions, times, ourselves—all change. So one plan is not good for all time. The above self-management structure, however, can transcend time, person, and circumstances. The self-management cycle of change blended with a sense of honor and integrity can lead to a job well done.

Stall Stopper Program

People who are stall stoppers look for ways to *get things done and out of the way*. The stall stopper program is a good idea for those who want to stop procrastinating. Here is the basic stall stopper action program:

➤ Be specific with yourself about your priorities. What are your short-term priorities that you can ill afford to put off until another day or decade? What can be done within the week or month? What are your important long-term goals? What detail would you wisely manage each day so that you have uninterrupted time to contribute to those significant life efforts?

➤ Keep your goals clear and measurable and your action plans as manageable and consistent as is reasonable, considering your temperament, interests, and style.

➤ Make a commitment to complete your priorities in a reasonable way and in a reasonable time.

➤ Focus on the most important thing for you to do and keep with it. However, allow reasonable time for reflection, relaxation, and replenishment.

➤ Apply the Seven Step Self-Management plan to stop stalling and stay going at a pace that gives you a sense of freedom of movement.

➤ Identify where your procrastination starts. Do you bog down at the *stage of inception* before you begin? Do you snare yourself at the *planning stage*, when you first start to think about designing your approach? Do you set up your plans and organizing scheme then *fizzle in following through*? Do you start quickly then *fade in the stretch*? Do you finish what you start but fail to capitalize on your accomplishment by *going the extra mile*?

➤ Determine how you stop yourself from acting effectively and productively in those zones of your life where such actions could lead to a desired advantage. Do you dodge discomfort?

Do you spend too much time doubting your abilities until the doubt feeds on itself and you hesitate, second-guess yourself, and doubt yourself even more? Do you look for certainty and guarantees? Do you tend to significantly over- or underestimate what you can do within a given time? Do you act as though you were living in a perfect world without interruptions and unpredictable impediments that can throw off your time estimates? Once you have diagnosed the catalysts for procrastination, focus on what you can do to get beyond these barriers and Do It Now!

➤ Get organized, especially with the everyday stuff. Find ways to manage the maintenance details such as paying bills, washing dishes, shopping for groceries, and so forth. Recognize that the need for such activities will probably not disappear, and so you'd better make a lifetime commitment to repeating some activities of daily living that you'd prefer not to do. The little things can sometimes trap and snare you. Even when you effectively deal with your major priorities, many minor "incompletenesses" can weigh on your mind and spirit. (See chapter 18 for strategies on organizing details and managing time.)

➤ Move forward through the "good" frustrations that often accompany productive pursuits that contain elements of displeasure. Use these experiences to build your tolerance for frustration and to more quickly get beyond the stalling stages that so often accompany purposeful activities that you feel reluctant to start, where you don't have all the answers, or where the outcome is uncertain.

You can build upon this preliminary stall stopper framework to truly free up your time. Time used to free time helps develop personal resources.

ACCOMMODATION

Once you've achieved an enlightened awareness and begun to follow your action plan, you may experience *conflicts of the mind against itself* when entrenched ideas contend with your positive new beliefs, such as when your voice of reason competes with your wheedler voice.

The accommodation phase involves organizing and integrating information into a harmonious whole where you feel a sense of connection between your thinking, feeling, and doing. In this process you will adapt your old, faulty beliefs to the facts and experiences that we call reality.

The Land of the Blind and Deaf

Consider this perspective. You visit the valley of the deaf and blind. You are the only sighted, hearing person. Can you picture yourself first feeling insecure in such a setting? If you become more comfortable in this land, what has changed? You have merely learned to accommodate to a new, and very different, circumstance.

The analogy of the land of the deaf and blind suggests that we can accommodate to a radical change. In some ways, we can create such radical changes for ourselves. People with a public speaking phobia, for example, can stop procrastinating about dealing with their irrational ideas about talking up in public by, say, practicing speaking before groups such as Dale Carnegie and Toastmasters or taking college courses in public speaking, and so forth. When we create a new environment for ourselves, we can learn to adapt to it.

Changing Realities

Accommodation is like the lens of a telescope. We make adjustments for objects at different distances. However, though the objects at the greatest distances are less visible, the perspective is the greatest. Going from closer to farther perspectives, and then back again, reflects the accommodation process.

This adaptive, adjustable accommodation process is basic to progress. If this mental accommodation mechanism was not part of the human condition, we'd still be roving the tundra gathering nuts and berries and running from predators.

Good and Bad

Shakespeare tells us that "There is nothing either good or bad, but thinking makes it so." We can clearly define some experiences as good, such as charitable work. We can define others as bad, such as when procrastination degrades your fortunes and the fortunes of others.

Accommodation to variability comes in other ways. We think different thoughts. We do different things such as inventing or creating. The issue is not that of *good* or *bad* but of how we adapt to new ideas and create new thoughts and understandings.

Accommodation has variable speeds. Sometimes a factual new idea may take hold and cause a quick shift in our self-concept. Sometimes the opposite happens. We stall in the phase of changing our self-concept during the accommodation process when a factual idea meets an entrenched, practiced, negative self-belief that evokes feelings of inferiority. At that point you may feel resistant to the new idea. In such cases, you may take many trials until positive divergent views crowd out false inferiority ideas.

ACCEPTANCE

After the awareness, action, and accommodation processes have been put into motion, *acceptance* is the next crucial stage. This stage comes about as you become aware that the ebbing and flowing of change is part of your human condition. As you are the only self that will experience change, you might as well accept that self and get on with your life.

The Diversity of Self

Robert Louis Stevenson created the characters Dr. Jekyll and Mr. Hyde to show the conflict that existed between moral ways of being (Jekyll) and base instincts (Hyde). This story showed that both dimensions of personality were necessary, as the moral drive gave direction and the basic instincts supplied the energy. However, once separated, the base instincts grew to dominate. This led to Dr. Jekyll's downfall.

Gestalt therapist Fritz Perls built his theory around the idea that when people try to disown part of themselves, they alienate themselves from themselves. The solution is to integrate all natural parts of a personality into a whole, or gestalt.

Stevenson and Perls speak to the risk inherent in separating off natural parts of the *self*. However, this view requires clarification. For example, our hardwired emotions are not going away, but our diversionary thinking is subject to change without destroying the essence of who we are. We can comfortably feel integrated and "whole" with fewer mañana ideas, addictivities, and avoidance indulgences.

The idea of acceptance involves an enlightened self-understanding and tolerance. Here you realize that any person, during development, cannot be perfect. Otherwise what is the purpose of developing?

As you adapt to the inevitable paradoxes and incongruities that exist within you and in the world around you, you recognize that you have only a transitory control over your thoughts and feelings. Because you have only a transitory control over your inner mental and emotional conditions, your thoughts will sometimes veer in unwanted directions. That is because the mind is active and versatile. It monitors what is happening around you. It selects what it sees. It associates what you now experience to what you have experienced. It is forgetful. It is expansive.

Acceptance involves recognizing and tolerating what is going on within and outside of us. Acceptance, however, is different from giving up or saying that anything goes. Indeed, acceptance is often an important prelude to growth, adaptation to reality, and an ethical bearing.

Self-Acceptance

We often make arbitrary choices when it comes to describing our *selves*. If you are going to review yourself, why not do so in a self-accepting way?

Psychologist Carl Rogers talks about the importance of openness to experience. By openness to experience, Rogers means a willingness to acknowledge and accept one's personal feelings and attitudes without judging the "self." This form of acceptance opens opportunities for change. If you don't judge your "self," you are better able to judge your attitudes and actions and change those that prove self-defeating.

Self-acceptance is an important part of developing an accepting style of thinking, feeling, and behaving. In a state of self-acceptance, you recognize that you are the only *self* you will ever be. You don't have to like everything you do, but you don't have to blame yourself for every lapse, error, or act of procrastination. Instead, you can make amends or try again, perhaps with a different plan.

Self-Ratings

For psychologist Albert Ellis, self-acceptance means you rate your thoughts, feelings, and actions but not your whole being. He argues that because your person is complex, and change is inevitable, static global self-ratings are both incomplete and wrong. As an alternative, you accept yourself as a fallible, yet valuable, human. In this context, you cannot be only one thing, say, a procrastinator. More accurately, you are a person who procrastinates in specific ways, and you can tackle the specifics.

You are on the way to *self*-acceptance when you recognize that it makes no sense to rate your total *self* on fragments of experience. However, it does make sense to rate specific instances of what you think, feel, and do without overgeneralizing to your *self*. You might, for example, rate showing up for meetings late as self-defeating, your charitable contributions as good, and feelings of depression as undesirable. If you did not make such evaluations, then you'd have no basis for trying to improve your life.

Responsibility

Acceptance does not negate the idea of accountability and responsibility. You are responsible for your actions. But accepting yourself is possible, and though you still may not like the idea that you are going, at times, to procrastinate, hopefully you will procrastinate less often after reading this book. Within this acceptant state of mind, you normally will have more control over what you think, feel, and do. You will have fewer reality distortions and, therefore, less to be defensive about. That frees time and energy for managing the details of daily living, anticipating future trends, and acting to gain positive advantages.

There is probably no attainable ideal state of self-acceptance. However, by working to maintain a fair-minded, tolerant, accepting, perspective on *self*, you are more likely to take responsible steps leading to greater enjoyment of living. You'll procrastinate less. Although it sounds like a paradox, this is normally true: acceptance leads to action.

ACTUALIZATION

Some portray the idea of actualization as similar to an emotional state of wonderment and unity with the universe. This pronouncement once fooled many into believing that they were missing something in life because they did not feel filled with a perpetual state of bliss or feel that they were achieving their full potential. This self-actualization ideal was an illusory state of mind.

There is another, perhaps saner, way to look at actualization. Consider that actualization is a process of portraying reality in a reasoned and realistic way. Here you engage in actions that further your desires, wishes, wants, and preferences. In an actualized state of mind, you are normally free of pejorative self-judgments but not of judgment.

When you feel *actualized*, you continually stretch your resources to discover more about what you can do. As you concentrate on what you are doing, you move away from concentrating on yourself. Paradoxically, through this focused process of learning and contributing, you discover more about yourself and about what you can do. As an unplanned by-product, you feel more authentic, capable, motivated, and alive.

You actualize yourself when you concentrate on actions that make your dreams and wants attainable. In this nurturing, self-renewing process, you become both intellectually and concretely absorbed in developing your resources.

People resist changes that don't "feel right." Sometimes these emotional signals are intuitively accurate and you can trust your feelings. Still, you can trust your "feeling judgments" better when you understand how what you are thinking and feeling fits with what is really going on around you. Such understanding is characteristic of an actualized sense of self. People who act from a simple, uncomplicated understanding of themselves are better able to acknowledge and articulate the obvious and to say how they feel.

The Pathway to Actualization

Perhaps the closest anyone will come to an actualized state of mind is through:

1. Voluntarily absorbing yourself in your purposeful and productive interests
2. Charitably contributing your personal time and efforts to good causes
3. Making products of social value
4. Reaching for higher values while keeping a practical eye on the reality that most others won't share this developmental goal
5. Finding a new way to develop yourself every day
6. Blending your subjective with objective views for purposes of extending your depth of self-understanding and of understanding others
7. Accepting that discomfort and other forms of pain are as much a part of the human condition as invention, joy, happiness, and enlightened self-discovery
8. Accepting that your purpose in life is found in the purposes that you give your life
9. Building perspective to strengthen the self
10. Believing and living the concept that you can modify and evolve and aid others in this same pursuit

When you reach a point of actualization, you will attain greater mastery over yourself and the ways that you use your time.

FLIES IN THE OINTMENT

For those who demand immediate progress because they have suffered long enough, a cruel fate awaits them. This irrational expectation slows progress. It is a symptom of the very type of strain most people needlessly place upon themselves when they think they have had enough manufactured miseries. Most have to take a few falls on this *instant mental health* idea before settling down to work out their real problems.

Throughout life we hear personal advice such as: be tough. Pull yourself up by your bootstraps. Don't let them get to you. Why don't you just stop feeling bad about yourself and get on with your life? If you are like the majority, you've heard this advice. At first, the advice may seem reasonable, but is it unrealistic?

Sometimes *get on with it* makes as much sense as advising someone to learn nuclear physics overnight. For example, those burdened by oppressive habits of thought, self-defeating routines, and self-concept disturbances normally have significant self-study and self-change work to do as they *get on with it.*

Willing yourself *into* a state of instant mental health is different, however, from willing yourself *onto* the pathway of enlightened change. Here you create opportunities to add to the positive, and to reduce the negative, conditions in your life. You can *will* yourself to *step* on the path of enlightened self-awareness anytime.

When you feel poised for a breakthrough change, you may still watch yourself go through the motions of repeating a habit that you know is self-defeating. Rather than see this as a discouraging sign, mark this as an interim process leading to a mental metamorphosis.

Well-practiced habits of mind stick like glue. This partially explains why people don't simply intellectually command their negative patterns of thought to change. Instead, time and well-directed experiences contribute to the formation of new perspectives. Knowing that this is part of the process can help to defuse premature conclusions of failure.

In a process of "getting better by doing better," you may have a temporary eye-opening experience where you feel relaxed, in control, and jubilant. These preview experiences are valuable when they show what life can be like without a pattern of negative thinking. However, like most movie previews, these experiences highlight the best points of the show. They often give an unrealistic picture of the movie as a whole. Nevertheless, a good movie, like an enjoyable life, may have parts that drag and prove unpleasant. But the overall experience will normally prove enjoyable.

Demand an end to your own procrastination, and the odds are you won't get what you demand. You normally have as much chance of demanding that your procrastination cease to exist as you would of building a solid self-concept overnight. Paradoxically, those who stop demanding instant change often make quicker progress. They are not continually paddling against the current by making unrealistic demands. They don't give up on themselves because they are not moving fast enough. They refuse to embrace irrational assumptions about what their pace of change should be like.

POSTSCRIPT

What do you want in the way of quality experiences? Without a vision of the possible, what is the incentive to do more than struggle with yourself, put things off, and promise to do better someday, somehow?

Telecommuters, for example, who work in flurries because they tend to postpone work efforts, face a special procrastination challenge. These are people who do much of their company work at home. They stay in touch with the office through the telephone and computer.

Setting goals, struggling with challenges, and maintaining a focus on taking necessary steps may sound like work. It is. There is a passage from the Koran that says it well: Do you think you can pass through the portals of the immortals without having done what others before you have done?

This is another of the great *procrastination paradoxes*. Emotional freedom involves a sense of guidance, restraint, purpose, and diligence.

PART TWO

Procrastination Contingencies and Wrong Solutions

What They Are and How to Recognize Them

7

In and Out
of the Quagmire

> **In This Chapter**
>
> ➤ Happiness contingency ploys

Happiness is a by-product of doing something else first. When we procrastinate, we pursue action, mental, and emotional diversions that are merely smoke screens that veil our self-doubts, discomfort fears, and other stressful inner conditions. The contingencies of control, success through perfection, approval, and comfort also hold out a false hope for a happier future. I call these contingencies the *happiness contingencies* because the person adhering to these principles tends to believe that when these contingencies are met, he or she will have a good life. These contingencies result in putting off the doable and involve primarily needs for control, perfection (success), approval, and comfort. These four contingency ploys add a complicating wrinkle to an already messy procrastination problem.

"Stop," you say. "Are not the experiences of control, success, approval, and comfort attainable, at least in some measure?" Yes they are attainable, but they are transitory states and are possible by-products of the effective things that you do. These desired states do not normally come into being on their own. At one level it seems to make sense to gain control, drive for success, win approval, or feel comfortable. But, paradoxically, a demand to attain these contingencies has the bearing of a *quixotic* undertaking—an "impossible dream." Those who devote their time and thoughts to this quest meet the fate of old Don Quixote, the major character in Miguel de Cervantes's book of the same name, when he challenged a windmill, believing the fan blades were enemy soldiers.

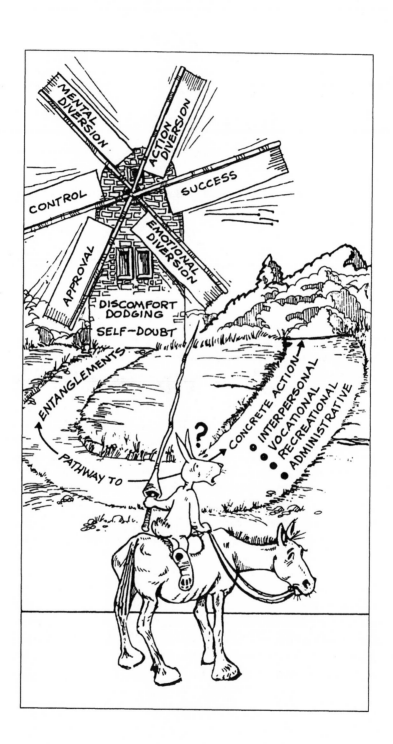

A NEW MAÑANA PLOY

The happiness contingencies are variations of the contingency mañana trap. If you make any one of these contingencies a necessity, the others will often follow. For example, if you assert that people must appreciate (approve of, love, respect) you, then you must act successful to get the approval. Without seeing the contradiction, you might also believe that you should have unconditional love and respect and then become anguished when you get less than what you expect. The eighteenth-century French writer Sébastien Chamfort wrote: "Eminence without merit earns deference without esteem."

In theory, attaining approval brings a sense of comfort and well-being. In an atmosphere where you believe your group approves of you, you would probably then judge yourself as in control. However, what if you are the subject of a false rumor, and lose that approval? What if you don't feel approval in the ways that you prefer?

Self-doubt spoils the contingency plan when this attitude of mind works as a defense against doing. For example, a Broadway actor's anxious questions about himself can be self-defeating: "Will I be in a smash hit?" (success); "Will people love or hate me for what I have to say?" (approval); "Can I stop feeling tense?" (control). All these questions suggest contingency thinking in which the actor views playing his or her part to avoid failure. But *time passes.* Today's victories or losses are mere preludes for tomorrow's challenges.

A pin in the seat of your pants quickly gets attention. Without some sense of urgency, we'll normally put off self-development, especially when we believe we *must* find happiness first.

Although the happiness contingencies sound authentic enough, in practice they float like balloons too airy to grab. Waiting for happiness is a poor substitute for action!

Contingency goals are false goals because they are too general. In this general state of mind you get caught in a psychological revolving door. You leave the revolving door when you actively create conditions that raise the probability of experiencing more happy moments. Constructive activities promise happier memories to balance off the less wanted variety.

Collectively, the happiness contingencies present another procrastination paradox. These vague demanding solutions for happiness heighten tension and stimulate more procrastination. Since procrastination bypasses purposeful and productive actions, the happiness contingency solution fails from the start.

The happiness contingencies, like *wolves in sheeps' clothing*, prove entangling and formidable. On the other hand, purposeful action goes along a completely different path. Over time, this preferred action path has fewer bumps.

POSTSCRIPT

In this impossible quest for perpetual happiness, the contingencies represent another wheedler ploy. We make promises to ourselves that we cannot meet. For example, how could any human exist in a state of perpetual bliss? Millions of years of evolution have discounted that possibility. Nevertheless, when the promise comes to the front of our thoughts, we make our foggy visions of happiness into a fantasy life that can't be real.

Happiness contingencies offer a false hope that someday, somehow, sometime in the future your life will turn around and feel wonderful. Since we build waiting into the contingency solution, our present passivity toward activity can be the result of delayed past efforts. We rarely develop ourselves by indulging in contingency thinking that entails needless delays.

Starting with control, let's get active unlocking these four contingency traps.

8

Control: The Pathway to and from Procrastination

In This Chapter

➤ Artificial needs for control
➤ Fear of loss of control
➤ Exercises to gain flexibility

You can guide a boat on an ocean tall, but where the waves go you cannot fore-stall. Given the opportunity, most of us would put off what we have to do but don't want to do. However, our will to regulate, direct, manage, organize, coordinate, and meet acceptable standards all represent disciplined assertions of inner control.

External social controls are everywhere and also regulate our lives in ways we often don't consider. Stoplights control traffic. The design of our towns and cities controls where we can live and where we can walk. Traditions influence our choices. We structure our lives by the clock. We phone our friends by following the rules that phone companies have built into their systems. Social practices control the way we write. Our folkways, mores, conventions, rules, regulations, and laws define a hierarchy of rewards and penalties to govern and control our conduct.

Social controls also come into play to enforce task completion. Students would probably not hand their term papers in on schedule without penalties or rewards. Writing reports is normally low on the list of the things most students prefer to do.

Even creative writers who put off writing can spoil their timing. The nineteenth-century American philosopher and author Henry David Thoreau warned us, "Write while the heat is in you. . . . The

89

writer who postpones the recording of his thoughts uses an iron which has cooled to burn a hole with. He cannot inflame the minds of his audience."

Despite social systems for controlling social responsibilities, we can normally find ways to procrastinate, including delaying important social tasks, such as returning library books, paying parking tickets, completing census forms, filing taxes, or obtaining automobile inspection stickers.

Reasonable controls are necessary in society to get reasonable things done in a reasonable time. Likewise, in our individual lives, a quiet sense of inner control has advantages. We are better able to focus our efforts on what to get done and can put aside many artificial distractions from daily living that twist and block the road ahead. True self-control and self-discipline offer advantages in getting things done.

ARTIFICIAL NEEDS FOR CONTROL

The artificial need for control is the idea that to feel whole, you have to be in full control and not subject to the control of others. In a strange way, this attitude of mind includes both establishing an authoritarian inner control while rebelling against the restraints and dominating influence of external authoritarian controls. Few of us like to be under the thumb of a demanding, irrational authority. Yet when we impose this autocratic control upon ourselves, we engage in a conflict in which we make our inner world feel like a pressure cooker with procrastination as the relief valve.

The need to exercise inner authoritarian control is fated to fail from the start. When we seek to completely control ourselves, our feelings, or our thoughts, we are really encouraging psychological malfunctioning in at least two ways. First, these demands create an impossible condition for gaining self-control. Second, these controls are really a form of the contingency mañana that has all the drawbacks of this wheedling ploy. We give priority to the need to gain control and relegate the real contingencies—the actual concrete steps for goal attainment, self-regulation, and self-stewardship—to the background. When you bend over too far to maintain control, you have lost the control you sought to claim.

CONTROLLING STYLES

A controlling style is a developmental procrastination issue when we overemphasize control to the detriment of our emotional well-being.

Here are some symptoms of *control procrastination* applied to self, others, and the environment.

Controlling the Self

We have many maladaptive ways to stiffen the self through excessive inner regulation.

Oversocialization. Some of us try too hard to control ourselves and, as our reward, feel stiff and uncomfortable in social situations. In this oversocialized state of mind, we try to do and say the right things. We avoid standing up for our rights when we frighten ourselves by thinking that the offending parties may not like our rightful assertions and retaliate by rejecting us. To control an outside world we fear we can't control, we follow unnecessarily restrictive inner rules.

Blind ambition. People who drive themselves to gain control often go into overdrive on *activities* to obtain money, a big house, or a beautiful or handsome mate in order to figuratively rub polish on their images. Despite their gallant efforts, they rarely succeed in proving their worth. Oblivious to the harm this overdrive begets in them, they move full steam ahead like battleships to a war. We recognize some members of this blind ambition group by their furrowed brows, health- and weight-related problems, and sometimes by the cigarette dangling from their lips. Most people who fall into this trap feel pressured to achieve and find it difficult to enjoy the accomplishments they produce.

Alien control. At the extreme end of this mind-control dimension, some people experience pervasive, invasive, intrusive thoughts they believe are crazy and alien. In this obsessive state of mind, you may have a vague sense of impending doom or more specific convictions about imminent disaster (e.g., you will surely have a heart attack and die). You might torment yourself for decades over these possibilities. By trying to force unwanted thoughts out of your consciousness, you only highlight them, and under these circumstances, you'll be inclined to put off much.

Controlling Others

Trying to control the conduct of others is challenging. In military-type situations, you can shape the selected behaviors and attitudes of others, providing you have the authority and you skillfully use the power of group pressures toward conformity to accomplish this result. As a parent, you can control the structure of young children's lives and shape some of their ideas through education. Where you are extraordinarily persuasive, you can influence certain outcomes. However, when you expect people to conform to your ideals, and you act controllingly to accomplish this outcome, you can create staunch resistance. For those who live their lives trying to control others, insecurity, intolerance, and distress mingle with this perfectionist picture.

Accusation-justification. When you act controlling, you risk creating unnecessary conflict. We see this in the well-known *accusation-justification-escalation control process* between couples bent on controlling each other. Here one accuses the mate, who then justifies and defends the self, and blames the instigator. The whole matter escalates as neither party gives ground. Each attempts to get in the last word, and by insisting on this, both parties show they have lost control.

The dominator. For some, controlling other people's time is a way of life. At a conference I attended, the speaker asked for comments. A psychologist from the audience took the microphone. She introduced herself, listed her credentials, and went on to talk about her own program. She spoke as though the audience knew who she was and all about her program. However there were murmurings from the crowd: "Who is she?" "What is this all about?"

Her speech went on for another five minutes. When the moderator attempted to regain the microphone, she barked, "Please! I am not finished."

It's easy to walk out on a controller at a conference, but what if this person is an employer, close relative, neighbor, or friend? What if *you* take on this role with an eerie regularity?

The dominator style shows in other ways. You talk over the voices of others or don't allow them to express their views because you are too busy expressing your own ideas. You interrupt with "yes, but." You change the topic. Although this communication style can represent a strategic decision to muddle communications, when you engage in these tactics because you *have to* have your own way, you signal a loss of inner control.

The adviser. Controller problems arise in other ways. You give your friends unsolicited advice. They get defensive. You get mad when they don't take your word. When you meet resistance—polite or otherwise—you counterattack by declaring that you are a caring person who is interested only in their good.

The scroll master. You attempt to gain control through acquiring knowledge and then using it to control. This is the world of the scroll master.

The scroll master is the person with encrypted knowledge, secret formulas, and mysterious information. Lawyers, doctors, tradespeople, financial advisers, spiritualists, even psychologists have a special language and use symbols to obscure the simple and to control the outcome of what they do.

The scroll master makes the simple sound complex and procrastinates on clarity.

The whiny manipulator. Telling a friend in a whiny voice, "Wouldn't you like to have lunch with me?" makes it difficult for the friend to refuse your invitation. You can try to accomplish this result in other whiny ways. You might try to make people feel sorry for you so that you might get your way. You also might use *guilt* as a tool to try to make others do what you demand, then whimper or get hostile if you don't get them to acquiesce.

The withholding procrastination style. I've met people with great creative ability who hold back developing their ideas because they believe they cannot fully control the product once it goes on the market; or they fear that other people might later imitate their good ideas. Demanding that this does not happen, they forget the expression "Imitation is the sincerest form of flattery." They also forget Miguel de Cervantes's warning, "Delay always breeds danger, and to protect a great design is often to ruin it."

Do It Now!

Withholding-Controlling Procrastination

Engaging in withholding-controlling procrastination is like mixing soap with your toothpaste to assure that no one else will use it. It is a self-defeating behavior. And in this process, the "withholder" often finds that someone else independently discovers and puts a similar idea to use first.

When you are 51 percent sure you have an idea worth exploiting, get started now. Test the idea in practice. Discover its real worth. Good ideas, like a fine spaghetti sauce, often take time to evolve, and you may discover new ingredients as you go on.

Controlling the Environment

If we can't fully control ourselves and other people, we can always control the environment, right? But after millions of years of trying, we have collectively advanced but have not succeeded in obtaining complete control.

You can change and modify the environment but only up to a certain point. We can't stop it from raining just because the hour has come for picnicking.

If you have a factory and a production line, you can find ways to improve the quality and flow of materials through the system. However, systems break down. Key people get sick. Electronic glitches appear. Fatigue sets in for both people and equipment. Customers return products you thought met standard. Today's state-of-the-art operation loses ground to tomorrow's. Time and change will not stop.

You can assert environmental control up to a certain point—which crops to plant, what product to produce, the method of production, the color of your house, the type of automobile that you drive, and so forth. However in situations where you make a product or provide a service, if you procrastinate on keeping up with the technology, relevant discoveries, and skill improvement in your field then you may have to figuratively hide behind sandbags, hoping to remain dry in a flood of new ideas.

GAINING CONTROL THROUGH PARADOXES

In really fulfilling your interests, you must focus on meeting challenges; as a result you will feel in command of yourself. When you are in this open state of mind, people will tend to describe you as energetic and approachable.

Control difficulties often block this outcome. You can use the following to identify symptoms of a control problem:

➤ Talking very softly or talking very loudly
➤ Agreeing with a "yes," then adding the word *but* ("Yes, you're probably right, but . . .")
➤ Not hearing what people say
➤ Working frantically
➤ Resisting new ideas
➤ Slavishly repeating the daily routine
➤ Making demands
➤ Consistently trying to get the last word in

➤ Bodily stiffness
➤ A sense of obsessive urgency (confusion about what to do first, coupled with an urgency to complete everything)
➤ Hostile feelings
➤ A sense of impotence

If you note that any of these examples apply to you, then select and do the appropriate exercise(s) to loosen up and feel more in command of yourself:

➤ Speak half as rapidly. Speak up in the groups in which you normally remain quiet. Make yourself heard. Tone down your voice. Let people have their say without defending yourself. Summarize and feed back to others what they have said to you.
➤ Work "planfully" rather than frantically.
➤ Experiment with potentially helpful activities you feel resistant to doing.
➤ Change one element in your routine each day, then go back to the old way if you don't find it satisfying.
➤ Instead of making one demand, have five alternate solutions available.
➤ Relax by concentrating your attention on your belly button; do this for five minutes every day.
➤ Among your many incomplete tasks, pick one at random and do it. (Write task titles on slips of paper, deposit them in a paper bag, and draw one.)
➤ Find three positive ways to view each hostility-provoking situation.
➤ Identify one strength per day; do this exercise for one year.
➤ Learn a new game or sport that you have to rely on others to learn; or if you generally rely on others, learn a game or sport in which you instruct yourself.
➤ Practice operating from concepts. Instead of worrying about the words that you use to express yourself, try to be clear on the concept you want to express (friendliness, dissatisfaction) and let the words flow from the idea.
➤ Visit a tranquil place and allow your eyes, hearing, sense of smell, touch, and mind to wander. Discover one new thing each day about your extended environment; do this every day for the rest of your life.

People who are in command of themselves are normally better able to control the events around them. When you feel in command of yourself, you'll procrastinate less.

COPING WITH FEAR OF LOSS OF CONTROL

A fear of loss of control is linked to the perception that you can't manage or won't cope adequately enough if things are out of your complete control. If you thought you could cope, you wouldn't fear a loss of control.

In this anxious state of mind, you are probably going to feel overloaded in meeting your responsibilities as you shift between trying to escape from threats and mobilizing your resources to cope. You can temporarily numb this anxiety through escapist activities such as watching television or mindlessly engaging in busywork, but this solution rarely helps.

Fortunately you have many positive options regarding building your coping capabilities when you fear a loss of control. Here are some ideas to bring this about:

➤ Look for evidence to show yourself you can cope. Chances are you'll find this evidence in situations where you have already coped with and survived unpleasant situations. Make a list of these coping strategies: what they are and how they work.

➤ Get advice from an objective and knowledgeable person about your options. This can help break a mind-set where you don't believe you can have alternative thoughts or possibilities.

➤ Recognize your cognitive signatures of anxiety, or what you tell yourself when you feel anxious. These signatures include ideas such as "I can't cope," "I'm trapped," "I can't stand this." Think about and begin activities that move you in a coping direction.

➤ Avoid making the magical jump from the possible to the probable and thinking that just because you can fail you will fail. What you have here is a hypothesis to test. A hypothesis is not a fact until it becomes a fact.

FLEXIBILITY EXERCISES

You can use the following sequence of exercises to help yourself increase your trust and flexibility and your will to take on challenging activities rather than putting them off.

➤ Place yourself in a situation in which having trust in someone is necessary for you—a situation in which you will have to momentarily depend upon that person for your physical well-being. A popular exercise is to ask a friend or family member to catch you as you fall backward. To do this, position yourself such that you are standing upright with ample room to fall backward. Your partner positions himself behind you, then signals you to fall backward, and you do so like a stiff board while your partner catches you in middescent. Naturally, if you weigh five hundred pounds don't expect a midget to support your weight. Exercise your judgment in the selection of a partner in this exercise. Repeat this exercise as often as required for you to feel relaxed as you fall backward.

➤ Turn your world around by doing an exercise in differences. If you are a shabby dresser, dress sharply for a day. If you are a sharp dresser, dress shabbily for a day. If you normally drive to work but can use public transportation, take the public transportation for a day or a week. If you avoid saying "Hello" to people where you work or go to school, say, "Hello." If you normally say "Hello," say "Hi." If you have relative freedom of choice about how to structure your workday, take some tasks you normally reserve for doing at the end of the afternoon and do them first thing in the morning.

➤ Do It Now!

Control Procrastination

Sensory-appreciation exercises are helpful for persons who focus on control to the exclusion of their sensory experiences. Becoming aware and appreciative of information from your sensory experiences provides a tranquil, refreshing experiential interlude that can motivate you to action. These exercises do not take any material time away from your getting your priorities done.

➤ Take a walk each day and be visually alert to new discoveries.

➤ Stop for five minutes each day to become aware of the varied sounds in your environment.

➤ Touch a new object each day. Close your eyes and concentrate on its texture.

➤ Find something new and pleasant to smell each day.

POSTSCRIPT

What is the answer to substituting a sense of command for the different forms of *control procrastination*? I find people who experience an earned sense of inner control consistently manage the things that take place around them including their deadlines. Those who ignore developmental challenges and experience inner disorder, do less well managing their daily lives and frequently fall into a procrastination rut.

The difference between trying to meet the contingency of control and meeting the challenge of productive activity is the difference between self-absorption and absorbing oneself in the concrete activities of living. Failing to meet the contingency of control, the person may falsely conclude—"I'm not in control. I can't possibly succeed. I can never be happy." When you meet the challenge of productive activity, you may feel as if you are organizing, regulating, and directing your efforts to achieve positive and purposeful results.

Some people really believe that they should have known what they didn't know and should have controlled what they could not have anticipated. For this group, here is something to ponder: how do you justify holding yourself accountable for matters outside your control? Now, let's take a closer look at how procrastination may relate to perfectionism and a desperate need for approval.

Perfectionism and Fear of Failure

Every garden has weeds. Daedalus, the builder of the Cretan labyrinth, had overstepped his bounds. He had placed wings on the arms of his son, Icarus, and given him the gift of flight. This act so angered Zeus, the father of the gods, that when Icarus ascended in the sky, Zeus caused the sun to melt the wax that bound the feathers to Icarus's flesh. Icarus fell into the sea, and Zeus made him into the island of Icaria.

This Greek myth inspired Henry Murray to call compulsive striving for perfection the *Icarus complex.* Murray saw that people have a drive to master their environment—a perfectly normal and quite desirable drive. He also saw that people could escalate this normal drive and become entangled in a pursuit of success through perfection, and when they did so, the fate of Icarus lay before them.

Psychiatrist Alfred Adler also insightfully noted that many people extend the normal drive for success by translating this quest into a *need* to heroically transcend themselves. Such attempts he saw as plainly vain, and vanity he saw as neurotic. The neo-Freudian Karen Horney said that neurosis is a state of imagining and then trying to live up to an idealized and glorified self-image. The founder of rational emotive behavior therapy, Albert Ellis, defined this perfectionistic state as a dire need "to be thoroughly competent, intelligent, and achieving in all possible aspects."

In this mental framework, what begins as a normal desire to achieve becomes a requirement for success. Persons *requiring* success preoccupy themselves with the pursuit of attaining the impossible dream of perfection and, as a result, procrastinate on accomplishing necessary, and achievable, tasks in the real world.

THE HEIGHTS OF PERFECTION

The false need for perfection is a joy-dissipating mental monster stemming from the false belief that perfection is achievable. Everyday observations repeatedly illustrate that there are limits to perfectability and that all humans are fallible.

The perfectionist is not necessarily the person with the squeaky clean house with all the pots organized according to size, nor is he necessarily the person with critical eyes who finds faults with unnerving regularity. For example, while traveling the *quixotic road*, we make unrealistic demands on ourselves and also on others. Some of these requirements may seem reasonable, such as expecting a friend to phone regularly. But in the perfectionist's world, what may seem reasonable is often not realistic. The friend may have a different schedule.

At the extreme, perfectionists have a contingency worth problem: be perfect and you are worthy; fall short and you're a loser—a big nothing! In this state of mind, life becomes a report card—a rating system in which fear of failure rises over normal self-interests and douses enthusiasm for doing what could bring satisfaction and a sense of accomplishment.

This habit flourishes under conditions in which the dominant members of a culture emphasize achievement. Many forms of religious training feed into perfectionism, especially those that employ guilt to control the flock. Educators whose minds are too structured attempt to channel children along perfectionistic pathways, as do parents who see a child as an extension of an ideal that they wish to mold. The media portray near-perfect presentations and lifestyles that few, if any, could hope to attain. At the extreme, these factors combine with a tendency toward perfectionism and result in the sort of paralyzing perfectionism that leads to procrastination. At various times in their lives, millions feel trapped in this process.

In an achievement-oriented atmosphere self-doubts burgeon. In this setting, you may not know whether to trust your instincts or to follow what you think are the lofty standards the crowd expects you to follow. You may feel unsure what to trust and what to believe; this perspective feeds self-doubts, and self-doubts commonly feed a pattern of procrastination.

Although people can develop perfectionism at any stage of life, and although we have the ability to self-induce perfectionism, in many cases perfectionism is a family tradition passed on from generation to generation. As a failed form of social control, this is a tradition worth breaking. Honor, responsibility, and a sense of personal dignity get people farther in life than perfection ever will.

THE DIRECTIONS OF PERFECTION

You can turn perfection inward, outward, or in both directions. We will look at same examples of perfection from different angles, much in the same way that we can view procrastination. *Absolute perfectionists*, for example, are a rare breed who define only the highest levels of attainment as acceptable. *Relative perfectionists* have lower standards that they believe they must meet. The student who sets B grades as acceptable may feel like a failure with a B– grade.

Individual Perfectionists

In the perfectionist's world, worth is contingent on achieving or exceeding standards. Achieve the standard, and you are worthy. Fall short and you are unworthy. In this black-and-white world of extremes, much mental misery is possible. Thus, *individual perfectionists* are their own worst critics. Whatever they do is rarely good enough. However, some do have moments of glory—when, for a short period, they reach a lofty level.

Some individual perfectionists believe that they need to be perfect to be average. That's quite a paradox! For reasons they cannot adequately explain, average is a state to attain. When pressed, these individual perfectionists, who think they are the lowly of the low, believe that what others do is right and whatever they do is wrong.

Procrastination, anxiety, indecisiveness, criticism of self and others, exasperated expectations, unrealistic goal setting, depression, difficulty dealing with feedback—all characterize an individual perfectionistic outlook. Fortunately, this is an outlook that you can modify through challenging the irrational beliefs behind this *manufactured misery. Bibliotherapy,* or healing through reading, also can prove effective in helping you to reduce anxiety related to perfectionism.

Social Perfectionists

Social perfectionists are the "know-it-alls" who criticize others for imperfections. These faultfinders cannot be consistently satisfied. Extreme social perfectionists act as if they really believe that their advice is better, their performance is better—that they are better. Often sulking because of a lack of recognition, this perfectionist fixates attention on the flaws of others while procrastinating on creating worthy personal achievements.

Since no one is perfect, social perfectionists can easily find imperfections and problems everywhere. They artificially make themselves feel superior by falsely elevating their stature at the expense of others, and they experience the sort of stress that invariably accompanies chronic dissatisfaction.

ASPIRING AND REQUIRING PHILOSOPHIES

We all have legitimate wants, wishes, desires, preferences, and yearnings. Doing well at work, getting along with our neighbors, meeting reasonable challenges, following our attainable dreams—all of these are signs of an *aspiring philosophy* toward life. Most of us also prefer to have our way and to have what we want with the least possible effort in the least possible time. It is when we *demand* these desirable things, and make them the requirements for our happiness, that our expectations exasperate our wishes and we follow the *quixotic road.*

Perfectionists who strain to contradict reality hold in common a remarkably similar set of *cognitive signatures* that evoke a predictable set of responses. These signatures include inflexible demands translated through words and phrases such as *should, ought, must, have to,* or *got to.* The perfectionist cognitive signature primarily includes the idea that if you are not what you should be, you are nothing at all. The shoulds, oughts, and musts in our lives represent *demons of duty.* When we coerce ourselves by demanding that we capitulate to these demons, we are likely to rebel. However, what are we rebelling against? Is it the activity or is it the *demon of duty?*

Psychoanalyst Karen Horney pointed out that when people demand perfection of themselves, they condemn themselves to obeying a rigid set of rules for achieving this idealized state. Cast in *shoulds, oughts,* and *musts,* these beliefs make for a tyrannical inner existence. For example, if you believe that you *must* be perfect and then don't perform well enough, you are apt to chastise and deprecate yourself for failing, even when most others think you've succeeded. In addition, as you continue to do less than perfectly, you may become cynical and defeatist and begin to characterize yourself as a total failure. When you do try and fall short of standard, you are likely to cause yourself to feel shame and guilt.

When your perfectionistic ideals waver too high above reality, you can have an emotional fall. The novelist Thomas Hardy wove this idea into *Tess of the D'Urbervilles* when he said that as the mighty fall, they make a more thunderous roar because they have a longer way to topple. So is it for those who reach too far into the perfectionistic stratosphere of life and find themselves ungrounded.

FEAR OF FAILURE

When you look at success and perfection as the solutions for resolving inner doubts, chances are you can link some of your procrastinating to a fear of failing. The person who believes in this contingency solution thinks that success is essential for creating a sense of self-worth and for making life meaningful. Not only does this belief prove wrong, but it also drains available energies and often promotes procrastination. The procrastination that results from this self-preoccupation increases your chances for more failure.

People fear failing because of the painful feelings of anxiety and depression they typically bring upon themselves when they believe they have fallen short of their standards. Instead of working to change their outlook to conform to reality, many who follow *quixotic quests* desperately cling to their stratospheric perfectionistic hopes. They repeatedly fall from these lofty heights because their beliefs clash with reality.

By setting perfect standards and then forging inflexible rules to meet those standards, you are apt to work hard at dodging what you think you'll fail at doing. To avoid facing the significance of this artful dodging, some use clever diversionary tactics. You wait until the eleventh hour (the proverbial last minute) to begin something that portends possible imperfection. Now we can explain the imperfect work: "I started too late; next time I'll do it right!"

Despite the self-con, a dim awareness exists that the time was available to do a better job. Even so, the con helps maintain a false sense of well-being. Though striving for perfection to avoid failure may sound noble, it is self-defeating.

ANTIPERFECTIONISM EXERCISES

These exercises will help build tolerance for making mistakes. After completing these exercises, use what you have learned to undertake a problem you've been ducking because you've feared failure.

> ➤ Eliminate perfectionism and failure from your life by redefining what you do. Within this tolerance zone you see your actions as

a series of experiments. You test your thoughts against reality and use the reactions you get to modify what you do. In this classic accommodation mode, you learn what works, what doesn't, what to quit doing, and when to do more.

➤ Carry out a dialogue with yourself on the topic of how people grow and learn through both mistakes and successes.

➤ Pretend you're a research scientist assigned the task of understanding and explaining why people can't be perfect. Write a one-page report summarizing your findings.

➤ Pretend you are an investigative reporter assigned to write an article on what success and fulfillment mean to you. Outline the article.

➤ List normally occurring impediments that could slow you from doing the best you can.

➤ Do It Now!

Perfectionism

Sometimes our quest for perfection is based on faulty assumptions about ourselves. Rather than anticipate failure and lament over not succeeding, try to get an alternate perspective by answering the following questions:

➤ If I'm not the person I "should" be, what is wrong with my being the person I am?

➤ What ten things do I appreciate most about myself?

➤ What compassion can I show myself if I don't act as I would like?

➤ What makes a less-than-perfect performance so unacceptable to me?

RISK-TAKING EXERCISES

Risk taking is helpful to people who try to cover up their faults. To break free from perfectionism, breaking down the conceited view that you must maintain a flawless appearance is important. Here are some exercises to get you there:

➤ Pick a project you can do without thinking less of yourself if you are not perfect. Carry through. Look at the range of activities that went into the task. Describe to yourself how each step has value.

➤ Purposefully make some of your work less "perfect" than usual. Ask yourself if a less-than-perfect performance in a specific situation will characterize you for all times as a less-than-adequate person.

➤ Undertake a difficult project that you've put off because you predict that your performance will fall below your standards. Now, think of yourself as a person who is simply striving to develop a skill. Analyze your efforts in nonjudgmental terms. Mark and measure your improvements.

➤ Admit some of your worst errors to a close and accepting friend.

➤ Compassionately support someone who seems frustrated with a poor work performance. Then apply the same principle of compassion to yourself.

A NEED FOR CERTAINTY

A gerbil, weak from hunger, chanced upon two heads of cabbage. Confused as to which cabbage to eat, the poor animal pondered the decision until it starved.

Some people who routinely procrastinate act like the gerbil. Faced with making a decision, they feel distressed over the possibility of not making the right choice. They wait for a guarantee that the decision will result in success (the "perfect" choice). While anxiously awaiting the guarantee, they put off trying to get the facts that might make for a more enlightened decision.

This *decision procrastination* leads to delaying relevant activities because of fuzzy direction and uncertain commitment. At least part of the indecision generates from the belief that one has to be sure before acting. This can lead people who procrastinate to have social problems.

Although no sure formula guarantees the correctness of the decision, you normally decide wrong when you choose inaction because of indecisiveness. Part of the indecisiveness reflects wanting to avoid any possible criticism that might result from making an error.

We have thus far highlighted indecisiveness as a problem. However, most people make decisions without a great struggle most of the time. If you are about to run short of food, you unhesitatingly go to the grocery store. If you want to go to the seashore, you decide when you will leave and how you will get there.

We feel comfortable about many decisions, like shopping for food, because we can predict the outcome. Practically everyone can and does make many decisions daily, and usually we render the decisions automatically. What complicates this decision-making process is the interjection of self-doubts, self-criticism, and self-doubt "downing."

Do It Now!

Indecisiveness

Instead of agonizing over decisions or delaying action until you've arrived at the perfect solution, try the Patton decision equation:

General George Patton believed that if you have a plan you are 51 percent sure of, execute it. If you are 80 percent sure, "violently execute it." If your options are such that you view your alternatives as equally desirable, then flip a coin.

THE ACCELERATING CYCLE OF INDECISION

Faced with an either/or decision, such as choosing between alternatives, an indecisive person can stall and stumble, fearing to decide. This indecisiveness can accelerate to a state where the person does nothing, becomes more dissatisfied, and worries about every imaginable problem that can result from a "wrong" decision. This perfectionist demand to make a failure-proof decision distorts perception and impedes progress.

The following Either/Or Cycle of Indecision Chart marks a familiar path of indecision. After examining the chart, we'll look at alternative ways to break out of a procrastination pattern of indecisiveness.

The Decision-Making Process

This decision-making process can help you discover the behavior patterns that cause you the most trouble and those that yield the greatest benefit. This process gets you most directly from where you are now to where you want to go. You will rarely get far with being indecisive because this quality overly complicates life.

Apply the following decision-making model to a procrastinated activity where you have been and continue to act indecisive. Test the decision-making model against this problem.

TWO DIRECTIONS TO CHOOSE

Decision-Making Process	*Decision-Breakdown Process*
1. Clear statement of issue	Vague and confusing statement.
2. Objective statement of alternative benefits.	Procrastination arguments.
3. Specification of personal strengths and limitations in carrying out the alternatives.	Envelopment in feelings of self-doubts or helplessness.
4. Identifying steps to reduce uncertainty and risk.	Escalating indecisiveness and inhibition.
5. Making decision based on best estimates for favorable . outcome	Making decision to avoid failure.
6. Testing steps through taking action.	Taking steps to divert from tension.

You can apply the following six-step decision-making process to answer a variation on Shakespeare's question: To procrastinate or not to procrastinate, that is the question. We'll use a health procrastination situation, losing weight, as an example and use both the decision-making and -breakdown process to compare each step.

1. Statement of issue. To take action or to put off making dietary changes to remain overweight.

2. Statement of benefits. Following through on weight loss and a weight-loss maintenance plan potentially reduces health risks, promotes energy, and yields a better body image. On the other hand, self-discipline is tough, and you may fail anyway. It's unfair to deprive yourself of those extra pieces of cake and other tasty goodies. You don't want to feel hungry.

3. Personal strengths and limitations assessment. Have displayed ability both to stick with a course of study and to overcome urges in other contexts. Limitations involve the fact that we need to eat to live and we will have temptations on the weight-loss journey. On the other hand, maybe you don't have what it takes to both lose weight and keep it off.

4. Identifying steps to reduce risk. Determine weight-loss steps to reduce weight in safe and healthy manner. Identify self-monitoring strategy to measure the efficacy of the chosen weight-loss program—that is, weekly charting of results. Joining a weight-loss support group can provide encouragement and the opportunity to contribute to the programs of others. A public announcement of the goal to get weight off and keep it off can stir a sense of personal pride. Purchasing only "healthy foods" and serving them in measured ways reduces some temptation. On the other hand, what if you were to fail? Think about the public censure and jokes. What if you didn't know what to do in a support group. You could make a fool out of yourself.

5. Making decision on best estimates. Modest weight loss and weight-loss maintenance are superior to a pattern of spiraling weight gains or remaining at the same unwanted weight level. Multiple interventions can support this program and improve the probabilities for achieving and maintaining the goal. On the other hand, putting this plan off until another date or time means that you have more time to gather information. Perhaps someone will invent a miracle drug to make dieting and weight maintenance fun.

6. Taking action. Start the healthy steps to weight loss and maintenance and keep this up for the rest of your life. On the other hand, you can read books and listen to commentary on how the "public" is too overfocused on health and weight. You can consider that the public "should" accept you even if you weighed six hundred pounds. After all, isn't that in the spirit of self-acceptance that you don't put yourself down even when you don't achieve your goals? (*Note:* The principle of self-acceptance implies self-responsibility. The above represents an adulteration of the concept.)

Although this decision-making process requires work, it can help to subvert the decision-breakdown process. Furthermore, in using this model, you keep yourself reasonably active. Even when you are not sure about the outcome, you are taking a logical pathway toward making that decision.

Use the following outline to map your decision-making process. Pick an area you've put off under the statement of issue. In this exercise stick only with the decision-making process.

1. Statement of issue
2. Statement of benefits
3. Personal strengths and limitations assessment

4. Identifying steps to reduce risk
5. Deciding best estimates
6. Taking action

What if, during this process, you start to anticipate "on the other hand" types of "disasters"? What if you thought, "What if I were to fail?" The solution to these "what if . . . ?" type questions is to add one word to the sequence: "*so* what if . . . ?" This simple step can place your decision to act or not to act into a clearer perspective.

You may encounter another difficulty with this process. Some people are great at doing the analytic work and creating plans, then they stop. This is almost like running a race: upon finding yourself ahead of the game, you stop when you are near the finish. Then you start fresh and repeat the pattern. This is the fall-back procrastination pattern. We'll look at this again in chapter 12 under behavior procrastination. For now, imagine yourself finishing the race by taking the steps to get there.

VINDICTIVE PERFECTIONISM

Wrath, fury, hatred, bitterness, rage, hostility, and resentment refer to different versions of anger. Our cognitions and the interpretations that we give to provoking events color these different forms of anger.

Anger is very much a part of life, and we can be both on the receiving and provoking ends. When we vex, tease, gall, irk, ruffle, offend, or push someone too far, we can evoke anger by the atmosphere we create.

Few can resist responding with anger under a legitimately provocative, inciting barrage. I do know some people who appropriately recognize that the taunter has troubles and often find ways effectively to undermine the validity of the other's position. When taunted some forcefully express a genuine sense of indignation that makes clear their intention to maintain their sense of integrity. Like most things in life, your response is a reflection of your perspective and personality.

Sadly, when you bait others into an angry response, you show a weakness in your own arguments. Perhaps you procrastinate on creating sensible dialogues and being on the right side of a principle.

In this section, we'll put aside the many levels and forms that anger takes and look at forms of anger that are generally the result of a perfectionistic view toward life.

The Jehovah View

The God of the Old Testament, Jehovah, punished those who disobeyed and offended him. So he evicted Adam and Eve from paradise for eating the apple from the tree of the knowledge of good and evil. Because of his disobedience, Jonah was forced to live in the stomach of a whale for three days. Noah's ark saved two of every species from drowning when Jehovah flooded the earth to destroy all other life in retaliation against those humans who disobeyed his laws.

Jehovah had an anger problem. He set down laws, expected people to follow them, and became wrathful and destructive when they failed to comply. Since humans are fallible, Jehovah was never without an excuse to exercise the prerogatives of a social perfectionist. However, Jehovah stories were probably intended to keep people in line.

Jehovah's attitude exemplifies the destructive urges within all people. The anger is irrational because it relates to the violation of personal rules that follow the sequence of expectations, intolerance, condemnations, and punishment. However, not all anger is irrational. We have a hardwired "fight" reaction that kicks in when we feel threatened and where we perceive that we can fight back.

We can wrong ourselves and others through the form our anger takes. However, as the Greek philosopher Aristotle taught, "We praise a person who feels angry on the right grounds and against the right persons and also in the right manner at the right moment and for the right length of time."

I-ANGER

Anger is a legitimate response to a threat to your health, economics, property, family, or survival. When you believe you were treated unjustly, you may also rightly feel angered. Anger under these conditions is normally a charged response to a specific event and short-lived. However, anger can reflect a lingering, irrational state of mind when you make up subjective rules and then decree that you or others should, ought, or must live by these dictates. Since the world is imperfect, your rules routinely will be challenged. This irrational anger (I-anger) is discretionary and unnecessary. It corresponds with low frustration tolerance, time urgency, intolerance, and a punitive attitude of mind. Floating in this cauldron of bubbling misery, you prime yourself to procrastinate as you heighten your risk for stress-related coronary heart disease.

I-anger follows a predictable pattern. First there is an expectation that others must live according to your expectations (social perfectionism). This illogical premise then demands that we force others to acquiesce to the "right rules"—namely, the rules we set. Third, people should know these rules, and if they act disobediently, or fail to properly interpret a subtle warning, they should be severely punished. To put this into perspective, pretend you have your own ten commandments for how people should act toward you. What are these commandments? Will everyone universally accept them as law and truth?

You can turn I-anger toward yourself. You condemn yourself for your failings and shortcomings as though such things should not exist. I-anger can develop out of a feeling of helplessness. When anger develops from helplessness, the first reaction is fear. But since fear might clash with your idealized image, a pseudo-anger erupts to cover up the helplessness. In other words, the person defuses the fear by acting angry and "sounding tough." The reaction is comparable to the puffing up of a blowfish who perceives danger.

When we internalize and repeat I-anger by obsessively reruning threat-evoking situations, we've entered an emotional torture chamber. Fuming over perceived self-weaknesses and entertaining destructive fantasies, we rage within. Chronic anger of this sort stresses our physical resources that fight disease, interferes with coronary functioning, and sabotages opportunities for doing the things that can promote happiness and contentment.

Sometimes you may position yourself like a Jehovah and feel good while feeling angry. For example, one day as I discussed the notion of anger with a group of psychotherapy trainees, one proudly reported that his anger felt good. The example he gave involved an incident in which he went to retrieve his clothing from the dry cleaner and noticed a tiny spot on his coat. In vivid detail he told how he had yelled and screamed and cursed the shopkeeper for the damage. He exclaimed how he had frightened this person, humbled him, and forced him to remove the spot immediately.

The trainee believed that yelling was the way to show power. He had learned this technique from an encounter group experience. He further believed that because he was on the customers' side of the counter, he had the unique right to be a glorious Jehovah. Like the judge in a kangaroo court, he indicted, tried, condemned, and punished the shopkeeper and believed he showed his power and strength in doing so. Instead he showed a lack of control and empathy.

As with the encounter group trainee, when you subvert a rule or desire, and you believe that you *should not* have to bear inconvenience or frustration, I-anger often erupts. As part of this process, you can devalue, dehumanize, and make punishable whoever does the unthinkable—violate an expectation. Who loses? Most probably everyone related to such irrational outbursts.

Chronic I-anger (hostility), generated out of intolerance for tension and irrational demands, can lead to a generalized pattern of vengeful impulses that raises the risk of personal harm. Retaliation by the adversary is one obvious outcome. There are other outcomes that result in self-harm. A hostile adolescent, for example, can get back at his or her parents by failing in areas the parents can't control. Thus the rebellious adolescent can fail school subjects, date people the parents disapprove of, become too thin or fat, and be chronically late. Although this behavior is equivalent to breaking one's toys so that no one else can play with them, the rebellious person is often too enveloped in vengeful thoughts and actions to consciously recognize the personal damage such rebellious reactions create.

The Futility of I-Anger

Overall, I-anger reflects a perfectionistic attitude. Furthermore, I-anger (hostility) is an exercise in futility because it potentially impedes progress in at least seven ways:

> ➤ We curtail enjoyment of living because of continual brooding or vengeful scheming.
> ➤ We expend time and effort blaming and condemning rather than in constructing.
> ➤ We maintain a high inner-tension level.
> ➤ Distrust becomes increasingly evident toward those who genuinely want to help.
> ➤ We invite retaliation.
> ➤ Life tends to be unpleasant.
> ➤ Hostile preoccupations distract from purposefulness and thus lead to procrastination.

Time expended in angry or hostile pursuits drains time from other activities. However, people engulfed in vengeful thoughts and vengeful actions divert time from the constructive challenges of life and often don't see the loss.

Sometimes called hostility, chronic I-anger is a manifestation of a maladaptive, primitive style of coping. So let's see how to build up some more "emotional muscle" to contend with this *vengeful perfectionism*.

Dealing with Hostility

The following hints to reduce anger obviously cannot result in the complete elimination of this I-anger challenge and of all the procrastination associated with it. However, your awareness of the challenge and the following "attack" strategies can add to your repertory of choices.

> ➤ When you feel hostile (I-anger), discern whether the feeling comes out of helplessness, intolerance for tension, or perfectionism. If the feeling represents helplessness (fear), identify what you fear. Then simulate a set of conditions under which you can

practice learning to act in nonhelpless and nonhostile ways. If the feeling represents intolerance for tension, explore what makes tension so intolerable to you. Face the tension. If I-anger stirs from the depths of perfectionism, work to change your demands to performance preferences and change your condemnations to considerations. Of course, I-anger can engage all three conditions of mind and emotion as well as other related outlooks.

➤ Identify situations in which you are likely to become hostile because of low tension tolerance, then imagine yourself in that situation responding in three constructive ways. Validate the three constructive alternatives by role-playing with an objective and kind friend.

➤ Define three alternative ways of stopping procrastinating in a situation in which you are procrastinating because you wish to punish somebody. Use the alternative that may be most effective in overcoming procrastination.

➤ Think of five positive qualities of each of your adversaries. When you encounter an adversary, keep these qualities in mind as you interact. This introspective experience can lend positive energy to your persuasive initiatives. When other people don't feel criticized, they normally will act more cooperatively.

➤ Face the reality that people are not born to abide by your rules, particularly if you don't tell them your regulations for living. Indeed, people have their own rules, and some will most surely conflict with yours.

➤ Irrational expectations lead to exasperation. So if you feel hostile, look to see what expectations you are holding. Then seek a tolerable alternative view of the situation.

➤ Substitute *expectancies* for *expectations*. Expectancies are probability statements. You think of how to increase the likelihood of bringing about desired results. For example, what is the probability that practically everyone will see life as you do and will accede to you wishes and preferences without causing you to make any major concessions in return? The expectancy attitude of mind takes nothing away from your sense of determination and adds to the likelihood that you will gain greater cooperation in getting things done.

GUILT TRIP THROUGH THE MIND TUNNEL

On his annual spring cave-hunting expedition in the Adirondack Mountains, Jack wandered far from the trail and chanced to notice a small, deep cave partially covered with scraggy shrubs. With rising anticipation he grasped his flashlight and entered. As he entered, his excitement evaporated. Suddenly the chill of apprehension hit him as memories of the past began to fill his mind. He recalled his third grade teacher, Ms. Brown, telling him that he was a dirty and bad boy for lifting Susie's dress. He remembered how horrified his mother seemed when Ms. Brown conveyed the bad news. "I feel like I will die," she said, "you've disgraced the family. We can never live this down." In rapid succession a barrage of images flashed before his mind's eye: how bad Aunt Tilly felt when he forgot to thank her for the handkerchiefs she had given him for his tenth birthday; his father's hurt when he failed math in high school; his first girlfriend, who told him he had "ruined her" and because of that he could never leave her; George, his first boss, who told Jack that he had let him down and that he didn't deserve the break he (Jack) had gotten.

The farther into the tunnel Jack went, the more vivid the guilty images, and the more quickly they came. Unfortunately, we'll temporarily have to leave Jack in the midst of his plight and take an academic look at guilt.

Guilt implies the violation of a moral standard followed by self-condemnation. Guilt is a vindictive perfectionism that takes the form "You *should* have behaved better. Now you're really no good—a real louse."

Although guilt is typically a useless, backward look, sometimes it is an anticipatory reaction leading to procrastination. This is when a person gets caught in a moral *double bind* by trapping himself between two moral opposites. For instance, suppose you believe that competing is wrong and simultaneously value the type of success that comes from effectively competing. This presents quite a dilemma: if you compete, you'll feel guilty for competing, and if you don't compete, you'll feel guilty because you haven't obtained the prize of the competition. Catch-22 strikes again!

Although there are many things to feel guilty over, we need not include procrastination on the list. In my view, if you must procrastinate, pointing the guilty finger at yourself will hardly serve to correct your behavior. Feel remorseful or feel regretful (feeling bad without self-condemnation). Consider corrective actions. This process can help you not only move away from guilt but also reduce the risks and negative fallout of procrastination.

Well, we left Jack several paragraphs ago suffering by going backward in the mind tunnel. Fortunately, he catches some pages flying by him with the heading "Getting Out of the Mind Tunnel." "What a strange title," Jack contemplates. "I think I'll read it."

GETTING OUT OF THE MIND TUNNEL

➤ Ask yourself what makes you a reprehensible person if you fail to live up to a subjective standard? If you fail a moral standard, then what can you do to make amends and do better next time?

➤ Try to collect concrete facts to help you learn the validity or non-validity of both elements of double-bind conditions.

➤ Give yourself five good reasons why you're not a terrible person even if you do procrastinate. Then give yourself five reasons that show the Do It Now! benefits.

➤ Accept responsibility for intentional or unintentional poor acts (like spreading false rumors or withholding affection) and try to spend more energy on preventing their recurrence than on backward looks through the mind tunnel.

POSTSCRIPT

Perfectionism mocks reality. In this world we try to turn quinine into sugar and vinegar into honey. Although our perfectionistic visions promote directions we can undertake, they are the visions of the impossible dream—a dream that lays waste to our emotional landscape.

With perfectionistic visions fixed in mind, we fear failing at every turn because whatever can get done will not prove good enough. In this atmosphere of mind, failure fears abound, and we wonder "why bother" if the results won't prove good enough.

Twisting our way through a desert of perilous perfectionist thoughts, we reinforce our own suffering. Our inner dictates that promise a better tomorrow make waking a nightmare.

Hostility and guilt supplement this way of perceiving and darken the barren road that supports a procrastination pattern. In that wilderness of crosscurrents and sand-blasted ideas, we have ample time to conjure up many false explanations for what went wrong.

In the world of the perfectionist, assumptions substitute for reality. In the perfectionist's mind, there should be no conflicts between rules and reality. But choice, by nature, means *chance, competition,* and *conflict.* Although trees compete for space in the forest, there is space for many trees. So there is room for many perspectives and views.

Perfectionism takes time from the important things in life. Of course, there is no universal law that says you have to change the path you follow, even when a perfectionist's path guarantees a strained and dry outcome.

10

Approval Seeking and Putting It Off

In This Chapter

➤ Eight approval-seeking myths
➤ Social anxieties
➤ Shyness

Present yourself as a maple and get sapped. It's very hard to be a hermit. In our daily lives we are in constant contact with other people—workmates, friends, family—and our greatest joys and problems often involve our relationships. Because people are so important, we make use of shaving razors, bath soaps, underarm deodorant, breath fresheners, beauty salons, fashionable clothing, manners, and other social devices so that we appear attractive and acceptable to others. And there is no doubt that getting along with others has considerable advantages. Some people, however, devote themselves to the idea that the way to feel worthy involves pleasing practically every person on this planet. But trying to gain universal acceptance is a *quixotic* undertaking—one that has all sorts of noxious consequences, including procrastination.

At the other extreme, some people have given up on improving themselves because of deep feelings of inferiority. But at the same time, they fear rejection. These people believe that others think as badly of them as they do of themselves.

The bottom line is that different people have different tastes, so you can't possibly please everyone. Universal popularity is a myth. If you try to live the myth, you'll probably end up displeasing yourself and everyone else. At its worse, this impossible desire to meet with

116

universal approval will paralyze you, leading to developmental procrastination.

PERILOUS IMPRESSIONS

When making a good impression on others becomes an urgent drive, you will probably procrastinate on developing self-assertion. Occasionally the urgent need to gain approval results in *confrontation anxiety*—fearing to express an unpopular opinion or an idea that might invite disagreement. Such confrontation anxieties can leave you looking like a wishy-washy wimp with few opinions or ideas.

Another negative result of a strong need for approval involves *compliance compulsion,* a mental state in which you believe that you can only gain acceptance and position by acquiescing to the demands of others and genuflecting at the right times. However, this mental state typically results in positioning oneself as someone whom others can walk over, rather than as a person whose actions command admiration and respect.

EIGHT APPROVAL-SEEKING MYTHS

Sometimes we act on approval-seeking myths to relieve social tensions. These approval-seeking habits of mind inevitably lead to procrastination as we wait for the myth to become real.

The following eight myths commonly appear in a *quixotic quest* to overcome social tensions. After each myth, I offer a rational alternative.

> ➤ **The myth of the perfect first impression.** This is the conviction that disaster follows unless you make a perfect first impression. Naturally, when you feel the inordinate pressure of having to make a perfect impression, you will be hesitant and uncertain. This hesitancy then ruins the impression.
> **Rational alternative:** Consider that though first impressions are often important, acting natural and showing interest in others is more important in creating a good impression than worrying about how you are going to come across.
> ➤ **The myth of the perfectly articulate person.** This is the notion that you should not express yourself unless you can do it in a highly articulate style.

Rational alternative: Although you normally do not want to stumble over your words, remember that ordinary conversations rarely translate into perfectly written text. Instead of a blind dedication to this ideal, find ways to develop your ability to express your ideas. The best way to develop this skill is by practicing it.

➤ **The myth of the perfect opening gambit.** You subscribe to this myth if you find yourself saying, "If I only knew how to start a conversation. . . ." Your perceived inability to start a conversation will inevitably distract you from ever trying to start a conversation.

Rational alternative: Consider that you will probably not find a universally appealing opening line, but you can find many acceptable ways to begin. The best way to develop this skill is to practice it by diving right into conversations.

➤ **The myth of perfect preparation.** This is the belief that you cannot speak up in groups until you have read all the latest "important" books and completely analyzed the most current news.

Rational alternative: While it's good to be informed, you can often learn and contribute more by talking to people about what they know rather than concerning yourself with discussing the thoughts of important writers and newsmakers. People are often flattered when asked their opinions.

➤ **The myth of complete comfort.** This is an idealized prerequisite to social interaction. When you follow this myth, you may avoid any social contact until you feel completely comfortable and at ease. In the end, you procrastinate until the opportunity passes.

Rational alternative: Consider that a certain amount of discomfort is natural when you meet people for the first time. For most of us, feeling awkward is more normal than being comfortable. Awkwardness, however, passes with familiarity.

➤ **The myth of the unassailable statement.** This is the belief that you should not speak up unless you state an idea that transcends criticism.

Rational alternative: Remember that the only unassailable statements are regurgitations of proven facts. If your contribution to a conversation is merely citing proven facts, you would be quite the boring conversationalist.

➤ **The myth of the savior.** This is the hope that a rescuer will take charge of your life and protect you in social situations. We often delay social interactions until we are accompanied by someone with whom we feel comfortable.

Rational alternative: Consider that it will be very difficult to find a guardian angel who will accompany you throughout your life. What you can do is ask yourself how you can become your own guardian angel.

These myths, when unchallenged, normally have a paradoxical effect. Because they are, in fact, nearly impossible criteria to meet, they can paralyze you into procrastinating. If you do try to live them, your social interactions are likely to be canned and boring, and you will appear to be a stuffed parrot.

WHO SEEKS APPROVAL?

Practically everyone prefers approval to disapproval. You normally will have fewer conflicts when you attempt to get along with others. Indeed, few people intend to act obnoxious or plan to alienate themselves from other people.

Most reasonable people recognize that there is a great diversity in styles, interests, and personal preferences among our population. We may really like some people but actively avoid or have mixed feelings toward others.

The approval seeker takes a normal human desire for affiliation and approval and turns this desire into a *quixotic quest* for being liked, loved, admired, and respected. By gaining the crowd's applause, the approval seeker expects to avoid the pain of rejection, gain control, achieve success, and experience comfort. You fall into this *social procrastination* trap when you sell out on yourself in a misguided hope that social approval brings worth. Although social approval is normally advantageous, worth is a gift that only you can give to yourself.

Like a chameleon, approval seeking takes different forms. If you find yourself using any of the following social styles, you problaby have a *social procrastination* challenge to face.

Love Lushes

Love lushes have an overpowering *need* to avoid rejection. They expect to have others think well of them—even strangers they've never seen before and may never see again. Love lushes want to get high on admiration. For a person in this painful state of *emotional drunkenness,* failing to obtain approval causes a tension hangover. Just as different people vary in their drinking habits, love lushism exists in varying degrees. In some situations—at work, for instance—love lushism will appear in full force for a person who concentrates on obtaining approval at any cost, though the same person may act differently in another situation in which approval carries less weight. But in any situation the overwhelming fear of failing to obtain needed approval has a crippling effect on that person's ability to get anything done.

The Compliant

Studies of pressures for conformity indicate that most people will comply with group pressures through the directives of authority. As a group we are, perhaps, too deferent to authority or to the symbols of authority. Titles like doctor, sir, officer, and mistress symbolize authority and make it easy for the approval-seeking members of society to know toward whom they should act particularly deferential. Uniforms imply compliance, and we may take direction from someone in a uniform who has no real authority.

Thoughtless compliance is an indicator of how low one places oneself on the social pecking order. Contrary to a popular belief that the meek will inherit the earth, we have no hard evidence that this will take place in the near future. In the meantime, when we are too eager to comply with authorities, we put off making important and necessary decisions about our own lives.

The Good Guy

Approval seekers have alternatives to acting meek and passive. One alternative is being the "good guy" who acts very friendly and eagerly grants favors at each convenient opportunity. This approval-seeking person will habitually consent to do favors for others often without realizing that being overzealous in granting favors steals valuable time from personal pursuits.

The good guy often takes on too much then procrastinates about keeping the original agreements and schedules. Some members of this *hate-to-say-no* group get people angry at them and defeat their original purpose—to appear good. In other cases, the good guy turns into *angry guy*. Anticipating criticism for procrastination, the approval-seeking person acts paranoid and resentful without justification. The animosity is often directed against people who have done little to apply pressure to get the favor done.

By actively expressing this resentment, people in this trap often lose sight of the fact that they created their own tangled web. They did it to themselves.

People who seek approval often procrastinate on healthy self-expression. If you think you may have approval-seeking tendencies, don't despair. Fortunately, you can correct this psychological hang-up as you will see in the section that follows.

DEALING WITH APPROVAL PROBLEMS

You can deal with *approval-seeking procrastination* in many ways. By desensitizing yourself to disapproval, you can become more sensitive to others. You won't direct your energies into mental machinations, or self-spying, and you can give more quality time to people who deserve your attention.

To become less needful of approval you can do uncomfortable, but temporary, actions (after a while, you may actually find them kind of fun). If your approval-seeking tendencies are based on·a fear of appearing conspicuous or fear of what others think, here are some approval desensitization exercises:

> ➤ Go to the local diner for breakfast. Ask for the unconventional one fried egg and one scrambled egg instead of two eggs the same style. You're bound to attract attention with this one! You may even find the exercise fun.
> ➤ If you are not quite ready for the two-eggs-any-style exercise, ask the food server to warm your cup before pouring your coffee, tea, or hot chocolate.
> ➤ Put on two different-colored shoes for a day.
> ➤ Wear your hair in an unusual fashion for a week.
> ➤ Stick a turkey feather in your hair for an afternoon.
> ➤ Whistle "Dixie" as you walk down the street.
> ➤ Step out of character. If you normally dress sloppily, dress sharply. If you normally frown, smile. If you don't compliment people, do so. If you normally act patronizing, be crisp and factual. In other words, try to change some of the external things that you do. As a result, you might find people responding more positively toward you.
> ➤ Make plans to go out in public with a person who you know acts silly. Use the opportunity to act silly yourself.
> ➤ Ask for change in a busy store with a sign reading NO CHANGE GIVEN. Ask the proprietor to justify his rule. You don't have to be hostile or aggressive, just matter-of-fact.
> ➤ If you feel dissatisfied with a product, return it. Make a mental note about how you handled the complaint. If you feel satisfied, repeat the process. If dissatisfied with your approach, modify it.

Although you may feel uncomfortable attempting these exercises, that's common. Furthermore, experiencing discomfort in the above situations makes sense. Some things are uncomfortable to do! Indeed, bearing discomfort helps you to build tolerance for discomfort.

If you feel embarrassed, however, you are putting yourself down or believing you are exposing a weakness. Now ask yourself: "What weakness am I exposing?" and "What is wrong with temporarily exercising my right to be less conventional than normal?" Well, what is wrong with that?

The following exercises extend the concept of overcoming fears of disapproval in areas of self-expression. They include saying what you mean, standing up for your rights, saying no, expressing opinions, giving feedback, and stepping into the limelight.

➤ Have a talk with yourself about the merits and disadvantages of saying what you mean and meaning what you say. Tape-record this conversation. Play it back. Note what you consider to be constructive ideas. Each day, for the next ten days, carry out a different idea.

➤ If you feel you get pushed around too much, practice standing up for yourself with some of your friends who are willing to help you role-play some new ways of responding. Next test these skills under real conditions where self-assertion is appropriate. Remember, others are not going to remain passive as you develop skill in being more self-expressive. However, if you speak from the heart, as the old saying goes, you'll be acting in truth with yourself. Also, the feedback you get from your interactions may prove that your opinions and ideas aren't 100 percent right in all circumstances. That's fine because that's how you learn.

➤ If you think the word *no* is naughty, get some practice saying the word. Go to a store with pushy sales personnel. Resist their sales pitches by using the word *no*. Examine what is wrong with saying no or maybe. What is so great in saying yes when you mean no?

➤ Formulate an opinion about a controversial news topic and present it to friends or colleagues for their reactions. If a debate results, stick to your point. Try to repeat this exercise at least once a week.

➤ If you feel dissatisfied with someone's behavior, consider if pointing this out to him or her would be helpful, and if so, put on your diplomat's hat and try.

SOCIAL ANXIETIES

You don't have to feel shy to experience social anxiety. Some generally outgoing people are socially apprehensive in some situations where they believe they are being evaluated.

Dating anxiety is common, especially among college students. This response is partially due to an oversensitivity to rejection, especially with initial face-to-face contacts. This form of anxiety sometimes results from sexualizing the relationship before it begins. Here sexual interests, sensitivities, and perhaps bending over backward to appear to have no sexual interests create added tension that leads to feelings of awkwardness.

> # Do It Now!
>
> ### Dating Anxiety
>
> To defuse this "dating" anxiety, it is sometimes wise to focus on companionship, common interests, and having fun with a potential date. A focus on friendship can do much to defuse sexualized tension and make love more likely. One way to get a new perspective on dating is through the Internet, which is a context without sexual tension where you can meet people and concentrate on developing your ability to exchange thoughts and ideas. However, be selective. The Internet has its share of unsavory characters.

Some people who procrastinate on overcoming their social inhibitions will engage in self-manipulations to compensate, such as using alcohol to lower their inhibitions and fears. At one level it serves as an excuse for negative social conduct: "I did it because I was drunk." However, drinking to get drunk is a choice that abrogates the excuse. And remember, when you use alcohol primarily to lower your inhibitions or to reduce stress, you are an alcohol abuser whether you *use* it once a day or once a year for such purposes. It's how you put alcohol (drugs) to use that defines abuse.

The different forms of social anxiety involve an irrational fear of rejection. This relates to the self-perception that you are not acceptable, have unworthy qualities, are not personable enough, or suffer another social affliction.

In this state, people channel considerable energies and powers of concentration into ongoing self-debates such as "Should I say or do this or that?" "What will he/she/they think?" "I wonder if he/she/ they like me, think I'm attractive, smart, witty, . . . etc." With all this mental turmoil going on, practically anybody would find it difficult to devote much energy to a conversation or interpersonal activity.

DEALING WITH SOCIAL ANXIETIES

You want to stop procrastinating on dealing with your social anxiety. You'd like to be able to meet more people, stand up for your rights, negotiate, relate, speak before groups—all with a minimum of irrational mental interference. Where do you begin?

The place to start is to listen to your own thoughts. What are you telling yourself when you experience a social anxiety? This cognitive map can quickly tell you about the connections among your thinking, feeling, and behavior. Chances are that upon examination some of your thoughts will prove irrational.

How can you identify irrational thoughts? Irrational thinking often involves perfectionistic claims and demands, demeaning self-comments, and self-defeating condemnations of ourself and others. Irrational thinking is overly generalized, circular, and unprovable. Such thoughts clearly detract from you enjoying your life. Yet the habits of mind behind these distortions of reality gain credibility through the emotions they generate and the results they create. For example, people in suspicious and jealous states of mind can cause themselves emotional upset while creating self-fulfilling prophecies that both result from and support the irrationality.

In chapter 14 we'll discuss varied irrational processes that correlate with procrastination. For now, you can apply the following basic idea to the task of keeping perspective on irrational approval needs.

Remember seventeenth-century French philosopher René Descartes's famous statement: "I think, therefore I am." This statement highlighted Descartes's way of opposing authoritarianism through skepticism. When you listen to your inner voices of fear, you may hear a wheedling voice. In this autocratic monologue, the wheedler tells you what you can't do, what you don't deserve to have, why you are unworthy, the terrible consequences of making a mistake, the perils of looking foolish, the disgrace of acting awkward, the woes of lacking polish, the crisis in coming across as socially inept, and so forth. This irrational mental interference is the stuff that fuels social anxiety.

To use Descartes's discovery, start to doubt the ideas but not the *self*. Write down each idea that causes you to feel anxious, and then preface it with the statement "I doubt that." Here are some examples:

➤ I doubt that I don't deserve to have congenial relationships because _____.

➤ I doubt that I am completely unworthy because _____.

➤ I doubt that the potential of making a social mistake is sufficient grounds for me to avoid social contact because _____.

Now, look at the statements you wrote after *because*. Would they hold up in a court of law? Could a good attorney take these assertions and muster a good defense in your behalf? If so, how? Take on the role of that defense attorney and beat the wheedler prosecutor.

SHYNESS: ANOTHER FORM OF INTERPERSONAL ANXIETY

People who appear shy may not be that way at all. Some individuals are quiet and prefer their own company yet act with social confidence. Others are reserved, modest, and prefer working alone. Indeed, millions of introverted individuals find that a little people contact goes a long way. They are happiest working with ideas, special independent projects, or doing other solo activities.

Shyness, a drawing back from others in a timid, inhibited, or fearful way, is different from quiet reserve. We see shyness in people who behave bashfully and freeze at social gatherings because they are self-conscious. Despite these feelings of social inadequacy, shyness sometimes appears to the casual observer as indifference, disdainfulness, superiority, coolness, aloofness, and distance—the very opposite of the way that shy people ordinarily feel. This social difficulty often results in procrastination in dealing with personal insecurities and inhibitions in social settings.

People with shyness problems believe that people are to be feared; they can hurt; I'm not smart or attractive enough for anyone to be interested in; attractive stable people will reject me because I'm not worth talking to; if I say anything, I'll make a fool out of myself. Preoccupied with these negative ideas, members of this clan shy away from interpersonal situations that evoke these lines of thought.

Overcoming shyness is a prime developmental procrastination challenge for the approximately forty million U.S. citizens who fall into this group. Since this number involves about 15 percent of the U.S. population, shyness represents an important developmental procrastination challenge. But shyness *can* be overcome. You may never fully rid yourself of shyness, but chances are that you can make solid progress by learning to become more self-accepting, relaxed, and expressive in social situations.

Discussing all aspects of shyness would require another book. I've limited the following section to a sample of methods for dealing with shyness as it relates to a fear of disapproval.

TACTICS FOR OVERCOMING SHYNESS

Develop a general plan for conquering shyness by doing the following:

➤ Identify those situations where you'd like to stop acting shyly.
➤ Rank the items on the list from least to most difficult.
➤ Begin with the least difficult project on your list.
➤ Use your imagination to create a mental picture of yourself as you would be socially if you were free of shyness.
➤ Pace yourself by gradually and consistently tackling your social challenges by following the list you made up at the beginning of this exercise. Start by taking the least anxious step, master that level, then move to the next step up. For example, if the first (least difficult) situation on your list involves going to unfamiliar department stores, enter and walk around such stores until you feel reasonably comfortable in that situation. Then move to the next level on the list.
➤ Consider an implosive method where you challenge yourself by exposing yourself to a difficult social situation. For example, begin with the top item in the list. This will have a ripple effect, making the less fearsome items easier to manage, that is, unless you procrastinate.

Implosive methods are less likely to be effective and can have side effects because you might feel more fear and resistance to moving forward. However, this is a matter of "knowing thyself." If your history shows that a graduated method has the greater potential, test those waters. If you've done better with more implosive methods, that approach bears consideration. When in doubt, ask your local friendly cognitive behavioral, multimodal, or rational emotive behavior therapist.

Now that you have the framework for a general plan, you can test these tactics to overcome social fears:

➤ First imagine yourself feeling a comfortable sense of self-acceptance and maintaining this mental image in social settings—even among strangers.
➤ If you fear expressing yourself in groups, plan to speak up each time you are in a group. You can support this initiative by asking questions, making a comment, asking someone to clarify a point, and so forth.
➤ If you fear eating alone in a restaurant, or fear going to a movie by yourself, live with the discomfort and overcome the fear by

going alone to a restaurant or the movies. Repeat this until you no longer feel self-conscious in those settings.

➤ Carry or wear an object that could be a conversation piece. A comic button or the latest novel will do. When you display such objects, someone may feel inclined to initiate a conversation with you.

➤ Be alert to conversation pieces others display. Casually comment about the conversation piece. Perhaps you'll start a conversation this way. You have more direct control over this procedure than waiting for someone else to discover your "conversation piece." Also, the person you speak to may pick up on your conversation piece.

➤ Ask three strangers a day to tell you the exact time. Persist with this exercise until you feel at ease asking this question.

➤ Practice acting friendly by saying "Hello" to people you barely know. Keep practicing until you feel natural greeting people.

➤ Try to maintain good eye contact with the people with whom you interact.

Improving your interpersonal skills involves developing not only positive behavior but also positive attitudes. As you work to develop both attitudinal and behavioral skills, sometimes you will feel discouraged if you backslide or if you don't right away achieve the results you seek. Possibly this retreat occurs when you first experientially "see" that you don't relate equally easily to all people, regardless of how interpersonally skilled you become. Bearing the occasional discouragement and disappointment, then rebounding to continue with developing positive attitudinal and behavioral skills, can give you a deserved sense of interpersonal freedom.

POSTSCRIPT

This chapter scratches the surface of a number of possible developmental procrastination problems related to people issues. For instance, while many procrastinators worry about what other people think of them, their procrastination may irritate the very people they wish to impress. But members of this procrastination set rarely see the incongruity!

Saddled with social challenges, approval seekers with procrastination habits can adapt some concepts and exercises in this book as part of a self-help program. They also can work with a counselor to develop such a program.

Discomfort Dodging and Procrastination

Besides physical danger, what else is there to fear? A proverb says that if you give a man a fish, you feed him for a day; if you teach him to fish, you feed him for the rest of his life.

Learning to tolerate discomfort is like learning to fish. It is perhaps one of the most important lessons to learn on the trail to doing it now. That is because so much needless psychological misery builds from an unwillingness to accept the frustrations of daily living. When there is an unwillingness to accept frustration, distress and procrastination frequently follow.

To help you learn this discomfort-tolerating process, we'll examine various aspects of the need for comfort and then suggest exercises to build tolerance for discomfort. We'll also look at the self-defeating need for immediate gratification and at methods for overcoming it.

These approaches represent a start to a frustration-tolerance training program, where you will learn to teach yourself to manage your frustrations and overcome this catalyst for procrastination.

LOOKING FOR THE EASY WAY

During the early 1950s, psychiatrist Abraham Low identified a "cult of comfort" whose membership worshiped comfort and indulged in an unwillingness to bear inconvenience and tension. Our tolerance for frustration may have worsened since then. However, this idea continues to have validity: Low pointed out that the act of accepting discomfort has a profound effect upon the intensity of the discomfort—it becomes bearable and less threatening.

People who believe that they cannot tolerate discomfort may procrastinate by substituting something else for a priority activity. This discomfort-dodging process is like distracting yourself from an itch by scratching, or distracting yourself from a headache by rubbing the area where you feel the pain—they create temporary relief but do nothing to address the root causes of our discomfort.

SATISFACTION SEEKING

Achieving satisfaction and happiness in life is a prime desire of every human being. Such pleasures may be anything—winning a chess tournament, dwelling in plush surroundings, talking with a friend, finding a cure for cancer. We can attain some with little investment; others require considerable work. Whether the investment is small or large, satisfaction is a common result of the human tendency to create and to construct.

Satisfaction seeking may become confused with the need for comfort, but they are different. Obtaining satisfaction requires making *efforts* that lead to goal attainment, and goal attainment often leads to satisfaction. Comfort seeking, on the other hand, involves avoiding effort or productive work and substituting the pursuit of a tension-free existence.

The very work necessary to achieve satisfaction may produce uncomfortable moments. If you say you want to feel a sense of satisfaction in what you do but avoid initially unpleasant tasks that might ultimately culminate in satisfaction, then the primary goal that drives your action is tension avoidance.

LEARNING TO BEAR DISCOMFORT

The fear of discomfort interacts with self-doubt in people who tell themselves they can't withstand stress; this fear leads to discomfort dodging, which in turn leads to procrastination. Unfortunately, discomfort dodging can eventually culminate in more intensely negative feelings like guilt—time passes, we put off tasks, we inconvenience people, we have a lot of explaining to do, we "down" ourselves for having procrastinated, and then we repeat the avoidance cycle. In this circular state of mind, no matter what you do to escape the pain, the haunting, inescapable frustration continues.

The comfort-seeking habit is tough to overcome. Most of us really dislike feeling uncomfortable, and we often feel considerable resistance in going against these resistant feelings. Part of this resistance comes from believing that one has to follow one's feelings—if hungry, one eats; if tired, one sleeps; if uncomfortable, one procrastinates. But there are exceptions to these rules: obese people who want to lose weight reduce their food consumption, even if they are hungry. They learn to restrict themselves, rather than indulging their desires. Like the overeater, members of the comfort cult believe that they need to consume comfort. Nevertheless, the solution for the comfort seeker is the same as for the obese person. Change requires restrictions.

► Do It Now!

Discomfort Tolerance

You can begin to teach yourself to bear discomfort by actively imagining situations you usually avoid. Think about a situation you find uncomfortable, like writing a report, doing the dishes, or asking for a pay raise. If after creating such images you feel uncomfortable, keep your attention glued to this feeling of discomfort. Now:

1. Try to detect where the feeling is localized (stomach, shoulders, legs, neck, chest, head).
2. Concentrate your attention on that tension zone.
3. If the feeling eludes you, try to bring it back by tightening that area of your body.
4. Maintain the tension for ten minutes.

When you conscientiously try to create a feeling of discomfort, you will familiarize yourself with your discomfort zone, and this zone will often feel less oppressive later.

Physical pain seems more acute at night and when we have fewer distractions. The same is true of emotional pain. However, with emotional stress, how you divert yourself can be good or bad. One poor solution is to try to control the feeling by demanding that it cease to exist.

Demands such as "I've *got to* get rid of the feeling" only escalate the misery. Another solution is to convince yourself that no problem exists when one definitely does. This form of denial rarely helps. A more workable solution is to *solve* the problem causing the anguish. The following procedure illustrates this approach:

> ➤ Describe the problem factually: "My fiancée told me she was considering breaking our marriage engagement."
> ➤ Describe *what you* would *like* to see happen: "To resolve her doubts in favor of proceeding with the wedding." Describe *how you* would act to try to cause the above result, assuming you were very tolerant of tension and discomfort. For example, strongly express feelings of love and caring while simultaneously supporting your fiancée's right to do what is best for her; allow time to work at trying to identify and resolve problems; convince your fiancée that getting "cold feet" is common just before a wedding.
> ➤ Test our your action plan and modify it with experience.

Another accomplishment exercise is to identify five accomplishments about which you feel a sense of satisfaction and then take these steps:

> ➤ Examine the elements they have in common.
> ➤ Assess the *effort* they required.
> ➤ What are the possibilities today of extending one or more of these accomplishments?
> ➤ What can you do today to begin?
> ➤ Begin.

HATING TO WAIT

Richard had a most unpleasant problem. His tension tolerance was very low, and he thought he had to have what he wanted when he wanted it to avoid tension. When faced with taking care of tedious details, he practically jumps out of his skin with tension. He can't wait to get done. In his frantic effort to blow away the details, he makes many mistakes and repeats the effort to correct needless errors.

Because of his demands for immediate gratification, Richard often acts against his own enlightened self-interests. For example, one day he decided to buy new furniture. Surveying his possible choices, he found some pieces he really liked. Unfortunately, the furniture store could not deliver those pieces for six weeks. So he decided to order furniture that had appealed less to him but that he could get the following day to satisfy his desire to fill some space in his apartment. Another time he varnished a set of bookshelves for his wall. He hurried through the varnishing so that he could see the completed job, and while the bookcase was still very sticky, he picked it up and positioned it against the wall so that he could see how it looked. Then he saddled himself with the unpleasant job of redoing the shelves to cover his finger marks.

Richard hates to wait, and so he leaves late for meetings, parties, and dates so that he doesn't have to wait if someone else is late. Because of this pattern, his popularity and reliability ratings are understandably low. Richard's rushing is a form of quality procrastination because it results in putting off working out the details to achieve quality.

Delays have many possible related causes in addition to pure discomfort dodging:

> *Fated-to-fail.* This is the false belief that whatever you do, you're doomed to fail. (So what difference does it make if you show up late?) It also includes the belief that you'd better play it very safe in your life to avoid getting emotionally whipped.
> *Rebellion.* You show up late, not so much because you hate to wait but because you are tired of being told to show up on time.
> *Testing.* You show up late because you want to test others' tolerance and to gain their attention.
> *Agoraphobia.* You're afraid of leaving the sanctuary of your home and therefore wait until the last possible minute to leave.
> *Mistiming.* You have a habit of expecting too much from yourself. In other words, you consistently underestimate the time it will take you to prepare to leave.

See if any of the above motives operate in your hate-to-wait problem. If so, plan to counteract these problems.

LEARNING TO WAIT

You have many ways to learn *delay of gratification* skills. Pick delay strategies from the following list that seem most helpful and try them out.

> When eating a meal, take small bites and place your eating utensils on the table between bites.
> When feasible, have dessert fifteen minutes after completing your meal.
> Plan a vacation months in advance.

➤ Finish a novel you once found interesting but only partially completed.

➤ Start a hobby, like needlepoint, that requires time and concentration to do well.

➤ Plan your morning schedule so that you can comfortably arrive ten minutes early for work.

➤ Put off the cigarette you usually smoke after breakfast until after lunch.

➤ Systematically put a predetermined amount of money into your savings account each payday.

➤ Take fifteen minutes before bed to prepare for the next day.

➤ Go for a three-hour stroll through a familiar area (your neighborhood, the local pond, the botanical gardens). Develop your observational skills by studying what you have not observed before.

➤ Take the same stroll and develop your observational skills by studying what you have observed before.

➤ Obtain a leaf. Study the leaf for six hours. During that time explore the leaf in as many sensory ways as you can. Note the many sensory qualities that are readily apparent. Then, when you think you have come to the end of your creative potential, try to discover fifty more.

➤ Be early for appointments with friends. Bring a book along to read if you have to wait.

➤ Buy birthday cards today for friends' and relatives' upcoming birthdays in the next year. Sign the cards, stamp and address the envelopes, and mail each out two weeks before the birthday.

FRUSTRATION PROCRASTINATION

Frustrations are natural. Few avoid feeling frustration when a tree falls on your garden or when you don't get a desired promotion or course grade. The major problem we have, then, is not frustration but low frustration tolerance. If you effectively manage the frustrations of daily living, procrastination is unlikely to be a major problem in your life. But if you suffer low frustration tolerance, procrastination usually follows.

Low frustration tolerance is the compelling urge to throw off the discomfort that follows frustration. This reaction usually involves the following:

1. You view a situation as frustrating when you cannot get or do what you want.

2. You magnify the tension by focusing on and then overdramatizing the feeling.
3. You feel an urgent need to act on your feelings of frustration.
4. Depending on how you view the frustrating situation, you might overreact, start stewing, and put off any unpleasant activities associated with the tension you experience.

Low frustration tolerance is a trigger for frustration disturbances. We suffer from frustration disturbances when our tolerance for the unpleasant is brief and the durability of our suffering is long. In this charged state of mind, you are primed to feel overwhelmed, distressed, confused, and disorganized.

Frustration disturbances are tightly linked to procrastination, so this problem habit state of mind warrants a closer look. A frustration disturbance normally includes three or more of the following:

1. A hair-trigger circular reaction characterized by sensation sensitivity, magnification of the tension, intolerance for the magnified tension, and greater sensation sensitivity.
2. An unrealistic fear of the feeling of frustration that stimulates discomfort dodging impulses and escapist and avoidance procrastination.
3. Ruminations of helplessness and powerlessness.
4. A distorted sense of self and of one's ability to cope with the stresses of normal daily living challenges.
5. Compensatory perfectionistic striving.
6. Negative emotional or physical states such as anxiety, depression, hostility, fatigue, and so forth.

Frustration disturbances are part of just about any major distress reaction and clearly are a part of chronic procrastination. This condition rarely exists in pure form. It commingles with many different cognitive signatures of distress. It is not necessarily a cause of, or reaction to, a situation as much as it is a part of an unpleasant emotional package.

The Chain of Pain

Imagine your frustration disturbance as a chain of interlocking ideas, feelings, and emotional reactions. The ideas involve thoughts of powerlessness, inferiority, intolerance, and so forth. Now, imagine this chain wrapping around you tighter and tighter as your tensions escalate. Suppose you decide to break the chain.

➤ Imagine that the chain of pain is like a hologram. It appears real but is different from what it seems. It's more a mirage than real.

➤ Pretend you are a scientist tracking the ideas that travel with your low frustration tolerance feelings and procrastinated activities. When in a low frustration tolerance state of mind, record your observations: what are the conditions, what are you thinking, how are you feeling, and what are you doing?

➤ Put your notes aside for about an hour. After that time, go back and critically review your notes. What assumption that underlies your frustration can you prove? For example, is it really true that your feelings of frustration are intolerable or do you make them so by magnifying their importance? Accept only verifiable assumptions.

➤ At another time, use the *right now* exercise to keep perspective on your feelings. For example, "Right now I feel stressed." By verbalizing how you feel in the present moment, you may paradoxically open opportunities for feeling better about feeling bad. After all, right now is not forever.

➤ Living through the feeling complements the *right now* exercise. When you feel tense, "go with the feeling." The way you "go with the feeling" is to allow yourself to experience the feeling. Although you may fear feeling tension, choosing to experience rather than divert from the feeling raises your chances of gaining a sense of "silent control." When you accept living through an unpleasant stressed feeling without escaping, avoiding, or procrastinating, this act of acceptance makes the unpleasant feeling more tolerable.

The purpose of these *chain of pain* exercises is to help defuse the sense of urgency that otherwise might become an impetus for impulsive responses that then add more links on the chain of pain. When you can repeatedly show yourself that you can cope with tension without ducking issues, backing away, overreacting, or procrastinating, you show emotional resiliency and a solid, constructive self-concept.

SIX POINTS FOR CHANGE

Additionally, you can both support and develop your frustration management skills by following these six steps:

1. *Build the body* through exercise to fortify yourself against stress.
2. *Liberate the mind* by challenging yourself to weed out irrational ideas and to develop a can-do attitude.

3. *Change the patterns* associated with low frustration tolerance and frustration disturbances.
4. *Nurture self-patience* by being hard on your procrastination problem while remaining kindly toward yourself.
5. *Use objective feedback* to improve coping skills.
6. *Continue the effort* to meet reasonable challenges.

By following this generic formula, the procrastination that results from low frustration tolerance and frustration disturbances will not permanently disappear. However, you might discover the truth in nineteenth-century French psychologist Jean Payot's observation: "Once you have chosen a constructive direction, you will find yourself drawing nourishment from everywhere to feed this process."

ATTENDING TO OPPORTUNITY, NOT ANXIETY

To test a young man's worthiness to marry his daughter, a king presented him with a difficult decision. Behind one door was the beautiful princess, behind the other, a tiger. The young man faced a choice between opportunity and certain death. Naturally, he was apprehensive.

Most choices in life do not have the tiger as a possible outcome. Nevertheless, some choices between opportunity and anticipated frustration seem equally ominous. For example, Wilma went to a dance, and when she arrived she began to *anticipate* that no one would ask her to waltz, so she returned home. The possibility of not having a dance partner represented a danger to her ego. The *thought* of sitting on the sidelines constituted a threat because she thought that she might be too homely and her personality too bland to attract a man. She concluded that she would remain sitting in the corner. Her self-doubts escalated to severe self-doubt "downing." She began to think that the people at the dance were noticing how isolated and how unworthy she was. A feeling of anxiety began to swell in her body, and so she left.

Threats psychologically equivalent to the tiger behind the door ignited Wilma's sense of vulnerability. Thus Wilma doubted her ability to attract a dance partner and felt distressed because she anticipated danger, not opportunity. She saw the situation as one that posed danger to her self-image rather than as an opportunity to meet new people and to develop her social skills. It was this fictional danger that clouded her consciousness, making her blind to opportunity.

Wilma did not define her situation as a procrastination or avoidance problem. Indeed, she engrossed herself in her anxiety and self-doubts such that she could not see beyond her symptoms. She was, however, developmentally procrastinating by not dealing with her anxiety.

The symptoms of anxiety can be severe enough to command full attention when you experience these symptoms. Some of these symptoms can be very startling. Acute anxiety, for example, usually involves symptoms like heart palpitations, sweating, tremor, shallow breathing, hyperventilation, flushing of the skin, and more. The symptoms can appear at a dance while fearing rejection, during an examination while anticipating failure, or choosing between two doors behind which is a tiger or a lady.

Not all anxiety has dramatic physical symptoms. A general sense of tension, apprehension, worry, and behavioral rigidity characterize contained anxiety. Nevertheless, whether contained or dramatically symptomatic, anxiety that continues over a long time eventually may become so routine that one cannot imagine feeling differently. The attention concentrated on the symptoms impedes awareness of the actual underlying problems, leaving the person feeling inadequate and helpless.

COMBATING ANXIETY

People with overactive imaginations can anticipate crises or "tigers" for themselves that exist only in their imaginations. But if we can conjure up crises with our imaginations, we can also conjure up opportunities. Thus, when you start worrying about the possibility of being rejected at a social gathering, for instance, try to imagine the best opportunities. Then decide *how to* make those opportunities actualities. Test out your plan.

You can combat anxiety by *humorous exaggeration.* In humorous exaggeration you purposely exaggerate the situation about which you feel anxious. So if you feel uptight about getting a report completed on time, take the consequences to a humorous extreme. For instance, imagine your boss jumping out of his clothing at the news that the report is late, and then reporting you to the United Federation of Planets. Then the starship *Enterprise* whisks you away to a galaxy far away and places you in a penal colony staffed by people who actively procrastinate. Pretend your sentence in the penal colony is ended when you get the procrastinating aliens to start processing papers for your release.

When you feel anxious, you make an emotional dwarf of yourself. You tell yourself "horror stories" about your inabilities, thus painting a small, restrictive mental picture of yourself. Fortunately, you are rarely as restricted as you think. So when you feel anxious, sit back and try to expand that mental picture of yourself to include a picture of you trying to do your best, and watch that dwarf grow. Consider alternative ways of doing your best and play out each alternative in fantasy. This positive fantasy trip adds ways to expand your awareness of your possibilities and thus creates an expanded self-picture.

DEPRESSION PROCRASTINATION

Like Joe Btfsplk in the old-time *Li'l Abner* comic strip, people who feel depressed act as if they have a cloud of gloom hanging over their heads. They have a sense of dejection, hopelessness, and helplessness. They pity themselves and believe they can neither stand the discomfort they experience nor tolerate the discomfort they anticipate.

Some depressions are physiological in nature and result from a biochemical or neurochemical imbalance. The imbalance fosters a listless feeling that the person often *interprets* to mean he is without energy and helplessly doomed to ineptness.

Depression can also be psychological and triggered by an external event, like the loss of a job, a divorce, or other life stress. Psychological depression starts through self-doubt "downing," and/or intolerance to tension. In psychological depression, the depressed person heeds a wheedler voice that repeats the equivalent of the following:

> ➤ Your situation is hopeless.
> ➤ You are helpless to do anything.
> ➤ It's unfair that you have to feel this way.
> ➤ The effort that you will need to pull yourself out of this malaise is just too much for you to handle.
> ➤ Poor thing. Why do you always have to be the one to suffer?
> ➤ You can't stand this tension.

A person giving in to this depressive wheedler voice feels increasingly hopeless and helpless.

OVERCOMING PROCRASTINATION DUE TO DEPRESSION

Clinical depressions characterized by a severe biochemical imbalance can respond to special psychopharmacological treatment. However, the cognitive therapies are slightly more effective and have a lower relapse rate. For example, a well-publicized National Institute of Mental Health study showed that cognitive therapy for depression was superior to antidepressant drugs.

You may help yourself decrease mild *psychological* depressions through self-help methods. These are the sort of depressions that do not have symptoms such as sleep and appetite problems, suicidal thoughts, and other equally severe symptoms of a major depression.

Depressions accompanied by sleep disorders, eating problems, or difficulties concentrating are normally not primarily a procrastination issue or the subject for a self-help project. This disorder frequently requires professional help. However, by reading this section you may get a perspective on depression, recognize that the cognitive signatures of hopelessness, helplessness, and worthlessness are phony, and realize that depression is highly treatable.

Most people who feel depressed feel hopeless and helpless and think they are unique in feeling this way. With good information, most can learn to change this perspective, which can lead to positive results. That is an empirical fact. From a logical perspective, helplessness is an ungrounded conclusion based on a major assumption that there is nothing you can do to change. You can challenge that assumption through this straightforward question: where is the evidence that you will live life without the opportunity to exercise choice? If you can exercise choice, even the choice of declining to do anything to break out from a depression, you're not helpless.

The following are a few suggestions to show those in a depressive mood the possibilities of what you can do to cope with the symptoms of depression.

> ➤ The founder of American psychology, William James, suggested a method for dealing with mild depression. As James suffered from many bouts of depression, he spoke from personal experience. James notes that depression is not continuous. From time to time your attention shifts momentarily from your depression. When this happens, you can use this brief interval to assert your will to mobilize and move yourself.
> ➤ The how-to technique, helpful in dealing with general discomfort dodging and anxiety, also applies to depression. Rather than wallow in thoughts of helplessness, hopelessness, and self-pity, identify the problem(s) you face and think about how to solve it (them). Next, actively test your plan.
> ➤ Can't muster enough energy to use the how-to plan? Try scrubbing your bathtub with a toothbrush. Chances are that the how-to plan will appear more appealing. Now this may appear on the surface to be a silly solution. However this method usually helps either because the toothbrush task proves tedious and most other tasks are viewed as pleasant by comparison or because the activity breaks the depressive stream of consciousness.

➤ Exercise helps diminish depressive symptoms. A half hour to an hour a day of reasonable aerobic exercise correlates with increases in self-confidence and decreases in depression. Though this takes a special effort at a time when you are likely to feel sluggish and uninterested in this form of activity, the results are normally worth the special effort. Many people who have followed this regimen reported to me that within six weeks they experienced a reduction in depressive symptoms.

➤ To contradict the wheedler, allow yourself to focus momentarily on happy thoughts or images: think about one thing that you did well today, or how pleasant taking a hot shower would be.

➤ Next, use this change of focus to mobilize yourself into an activity that you might enjoy: call a friend, take a walk, read a poem, observe a beautiful work of art or nature. Allow yourself to really "get into" whatever activity you choose. Engaging in an enjoyable activity can play a part in counteracting your depression because: 1. such experiences create opportunities for you to think productive (rather than sad and hopeless) thoughts; 2. you will have counteracted your discomfort dodging tendency; and 3. you will have proved that you are *not* helpless or hopeless. However, since depression can be such an energy-draining sensation, professional help often provides the most effective solutions.

POSTSCRIPT

A *preview experience* is when you act the way you want to act upon one occasion. For example, you are normally very late for parties, but one day you arrive on time and feel good about your accomplishment. You are delighted with the change and expect that the change will be durable. Actually, the change most probably is a good illustration of how your life can improve if you sustain the change. That's why the experience was a preview experience.

A positive preview experience is particularly helpful, as it is a strong cue signaling the possibility for change. Imagine experiencing a tension-free moment after having been chronically anxious. Clearly, the preview experience can help establish a positive anticipation for resolving tensions and for dramatically reducing the various forms of *discomfort avoiding procrastination*.

PART THREE

Strategies for Overcoming Procrastination

At first procrastination may seem to have remote consequences, but eventually serious repercussions materialize. People who procrastinate in different areas of their lives and in different ways produce different backlashes for themselves. But the backlash is inevitable.

I start this section by describing nine procrastination styles. I'll tell you about some specific ways to handle each and a general strategy for handling all. Then, to cut through other thorny procrastination barriers, the next four chapters focus on strategies for change that include using your imagination, voice of reason, emotional resources, and reward systems to overcome patterns of needless delay. The remaining chapters deal with planning and organizing for change where we'll look at structured ways to pull your Do It Now! program together.

12

Procrastination Styles: A Fresh Look at an Old Problem

Some friends and I once took a series of karate lessons with a talented Korean instructor who spoke broken English. One day the instructor was teaching us how to defend against an assailant who grabbed your shirt or jacket. To demonstrate, he asked me to grab his karate jacket, and as I did so he skillfully bent my thumb inward, easily bringing me to the floor. Next, he reversed the exercise by attempting to grab my karate jacket. As I fumbled around, engrossed in grasping his left thumb, he adeptly drew back his right fist and positioned himself to clobber me. When I finally looked up to see what was happening, I heard the instructor say, "Many way do same thing." He had taught his lesson well!

When developing a means of attacking a problem, knowing what is happening and having a variety of tactics from which to choose is helpful. Toward this end, I'll describe nine procrastination styles: New Year's resolution procrastination, fantasy procrastination, mental procrastination, drifting, behavioral procrastination, frustrated artistry, competitiveness, bureaucratic procrastination, and intrigue creating. Each style has solutions that overlap with the others so you will find *many ways to do the same thing.*

NEW YEAR'S RESOLUTION PROCRASTINATION

January 1 arrives and you decide to "wipe the slate clean" as you enter the new year. So, you make a resolution to stop procrastinating, to start exercising, and to lose weight. This year, you think your intentions are better than ever before.

Four months later, you nag yourself for not having started on any of your promissory projects. With summer coming on, it sure would have been great to be ten pounds lighter and in shape. You also feel unhappy about the extension you filed on your taxes and the fact that your garage continues to have so much clutter that you have to park your automobile in the driveway.

New Year's Day can trigger a covert process that leads to a decision to make a change followed by a decision to delay the promised action. If you are like most people who make New Year's resolutions, this promise will have a life of about twenty-four hours. After that, you procrastinate on overcoming procrastination, find an excuse not to exercise, and then overeat because you really don't have to worry about dropping weight until the spring. Is this annual retreat from New Year's resolutions a serious matter? It depends on your situation.

New Year's resolution procrastination is a *promissory procrastination* style. This promissory approach to life often promotes episodes of frustration when you realize that your commitment to make necessary changes lurks in the past and only emerges, like the proverbial groundhog, on special days. But it goes away after the special day ends, to be taken up at another day or time.

Promissory procrastination can pop up whenever you have an event that causes you to pause and contemplate the direction your life is going, and where you feel tempted to resolve to do better. You'll diet after the holidays. You'll commit to a new exercise plan on the first day of spring to prepare for beach weather. When birthdays come, you swear you'll be more attentive to your family.

The promissory note ploy points to some interesting questions about the ongoing mental process that supports your procrastination. By answering the following sample questions you can clarify the covert ingredients in a procrastination decision to put off exercising and weight loss until another day or time:

1. Does your New Year's resolution to lose weight represent a weak commitment—that is, you never took the resolutions seriously?
2. Do you have an anticipatory anxiety in which you fear that you will look out of shape at the gym and be criticized?
3. Do you resent using time to keep yourself in shape?
4. Do you doubt that you have the will to succeed?
5. Do you feel an inner sense of resistance to your own idea?
6. Do you think you lack the will to sustain the effort and give up on yourself before you start?

Whatever the answers to the questions, you can tap into some covert ideas that promote procrastination.

RESOLVING THE RESOLUTION DILEMMA

The promissory note style of procrastination flourishes when the person doesn't appreciate the trials and tribulations that commonly come about when facing any change—even minor ones. Consider changing your brand of sunglasses, buying a new brand of soup, changing your normal style of clothing, or buying a foreign car when you've always bought domestic. You may feel some sense of unease, discomfort, or resistance making these changes. There is a discomforting element in making changes in even minor day-to-day matters. Why would a major change prove any different?

Here are some ways to overcome New Year's resolutions or promissory note procrastination and get it done:

➤ Accept some strangeness and discomfort in a change of routine. As creatures of habit, we often prefer the old to the new, even when the new is better than the old.
➤ Resolve to live through the discomfort of change while in the process of making the change. You're now targeting a primary developmental procrastination issue that can pay dividends.
➤ Work against pessimistic outlooks where you believe you are fated to fail before you start. Sure you'd like to change, but you know you don't deserve it or can't do it. Think again. Who says?
➤ Pick a date to start. You could arbitrarily pick ten days after you make the resolution. Mark the date on the calendar. Take

reasonable preparatory steps before that date: read books on the topic, make public announcements—do anything to get comfortable with the idea and to start some momentum.

➤ Accept that it will probably take time to develop a new routine to replace the old, and allow yourself to feel some internal resistance, clumsiness, or discomfort until you develop your new weight-loss routine. Relapses are possible, but they represent temporary stumbling blocks rather than permanent obstacles on the path to change.

➤ Avoid making promises to yourself that you don't intend to keep.

FANTASY PROCRASTINATION

Some people live in a world of dreams, fantasies, and memories. Preoccupied with a life that exists only in their minds, they put off dealing with what affects them in the real world.

Walter suffers from a bad case of *omphaloskepsis*—contemplating his navel. On a typical evening we can find him sitting listlessly in his apartment ruminating about his old friends and all the fun he used to have. He plays his favorite old songs on the stereo, practices a few outmoded dance steps, and imagines himself a Byronic hero, sweeping some beautiful, breathtaking young maiden off her feet. But alas, these are pipe dreams. Walter's old friends have long since married and moved away.

Nowadays Walter rarely socializes. On those few occasions when he gets out of his apartment, covers his navel, and makes an attempt to meet new people, he normally returns home feeling discouraged and forlorn. His aloof, silent glares have again failed to attract the fair damsel, or even the not-so-beautiful wallflower.

During his workday, Walter maintains the same "woe is me" outlook, hiding in his cubicle to avoid having lunch with colleagues who he thinks are unfriendly bores. So he spends hours of his days and nights feeling bitter while negatively ruminating about heartless people in a cruel world.

Walter's thoughts wander. With the swiftness of light, Walter's mind switches to a grand life. This time he places himself in medieval England. He is Prince Charming and can have any woman he chooses. Oh, what a wonderful life of knightly courts and love-struck maidens.

Walter *fantasy procrastinates*. He puts off identifying his real problems and developing solutions to them. He won't admit to himself that he is afraid of people and fears that others will find him unacceptable. Instead, his time and life evolve around the myths in his mind.

RECOGNIZING AND CHANGING FANTASY PROCRASTINATION

Throughout our lives we will have productive fantasies that become visions for attainable goals that we make real. Fantasy procrastination, however, is a nonproductive fantasy that diverts our awareness away from our real problems. Thus, the first crucial step in overcoming fantasy procrastination involves using your reasoning ability to unmask your real problems, override your fantasy impulses, and do something sensible to create changes. So if you think you suffer from fantasy procrastination, consider the following exercises:

➤ Eating your favorite meal is normally preferable to fantasizing about eating. In the same way, living a real life is generally preferable to being absorbed by whimsical pursuits that lead you into a procrastination zone. If you find yourself too often in this zone, consider this question: what does your *fantasy procrastination* mask?

➤ To help yourself answer this question, write your autobiography. Use as stimuli old photographs from different periods in your life. Try to remember colors, smells, textures, and other sensory impressions that could help you to recall additional experiences. Ask friends and relatives to recount memorable anecdotes about you. Look for positive outcomes where you have acted and enjoyed the results. Once you have completed your personal history, look for qualities, features, and experiences that will help you promote a sense of empathy and appreciation for yourself.

➤ As a second phase in this autobiographical exercise, look closely for gaps—things that you may have once wanted to do that are conspicuously absent from your history. Also, look for dead-end patterns—important things you once started that you didn't finish. Lastly, look for anxious or otherwise uncomfortable times where you had problems that you put off resolving that later mushroomed. Within a context of empathy and appreciation for yourself, finding these patterns can help you uncover stimuli for nonproductive fantasies.

➤ Next after you've identified your procrastinating patterns, use them as a red flag to signal trouble spots that you can then examine for discomfort dodging, self-doubts, or other mechanisms for procrastination. Pick a fantasy procrastination problem. But now enter a fantasy where you see yourself going through the steps to create positive concrete experiences that you can achieve to replace the procrastination fantasy experiences. Start taking the steps.

In the world of *fantasy procrastination* anything is possible. However, living in this world is like denying that you have diabetes, then bingeing on sugar and wondering why you feel so bad.

MENTAL PROCRASTINATION

I doubt that we will ever find a person whose mind does not wander at times. We naturally have a lot of distracting and intrusive thoughts, especially when we experience multiple forms of stress. However, some people habitually distract themselves and lose focus when confronting practically any uncomfortable situation. Then they delay and procrastinate when they lose attention and concentration. This *mental procrastination* style can come over people quickly, and the procrastinators who fall into this group are inclined to minimize their problems and shift their attention from the troublesome task in order to avoid discomfort. Thus, whenever they start to think about why they don't get started or why their problems persist, they then switch their thinking to a different topic. Yet they cannot escape a chronic nagging tension that accompanies this avoidance prance.

Members of this mental procrastination group typically get defensive and act like ostriches with their heads in the sand. They normally tune out their rational thinking. Failing to make the connections among what they think, how they feel, and what they do, they dizzy themselves following the same circular pattern.

Despite their defensiveness, denials, and "know-nothing" attitude, people in this group have more than their share of negative feelings and crises. Since they normally focus on the wrong problems, they habitually follow the same procrastination patterns. The following example describes this pattern.

Betty is married to an alcoholic husband who routinely beats her during his drunken fits. When asked why she stays with him, she answers, "I don't know." She excuses his behavior, saying that he grew up in a dysfunctional family. When asked about her life, she says she is doing okay. When asked about the relationship between her husband and their children, she remarks, "He is their father."

Betty is noncommittal about the tragic course of her life. She speaks in generalities. She admits to nothing. She mentally procrastinates by refusing to face the overwhelming evidence that her marriage is sick and harmful.

Mental procrastination appears in other disguises. When these rationalizations and denials of reality flip-flop your life from action to avoidance, and when you avoid facing and neutralizing these mental delaying mechanisms, you *mentally procrastinate.*

TURNING ON THE LIGHT

Beneath mental procrastination blockages we find a network of raw nerves and a strong incentive to keep these nerves from view. However, putting gauze before your eyes doesn't prevent the nerves from feeling raw.

The way to change a mental procrastination pattern is to turn a spotlight on your problem areas. What is happening in your life that you put off facing? What problems do these events represent that you don't deal with? What part do you play in creating them? What short-term benefits do you get by this avoidance? What *thinking* do you turn off when you get to one of these procrastination flash points?

This problem-mapping process features *thinking about your thinking.* You develop this *cognitive map* by showing yourself the interconnections between avoiding certain thoughts about reality and procrastination. Because many mental procrastinators tune out unpleasant awarenesses, this is a challenging self-help project. However, if you have a pattern of mental procrastination, you can assume that you are shutting yourself off from rationally thinking about your situation.

Your thoughts reflect many different experiences and sources. In searching for truth, you don't have to protect any of these sources. The idea is to get a clearer picture of the "enemy within." This may include doubts, fears, resentments, and resistance.

Now, what do you do when you catch a glimpse of the wheedler pulling the mental blinds down over your reason? Challenge those wheedler thoughts. Override the wheedler's ploys by asserting your reason and making it stick. Support this willpower by planning and then following through on a behavior change. Adjust your sights as you gain new experience that invites a different perspective. Persist. This cognitive override is natural to do. For example, we cognitively override behavior habits when we drive on the right side of the road in our country and then must drive on the left side in another country. We can do the same with procrastination habits. It is a question of *making* reason prevail over habit.

Mental procrastinators who force themselves to see the relationships among their beliefs, feelings, and defensive reactions open opportunities for making meaningful changes. However, we will be naturally limited in this self-observation exercise because our wishes and motives limit this process. It often takes time and experience to turn on the light and recognize that a problem may clash with our idealized image, and that we have to make an effort to resolve the conflict.

Recognizing a mental procrastination problem doesn't necessarily change this self-defeating pattern. Problem awareness does, however, open opportunities to exercise options and choices.

DRIFTING

Neo-Freudian analyst Karen Horney tells us that drifting involves a pattern of routinely failing to identify life objectives. I find that *drifting procrastinators* have only vague and indiscriminate goals and plans. As a consequence they feel hounded by thoughts of purposelessness. Blocked by feelings of sadness, they succumb to having a barren life brought about by a blanched mind and spirit.

Drifters normally act blandly and indifferently toward life. Rather than initiate, members of this group *react* by avoiding being responsible for charting the direction of their life. Making feeble gestures to pretend they have a direction, drifting procrastinators go through the paces of living without enjoying the journey. Something seems missing to them.

People who drift mostly settle for what life has to offer. They rarely select what they want. That is why they move from job to job or get into dead-end careers or moribund marriages.

George is a security guard at the Third National Bank. He's a bright, sensitive man who "drifts" along, doing a job he secretly loathes. He feels stalemated and stagnated because he can't think of what other job he would prefer doing.

George worries about his future and what his life will be like later. He feels a sense of aimlessness or purposelessness, and this adds to his worries. He feels trapped in what the existentialists describe as a vacuum of meaninglessness. Indeed, he is not even sure what his problem is. Occasionally, however, he has a dim awareness that he doesn't seem to make commitments easily, is confused, and wanders without meaning or direction.

DEALING WITH DRIFTING

Drifting is an evasion of self-responsibility. So when you drift, you act irresponsibly toward yourself.

Commitment is the key word in breaking a drifting procrastination pattern. The question is, commitment to *what?* So, the first step in disrupting drifting is to appraise your current situation. Learn what you would like to have that you feel is presently lacking in your life.

Working to take yourself more seriously—viewing yourself as a worthy person—can help create conditions for a change in direction. You can readily accomplish this task by doing a functional analysis of yourself. Examine activities that you perform well. For example, if you play bridge skillfully, examine the qualities that contribute to your skills. Do you have a good memory, strategic sense, judgment, intelligence, concentration, or good communication skills? Do you have all of the above and more? By making this *functional analysis* of other activities you perform well, you'll begin to recognize qualities that keep repeating themselves—qualities that can define a bright new direction. Enlightened self-knowledge of both your skills and positive qualities can help you to define your career and interpersonal objectives, and to provide a foundation for making commitments.

BEHAVIOR PROCRASTINATION

Behavior procrastination occurs when you develop plans but put off carrying them out. The person with a behavior procrastination style avoids the possible discomfort and tension associated with actually following through and delays until the plan goes stale. In the following example, you'll see how this works.

At first glance Sally looks like one of those utterly organized, efficient people whom we all envy. Outwardly, she really seems to have her act together. She methodically decides what she wants and how to get it. For example, she recently obtained books and other information about setting up a freshwater aquarium. She passed the exam to become a real-estate broker. She formulated a step-by-step plan to get a promotion and raise in pay at her job. Her office desk and apartment are so marvelously organized that she can find anything at a moment's notice. She has a carefully written calendar of her appointments, outings, parties, and birthdays for the upcoming year.

As she arises each morning, Sally makes a long, annotated list of things to do during the day and the approximate times for each activity. The big catch of this organizational genius is that she doesn't follow through, or she waits until the last minute. Thus, we find Sally at the convenience store at midnight buying items for tomorrow's family outing.

Sally constantly distracts herself with a myriad of projects and plans. Thus, an aquarium tank sits empty in a corner. Her plans for career advancement drift into the recesses of her brain. Her friends and relatives rarely get a birthday card from Sally. Many other items on the daily to-do list get put off to tomorrow's list of things to do. Figuratively, Sally runs a swift race but sits before reaching the finish line, then waves the competitors onto victory.

Behavior procrastination can affect other people besides the procrastinator. We most often see this in "omissions." The student who starts but doesn't finish a term paper may cause the professor to have to do extra work. The manager with great ideas who maintains the status quo may burden others by continuing an inefficient system.

BEATING BEHAVIOR PROCRASTINATION

Behavior procrastination is often a symptom of well-hidden fears and self-doubts as well as a strong urge to avoid the uncomfortable. This process also has many of the features of a problem habit. If you operate with a behavioral procrastination style, the following exercises can help you overcome it:

➤ Some people are naturally more temperamentally suited for planning and organizing a project. This preference need not lead to behavior procrastination, provided you can delegate follow-through activities and don't procrastinate on passing them along. It also need not lead to procrastination, provided you accept responsibility for completing the process involved in each project. Although finishing may feel anticlimactic compared to preparing, finishing is the payoff of preparation. Why deprive yourself of the advantages of completion?

➤ To build awareness of behavior procrastination, look for cues— projects or tasks that you have put time into planning but have put off completing.

➤ See if self-doubts are hampering your progress. For example, if you were to follow through with your plans, are you afraid that your work would not be perfect?

➤ Tune in to your thoughts to see if you aren't believing in "magic." For example, do you believe follow-through should be effortless? Do you think that preparation is worthwhile but that action has secondary value?

➤ Recognize that behavioral procrastination is a problem habit supported by a psychological barrier to finishing. This inertia is often caused by no more than a barrier of task-resistant feelings (low-grade procrastination).

➤ # Do It Now!

Behavior Procrastination

Sometimes behavior procrastination can result in physical symptoms. For example, at the thought of a specific action, your left arm can appear heavy and dull. Next you notice that you feel a resistance from your stomach up through your chest and neck. Your head and mind feel tight. Then your whole body recoils. To see if you fall into this group, pick a project you started but stopped due to procrastination. Think about finishing. If you feel a strain, you are feeling resistance.

If you have these feelings of bodily resistance, override them by acting on your best thinking. Your mind can command your body to carry through with actions despite feelings of physical resistance.

THE FRUSTRATED ARTIST

Do you have a creative mind but persistently fail to take the time to organize and coordinate your imaginative efforts? Many of these people feel like frustrated artists who "don't have their act together." People operating with the *frustrated artist* style cultivate their doubts about their creative ability. Instead of following their creative urges and developing their talents, they fritter away their time.

Frustrated artists avoid the very activity they enjoy because of the low-level discomfort in starting. They put off creating their art and instead wander in a mire of uncertainty, wondering what to do with their free time. This is their eternal plight—waiting for moments of inspiration while suffering from a lack of accomplishment. The misguided belief that inspiration is the ticket to creative involvement often results in a renewal of self-doubts and increased frustration.

The frustrated artist waits in the same old well-known corner of restricted existence, rarely risking the frustration and tension that might accompany the real expression of inner creative drives. Ignoring the important truth that positive self-expression liberates the mind, the frustrated artist follows "safe" but restricted corridors.

Being creative is not a hobby or avocation; it is a lifelong process that can constantly open new experiences for the creative individual to explore and to enjoy. Even if you don't completely identify yourself as being a frustrated artist, you may procrastinate because of similar restraints. Let's see what you can do to liberate yourself.

SPRING FREE

You can break the chains of creative suppression. Try the following activities to free your creative abilities:

➤ Think back to times when you felt that your creative expressions flowed freely from your inward feelings or ideas. This gives you a point of reference for the mental state when your creative thoughts and actions connect. Writing, acting, painting, programming, singing, organizing, counseling, talking, diagnosing—all of these and more provide opportunities for this creative reference. Think about this connection when you have a creative idea that you think is worth pursing. Use this framework as a platform for action.

➤ Schedule a time to do the artistic activities you normally put off. Pick a time of day, each day, when you will involve yourself in your creative project. Persist even if you feel discouraged.

Many artists, like baseball players, periodically go into slumps. They say they have run out of ideas. However, even players who slump normally continue playing.

No law says you should have a guaranteed exemption that you will never have a mental slump. Nevertheless, the *slumping mind-set* is an illusion when it comes to being creative. You don't have to be in a creative mood or wait for the moment of inspiration to create. Even when you don't feel in the mood you can play with ideas, experiment, free-associate, or play games of opposites where you flip ideas upside down and around and around. To get your creative project started you also can pretend you have a ten-minute deadline.

Artists are born. But skill or technical competency needs developing. That skill is necessary to give full expression to that creative drive. Procrastination warps that drive by preventing us from developing this competency.

THE COMPETITIVE PROCRASTINATION STYLE

Jack is so aggressively competitive he sees casual conversations as opportunities to have a contest to prove his superiority. However, rather than compete with people who are his equals, he competes with people he can beat. He subsequently spends much time congratulating himself for his victories.

Jack plays what author Stephen Potter terms one-upmanship games. He tries to upstage others and show that he is smarter. In Jack's world, we find only winners and losers. Indeed, Jack's T-shirt reads THE GUY IN SECOND PLACE IS THE FIRST LOSER. However, unlike a footrace, which has only one winner, life provides many ways for many people to win.

Competitive procrastination has its flip side. Jill, for example, associates competitiveness with aggressiveness. She fears appearing non-feminine if she expresses her competitive desires. More important, she fears that exposing her talents will cause others to retaliate aggressively. Because she worries about retaliation, she slams on the brakes when it would be wiser to accelerate.

Jill compares her abilities with the talents of others, and this compulsion to compare is what I term "comparativitis." In this process, you take the normal tendency to compare and turn the process against yourself. You match your qualities against others' better qualities and declare yourself the loser. In this state of mind, you operate well below your capabilities and abandon the field to others. Paradoxically, people who suffer from comparativitis feel competitive while fearing competition.

People involved in *competitive procrastination* believe they *should* continually work at top speed and they suffer from repeated frustrations when reality tells a different story. This demand invades their conceptual system, weakens their judgment, and soaks their spirits with inane ideas about how things are supposed to work.

When you set internal performance standards excessively high then fail to meet those standards, you risk tripping the comparativitis trap. The more common crises we create for ourselves through this comparativitis debacle involve setting unrealistic time-performance standards. In this mode you can declare yourself a procrastinator for not operating with alacrity. Nevertheless, this may be false reasoning. Arguably, we could say that this process exemplifies *mental procrastination.* By putting off reading the urgent messages we deliver to ourselves, we stay in a twilight zone of awareness, or in a state of nonawareness. Nevertheless, in the end the time it takes to complete a job is the time that it takes.

CONSTRUCTIVE COMPETITION

The forces motivating *competitive procrastination* often interact. Sometimes competitive procrastination grows out of a perfectionistic fear of failure, fear of aggressiveness, or the desire to hold back because of a chivalric notion that others should precede you.

Whatever the causes of competitive procrastination, you will find a clear advantage to developing and maintaining a healthy competitive spirit. Following through in this spirit yields dividends. In contrast to the competitive procrastination style, a healthy competitive spirit gears toward building rather than comparing. This spirit leads to growth, efficiency, and productivity. Now how do you promote this constructive competitive style?

Creating and meeting *productive challenges* direct your mental, emotional, and physical energies to flow along productive channels. Focus on developing your interests, talents, and resources where competition can challenge you to do better. You can often learn more from people who have demonstrated talents and skills.

Compete against your prior performances. When you attempt to do better than before, you stretch your resources. Winning and losing then give ground to self-development and progress. Sometimes you'll succeed, and sometimes you'll fall short. It's all part of making progress.

Most people periodically require new competitive challenges. If these challenges are healthy and routinely met, the person learns more about the *self*. This concrete information derived from experience feeds into a healthy self-concept, weakens the foundation for self-doubts, solidifies frustration tolerance, and helps put the wheedler out of business.

BUREAUCRATIC PROCRASTINATION

Bureaucracies normally have procedures and regulations that can promote the status quo. Although some bureaucrats operate with alacrity and efficiency, *bureaucratic procrastination* is a long-standing joke. For example, during the summer of 1996 a deer lay dead on a road in Pennsylvania for several days or weeks, depending on the report you believe. Officials seemed confused about what to do and put off making a decision. Meanwhile, the paving company they hired to blacktop the road covered the animal, leaving its antlers sticking above the new pavement. (The bureaucrats chided the company, saying that it was against state regulations to pave over a deer.)

Bureaucratic doublespeak, red tape, insincere speeches about change, snafus, cover-ups, finger pointing, and deflecting attention from salient issues are examples of how some folks turn procrastination into an art form. These bureaucratic procrastination ploys engage us in other ways. In the bureaucratic procrastination world, we often hear the passive tense. For example, bureaucratic statements such as "it was decided to process this form differently" clearly obfuscate accountability. Who decided? What makes the process different? How does the efficiency of the new process compare with that of the old? What is the measure of efficiency? Bureaucrats rarely publicly present or answer these questions. In this avoidance dance, procrastination serves these purposes: no accountability; no responsibility; no change.

The bureaucratic procrastinator has many mottos and sayings that have become a tradition: for example, delay pays. Wait until the problem goes away. Doing nothing is better than taking a risk. Keep a low profile. Blame the victim for the problem. Spread the risk—use a committee. Use loopholes to avoid getting pinned down.

In the bureaucratic world, uncomfortable unresolved problems get relegated to the category of "old news." But these problems still fester. Because the procrastinated problem ages, the bureaucratic procrastinator implies that "the problem *is* resolved" because the matter has gone stale.

Bureaucratic procrastinators are resistive and reactive. They rarely anticipate problems. They expend too much time and effort in being defensive, avoiding responsibilities, and trying to polish their images, and too little time following through on solving problems. Because bureaucrats often have little incentive for change, they are the consummate procrastinators when it comes to change.

OVERRIDING A BUREAUCRATIC STYLE

The secret to changing a bureaucratic procrastination style lies in the word *accountability*. President Harry Truman's motto was "The buck stops here." In the world of bureaucratic procrastination, you make yourself unaccountable for matters under your control. To get out of the bureaucratic quagmire, look for ways to get things done rather than use time to concoct excuses for delay.

Beware of the bureaucratic loophole. Statements using phrases such as "hopefully," "I anticipate," or "perhaps soon" all provide avenues for delay. Instead of loopholes, make realistic time and performance commitments and attempt to stick to those commitments.

INTRIGUE CREATING

Intrigue creating, the ninth procrastination style, involves making a decision today that leads to a crisis tomorrow. For example, deciding to put off paying the telephone bill results in a crisis several weeks later—a needless hassle that drains much more time and energy than if you had paid the bill on time.

Some students have developed the intrigue-creating style into a fine art. They cut classes, goof off during the semester, then come up with a stupendous excuse for enticing a professor into giving a makeup exam or an extension on that term paper. The plot for this suspense is defying authority, testing the professor's tolerance limits, and flexing one's skill in turning a bad situation around to one's advantage. This intrigue has all the stimulating elements of a come-from-behind victory.

A person may also play the suspense game. By threatening his collaborator with quitting in the middle of a project, the procrastinator stimulates long, dramatic discussions to resolve the crisis. This intrigue-creating (crisis-creating) pattern involves risk and some danger and is generally initiated to create a sense of excitement and a feeling of stimulation.

Stimulating as intrigues may seem, these artificial psychological stimulants divert us from productive activities. Energies invested in intriguing shift our emphasis away from constructive activities that provide a source of genuine stimulation and excitement.

PRODUCTIVE STIMULATION

The following ways to rid yourself of intrigue creating give you a brief hint of the possibilities for creating change:

➤ When deciding to put something off, first pause to check the long-term effects of that decision. Could the decision, for example, end in an unnecessary crisis? This *stop—think* technique, used consistently, helps clarify the impact of putting things off and the advantages of doing it now.

➤ Intrigue creating reflects not only a need for stimulation but also a fear of failure. Why do you think you need the sort of stimulation derived from intrigues?

➤ Intrigue creating sometimes involves an attempt to get a quick emotional charge. Threatening to quit a job or dissolve a relationship may provide that quick charge. As a constructive alternative, find out the important and worthwhile challenges facing you and pursue them. You'll still get that energizing spark, and the consequences will be positive.

ENACTMENT EXERCISES TO ALTER YOUR PROCRASTINATION STYLE

One way to change a procrastination style is to replace it with a Do It Now! style. Using this technique, a drifter, for example, would develop and enact a new role of creating positive life objectives and following through on goals that support those objectives. No matter what your current style of procrastination, you can formulate and act out a new role for yourself.

The idea of role enactment has a long and fruitful history. Behavioral therapists use role-playing techniques to help their clients develop effective communication or assertion skills. You can effectively use fixed-role therapy, developed by psychologist George Kelly, to break your procrastination style and get into the Do It Now! style. Here is how:

First, write an autobiographical sketch (or use one that you may have started earlier in this chapter under Recognizing and Changing Fantasy Procrastination). Next, examine your sketch closely for your patterns of procrastination.

Once you have isolated these procrastination patterns, use them to write a new script for yourself—one in which you have replaced procrastination with purposeful actions. For instance, if one of your procrastination stumbling blocks involved avoiding expressing your opinions at executive board meetings, you would create a new script in which you clearly and constructively express your opinions at such meetings.

Before writing your new script, read over the following guidelines:

➤ Write biographical sketches and new role scripts as objectively as possible. When composing your script, use the third person ("he," "she") as if someone else were doing the writing.
➤ Make the new script much more than a modification or minor adjustment of your biographical sketch. Make your new role the antithesis of your old procrastination pattern of behavior.
➤ Write the new script with an awareness of how the new role will affect other people. Specifically design the role so that you have a constructive impact on others.
➤ Keep your new role flexible and realistic.
➤ To add to the make-believe element of the new role, make up a new name for yourself.

Kelly points out that we have no concrete formula for writing the new role script. Ingenuity is left to the writer. However, beyond Kelly's suggestions, the following list contains items you may want to include in developing your new life script:

➤ Style of clothing
➤ Manner of speaking to bosses (tone of voice, content)
➤ Manner of speaking to colleagues
➤ Manner of speaking to strangers
➤ Body posture

- ➤ Use of leisure time
- ➤ Manner of handling problems
- ➤ Reaction to criticism
- ➤ Reaction to others' negativism
- ➤ Types of risks taken
- ➤ Opportunities sought
- ➤ Style of interacting in groups
- ➤ Manner of expressing feelings
- ➤ Future planning ability
- ➤ Energy level
- ➤ Awareness of others' feelings
- ➤ Manner of getting work done
- ➤ Relations with members of the opposite sex
- ➤ Relations with same-sex friends
- ➤ Interests
- ➤ Values
- ➤ Positive beliefs

Now write your new script. Test it. Modify it. Live it.

POSTSCRIPT

Procrastination, like weeds in a garden, periodically spreads too far. However, like pulling weeds to save the garden, if you deal with procrastination swiftly by returning to your constructive challenge, you gain more Do It Now! competency for your efforts.

Because procrastination can weave through so many thoughts, feelings, and patterns in our lives, there will probably never come a time when we can have a garden that is free of weeds. However, by making a life plan of preventing more weeds by keeping after them, many "have to," "don't want to," and "won't do" types of priorities will get done sooner rather than later. This shrinks the accumulating burdens we feel when unpleasant tasks pile up.

Developing the desired plants and keeping the procrastination weeds out of your perennial garden involve developing or refining your productive style and sticking with it. Once you resign yourself to this reality, vigilance and follow-through are the price you pay to keep the procrastination weeds out of your garden. Commitment, involvement, and accountability fertilize the desired garden plants and reduce the weed competition.

13

Your Imagination Can Help You Get It Done

In This Chapter

➤ Ten visualization techniques

In the world of dreams, anything is possible. When you fantasize, you become emotionally and intellectually involved in a pleasant or unpleasant, exciting or relaxing, imaginary experience. Furthermore, you have no limits to the types of fantasies you can experience. Among the many varieties of fantasy, one bears special consideration: productive fantasy. Most important artistic or scientific creations first existed only in the imaginations of scientists, artists, and inventors. Some fantasies have even anticipated future inventions. Jules Verne's *20,000 Leagues under the Sea* illustrates how a fantasy was a rehearsal for the development of the submarine.

In this chapter, I'll use word stimuli to produce ten mental images that you can use to create a Do It Now! outlook. These images can help power your motivation for overcoming various forms of procrastination and getting it done.

Before we go on, see if you can produce pictorial images. Create a mental image of a watermelon, ripe and oozing with sweet juices. Can you see the picture in your mind's eye? Is the color vivid? Can you almost taste the fruit? Perhaps your mouth is watering. If so, you are very good at creating mental images.

Some people don't create pictorial images well. Maybe you are somebody who has trouble creating such images. If so, then obtain a sketch pad and some colored felt-tipped pens or watercolors. Use these materials to sketch the images. As you draw or paint, try to get into the feelings these pictures create. Don't worry if your efforts won't win an art award. Your purpose is to create a positive, fertile mental atmosphere. Even if you can only draw stick figures, if those stick figures help you to create an atmosphere, you are accomplishing the purpose of this exercise.

As you finish reading each example, close your eyes and play out the image in your mind. Replay those images that might simulate situations that apply to your own special brand of procrastination. However, before you begin, find a comfortable spot where you are likely to be free from interruption and free to use your imagination. Then let your actions tell you if creating constructive mental images can aid you to get it done.

THE TIGER AND THE PUSSYCAT

Are you afraid of the unknown? Does this dread spread to other activities that you see others fearlessly doing? If so, do you put off embarking upon doing something new if the territory is unfamiliar? Do you believe there is danger to your self-image if you are not immediately an expert in a new field? Do you immobilize yourself because of these preoccupations? If the answer to any one of these questions is yes, then the first imaginary journey can help you to develop motivation for dealing with a developmental procrastination challenge.

Pretend you are walking through a desert in a foreign land. You have lost your way and are hungry and tired. You finally arrive at the base of a tall stone wall. You look to either side, and it extends to each horizon. You look behind you and see nothing but the arid desert you walked through to get to the wall.

Suddenly you hear very faint sounds on the other side of the wall—a sort of rumbling or purring sound. Is it the sound of a tiger or the sound of a pussycat purring in the sun? Do people live behind the wall? Are they friendly? Will they help you? Will they seize and imprison you? What will these people be like—tigers or pussycats? Will you find both tigers and pussycats among them?

Now, in your mind's eye imagine yourself going over the wall and seeing what is there to see. What do you find on the other side of that wall? When the unknown becomes familiar, imagine yourself adapting to this new territory and coping with whatever challenges you find.

WHAT DOES YOUR ANXIETY LOOK LIKE?

Each of us feels anxious from time to time. When you feel anxious, you generally concentrate on both threats and your bad feelings. Anxiety can definitely influence what you do, but what if you could influence your anxiety to stop pestering you?

Imagine giving your anxiety a form. Draw a mental picture of anxiety. Does your anxiety take a humanoid or an animal shape? If it's humanoid, dress it up in a Little Lord Fauntleroy outfit and place a red-and-gold-striped beanie with a pinwheel on its head. Now do you feel a greater sense of inner command? Do you still take your anxiety so seriously?

Sometimes anxiety becomes a mask that we put over our perceptions, perspective, memories, anticipations, vulnerabilities, and moods. The anxiety distracts us from the real, but manageable, underlying problems. Now pretend to take off the mask. What do you see? Do you face real dangers or dangers created by your mind? Armed with your clear-thinking tools, imagine yourself facing the anxious myths of your mind that roam through your mental jungle.

Think of a task that you put off because you feel anxious. Imagine the task and imagine that silly anxiety trying to stop you by frightening you. Imagine yourself gaining control by doing it now. Then, Do It Now!

MAKING OIL AND WATER MIX

Do you think you can make your life wonderful by getting your friends and family to do things your way? Have you noticed that the more you push them to change, the more resistant they become? Perhaps you can find a way to see this *control procrastination* process in a different light.

If you try to exert control over others, the following image has special merit. Imagine yourself trying to blend motor oil and crystal clear springwater.

You've decided that you want to stop light oil from floating on the top of your crystal clear water. So you devise a technique to drive it down to the bottom. To accomplish this feat, you obtain a trough of springwater, a gallon of oil, and a large wooden paddle. You pour the oil on the top of the water and begin vigorously to slam it down with the paddle. Imagine yourself working hard at this task, and imagine the oil bubbles floating leisurely back to the surface. Now you slap even more vigorously, thrashing the oil and water together.

After you've rested from this tiresome fantasy, try to imagine three people you would most like to change (other than yourself). Can you force them to act exactly as you want them to act? Imagine continually and directly pounding at these people to force them to match the way you want them to be. Can you imagine an alternative to control that doesn't involve mixing oil with water?

WHAT WOULD YOU DO IF YOU WERE SOMEONE ELSE?

If you could be the ideal you, in what ways would you act differently from the way you currently do? Imagine what that ideal *you* would really be like. (Would you be like someone else or like an improved version of yourself?) What would you be doing with your life that is different? What would your interpersonal relationships be like? What type of work would you be doing to earn a living? What type of hobbies would you enjoy? Would you travel?

As you imagine this other *self* in operation, what positive parts of the fantasy can you turn into reality? What would you do to make this translation real? With any change, you might find some unplanned results and consequences. How would you respond positively to reestablish a balance? Imagine yourself managing, persisting, and eventually prevailing.

IMAGINE WHAT DOUBLE TROUBLE IS REALLY LIKE

Double trouble occurs when you make more of a situation than it is. When you procrastinate and then become depressed, angry, or worried over the consequences, you create double trouble for yourself. For example, worrying about procrastination and then worrying about why you worry so much can churn up much mental misery and result in more procrastination.

This double trouble process is like layering a problem onto a problem. The secondary worries and procrastination greatly magnify the original problem and can trigger panic attacks.

In using imagery to combat *double trouble procrastination,* first try to imagine what double trouble looks like. Here is one example: think of yourself running through a well-worn pathway and coming to the start of a long flat steel bridge across a deep ravine. Heavily layered with warm green grease, the bridge looks uninviting. Yet you want to get to the other side. Imagine yourself walking on the slippery path, wanting to get to the end quickly. Now pretend that you decide to run fast to cross the ravine as quickly as possible. Imagine your feet starting to pound ever harder against that oozy stuff. Imagine how the harder you run, the more you slip and fall. Your body is now covered with that warm, gooey green grease. Now you worry about whether you'll slip and fall into the ravine.

This imaginary run describes what double trouble means. In this developmental and mental procrastination mind-set, through our haste and urgency we create mental miseries and put off establishing a stable quality in our lives. We slip and fall for no good reason at all.

It often takes time for new habits to replace less functional ones. Now imagine yourself getting off the double trouble track onto a path of graduated changes. What does that path feel like? I'll bet it feels like a better place to tread.

IF I WERE A PRIVILEGED CHARACTER

If you *socially procrastinate,* you'll eventually earn the reputation of being undependable, and this can cost you opportunities. To exempt yourself from onerous consequences due to your omissions and procrastination, imagine getting a law passed that exempts you from the trials others face in meeting their social responsibilities.

Let's look at the image of the privileged character. To put this self-defeating fantasy into perspective, imagine the president of the United States working to grant you the legal right to put off whatever you wanted without you having to pay any consequences.

Now imagine the president pleading your case before a joint session of Congress, begging that you should have repeated extensions on everything, including paying your taxes. You should never again have to suffer the pangs of feeling bad for putting things off.

Congress grants this request. A special emissary presents your case before a council of world leaders, asking that wherever you travel in the world, you be granted immunity from responsibility.

In a special series of meetings the president makes major military and economic concessions to the United Nations. The work pays off, and the president signs an agreement with this esteemed body to put the issue to a vote before the peoples of the world. Imagine people pouring out of straw huts, country mansions, and Midtown apartments to vote on whether to grant you such a universal privilege. When they count the vote, it's unanimous that you should have endless reprieves.

Now pause and reflect upon the meaning of the reprieve. Do you require endless automatic reprieves because you are extremely powerful or extremely helpless?

Next imagine doing something to help yourself with each of your priority activities. Take a step to translate the imagined action into a real act. Through enacting this fantasy you've enabled yourself to *earn* the privileged status of a doer.

THE GETTING-IT-DONE TRIP

Suppose you had a unique opportunity to be superefficient for one week—would you take the opportunity? Here is the situation: imagine that a magic genie that you've released from imprisonment in an old cola bottle has granted you a week during which you can accomplish all that is humanly possible within the time and with the resources available. Here is how the deal works. You have an hour to identify what you want to accomplish during that week. For the rest of the week, apart from sleeping, you will be in a state of complete command over your desires and actions. In this state, you can move effortlessly from one project or desire to the next. As you progress, you will use your time effectively to get your projects done right.

During your week of maximum efficiency the usual diversions will not detour you. In effect, your actions will be realistic and your timing excellent. In other words, you will not suffer the disillusionment so many suffer when their minds seize upon ideas their abilities can't equal.

What would you like to see yourself getting done during this week of efficiency and effectiveness that the genie has granted? Pick one of those activities and imagine the steps necessary to follow through. Now, in the real world, take the first step.

MAÑANA CONFRONTS TODAY

Pretend you are Mañana waiting with clenched fists to take what Today will have needlessly put off. Today has lots of confidence in you. Nevertheless, you suspect that despite Today's glorification of your capabilities—and how flattering that glorification is!—you will still have something nasty to say to Today for passing on to you what you do not want to do.

So there you are, the great Mañana, anticipating feeling swamped under the remnants of Today's procrastination. Knowing what is in the offing for you, you decide to try to change the course of your history. You unclench your fists and decide instead that you will not blame Today. Rather, you will try to convince Today to leave good memories of things well done.

You recognize that you want Today to do a favor for the self that Today will become tomorrow (which is Mañana, you). Like a tolerant and helpful teacher, you lend aid and support and knowledge. You do this because you recognize that when the great Mañana becomes Today, you will have plenty to do without having to contend with debris from the past.

So entertain this zany fantasy where you are both Mañana and Today. Carry on a debate with yourself for approximately fifteen minutes and let both Mañana and Today work out their getting-it-done challenges to mutual satisfaction.

The Hay Image for Combating Mañana

Here is an image for what happens when you continue to roll over projects and activities into the future. Imagine that each of the activities that you delay or put off is like a block of baled hay. Each bale is manageable, and you can push it forward without too much effort. However, when each bale is joined by another, the load gets heavier, and there comes a time when they pile up before you and block your sight from seeing the things that you normally enjoy. Indeed, you may feel overwhelmed.

This image describes the differences between short- and long-term benefits of putting things off. With a pattern of piling up the problems of the past and present, the future dims. This is not logical, but then, humans are psychological and do not necessarily follow the rules of logic.

How do you break this pattern? Imagine yourself putting the bales aside by finishing what each represents. This leaves the field to the future open. Consider, without a pileup of bales of hay, you have less to distract you and you can see more options and choices. If you fear these options, you can always go back to push the different bales forward. On the other hand, if you decide to face the future clear of the leftovers from the past, you'll have little time for procrastination and more time to face and overcome your fears.

SING A MERRY TUNE

Imagine yourself a concert singer on the stage with national TV cameras focused upon you. The orchestra strikes a chord. You start singing the following procrastination song.

Whenever you think of putting things off, think of this song and let your natural spirit of determination march to a Do It Now! tune.

POSTSCRIPT

Nightmares can leave us feeling cold and sweaty. We don't have much control over their occurrence, but even in sleep some of us can influence the direction of these nightmares. During the day we also can invent demons and cower before our creations.

In the world of procrastination, we often begin with reasonable fantasies. First we believe we have more time later to do what we don't want to do now. This "later is okay" image eventually dampens our enthusiasm for the present and casts a pall on the future. When we visualize a Do It Now! pathway, we hold a contrasting mental image that clarifies choices and suggests ways for achieving our goals.

Procrastination

continued next page

Clear Thinking Gets It Done

The situation changes in the mind of the beholder. Joseph K. in Franz Kafka's *The Trial* was arrested one morning and didn't know the reason. Although the authorities released him on his own recognizance to await trial, his life revolved around trying to discover the charges brought against him and how his defense was progressing.

Many people who procrastinate place themselves on trial daily. They act as if they suffer from some unknown but fatal personality flaws. They search for this flaw in much the same way that Joseph K. searched for the reason behind his indictment. So the search goes on for the fatal "flaw."

Faulty thinking is one of those flaws that can lead to procrastination, which results in making you feel as if you were in emotional trouble. Learning how to recognize and correct this biased thinking opens opportunities for constructive actions.

Knowing the pitfalls that interfere with straight thinking is often not enough to change procrastination patterns. Some procrastinators delight in such self-revelations but still fall into the *behavior procrastination* trap.

Let's look at extremist mental traps that support procrastination practices and at the clear-thinking action steps we can use to unlock our minds when in these traps. In this chapter I'll emphasize self-concept issues because *self-doubt procrastination* often gains momentum from these problem habits of the mind.

EXTREMIST THINKING

Remember the story "The Little Boy Who Cried Wolf"? He too often made up a story that a wolf was coming. When the wolf finally came, no one believed him.

From time to time, practically everyone will exaggerate or embellish reality. However, some of these embellishments become problem habits when what we imagine evokes distress, disturbs our relationships, and promotes delay. When you enter this jungle of extremist thinking you will surely entangle yourself. Wandering through the mental jungle, our thoughts and beliefs echo through our language, and our language, in turn, colors our thoughts and beliefs. We still think we are perceiving reality but are actually perceiving distorted ideas.

Our thoughts and language represent our interpretations of reality, but reality is different from them. This is an important yet not so obvious idea. For example, the two words *lemon drop* are different from the taste of a real lemon drop. Nevertheless, the words anticipate and describe an experience others can understand.

Our choice of language has evocative power that reflects, anticipates, and defines experience. This partially explains why we procrastinate. The mañana ploy, for example, involves interpreting the task, anticipating the effort, and coming to a *better-to-delay* conclusion. We can find many other time-robbing, overgeneralized, problem habits of mind that reside in our mental jungle that delay Do It Now! opportunities.

ALLNESS THINKING

General semanticists describe *allness thinking* as an overgeneralized communication. When a person has a problem with his or her self-perception, for example, allness thinking generates statements about the self such as: "*Everybody* thinks I'm a failure"; "I *always* alienate others"; or "I can't do anything right."

These vague value terms and phrases mislead. People who define themselves as strong or weak, good or bad, often forget that they use limited-value terms to describe the whole *self.*

Skewing our definition of reality by oversimplifying the *self* distorts perception and perspective. Nevertheless, some people believe that they are strong when they follow through, and weak when they don't. When they apply this strong-weak dichotomy to themselves they often go through the day feeling like the ball in an aggressive game of Ping-Pong.

An Allness Perspective

Let's put allness thinking into perspective. Instead of judging the *self* like a Ping-Pong ball, why not judge your performance on a scale of one to one thousand. Since you perform in hundreds of ways each day, and since some are of greater and lesser importance, we need to judge our ratings situation by situation and give a different weight to each situation.

Because not all performance categories have the same priority value, you may give different weights to each. But how are we to come up with a daily score if the numbers have different weights? We'll use a weighted transformation to make the separate scores equivalent. Now you have a performance rating for today that you can also use tomorrow.

Is this rating system exercise worth doing every day? Should you put your performance categories on an electronic spreadsheet, input numbers, and make a running tally for the next several years? That's impractical. Nevertheless, the weighted rating system does show the folly in using allness thinking to give yourself a global self-rating. If you need to convince yourself that you have the power to negatively overfocus on one of your performances, and to foolishly turn this focus against the *self*, this rating concept is worth thinking about each day.

This is the point. Life is not a photograph frozen in time any more than the *self* is fixed in only one way for all time. Our personal lives are more like a movie in the making that goes on until it stops. We move through time and space with our basic temperaments as we develop, modify, and carry our experiences and anticipations along with us.

It is also a practical reality that the structures of our present lives are cast from the materials of our yesterdays, and our responses today are often shadows of what happened before. Our insights and changes take place in a few of the many compartments of our lives. We react according to our perceptions, and they change as we act. Calamity, of course, can causes radical transformations.

If you wish to cast a different shadow in the tomorows that are coming, you must prepare for those shadows today. Cumulative effectiveness casts a different shadow than cumulative procrastination.

Allness Indictments and Defenses

Allness thinking represents a sweeping indictment of your *self* in cases such as when you think "Everybody thinks I'm a failure." The defense translates this perception by giving it a more concrete perspective: "John said I acted poorly when I delayed submitting my recommendations for improving our company's public image." With the problem translated and made more concrete, you can better deal with the challenges this description represents.

Complete any allness statement and learn what results. The allness statement "I'm no good" is incomplete when you don't objectively list the reasons for and against this proposition. The simple addition of the word *because,* and the reasons that follow, help to complete the statement. With a completed statement, you can objectively scrutinize the criteria for worthlessness: "I'm no good" becomes "I'm no good because Joan said she did not want me to be one of her friends." Once you put this statement into perspective you can see the flaws in the logic.

Now you try it. To finish incomplete allness statements, such as "I feel helpless," add the word *because* to help flesh out the issue. For example, I feel _____ because _____. You fill in the blanks. The completed statement can now be rationally evaluated.

BOOMERANG QUESTIONS AND DISGUISED DEMANDS

Boomerang questions are those with a built-in answer that is not good. Some examples of this boomerang line of questioning include: "When was the last time I did anything right?" or "Why did I act so grossly?"

A rhetorical question such as "Wouldn't it be better if I didn't procrastinate?" can lead to a monosyllabic "yes," which has, at best, a neutral impact. But it can translate into guilt and resentment when the answer translates into something like: "I shouldn't procrastinate; I'm a loser." These questions and answers are the opposite of problem-solving questions such as "What do I procrastinate doing?" and "What can I do to get it done?" This language gives direction, which leads to solutions.

Disguised Demands

We've all seen the type of children's pictures in which various figures are hidden. At first we may not see the figure. After a while, we discover what and where they are. Like embedded figures, disguised demands are often in hidden parts of the mental jungle. We may not see them unless we look.

We've visited the world of absolutist statements that use *should, ought,* or *must.* When these words represent an irrational negative demand, they signal a faulty judgment. For example, you may believe that people *should* treat you fairly, and then you get yourself angry when they don't understand your script. Unfortunately, no law says that others should treat you according to your idea of fairness when that notion is both discretionary, arbitrary, and possibly counter to the interests of others.

The negative power of absolute statements translates into other forms, some that are embedded in our thoughts in a way that makes them less available to scrutiny. Watch out for these *disguised demands.* Here absolutist statements using *should, ought,* and *must* appear in sheep's garb.

The statement "I don't understand why I acted that way" *could* reflect a genuine question leading to self-exploration. Nevertheless, when anger or anxiety feeds off such questions, you might consider that a disguised demand could be embedded in the question causing a boomerang effect. For example, when the statement feels like a put-down, perhaps it has a built-in answer: "You should not have acted as you did." This conclusion often supports another such as, "You deserve the worst for this failing." Such absurd assertions are twice removed from reality and waylay the seeking of truth.

If you snare yourself in this part of the mental jungle, you have a logical exit. As with allness thinking, disguised demands are irrational. You can quickly undermine their logic. The implied *major premise*—I should not make mistakes—violates common sense and experience. The stated *minor premise*—I made a mistake and should not have done this—falters before reality. No universal law says that humans, who make mistakes and are fallible, should never err. That *conclusion* is irrational, untenable, and disputable, as the *self* is more than an oversimplification.

Does substituting the meaning of words such as *prefer, desire,* and *want* for demand terms such as *must* generate a different emotional tone? Probably. But of what value are wants and wishes without concrete actions to make them possible?

VERBAL VAGUENESS

Vague verbal abstractions such as *terrible, disgusting, bad, sickening, disgusting,* and *awesome,* when used at flash points of experience, can both promote and reflect distress. But this depends on what they mean at the flash point.

These shock words can reflect emotional intensity that is not irrational but this depends on the person using these expressions. For example, when these verbal vagaries occur in a ruminative state of mind, they can set off a chain reaction of negative feelings. Albert Ellis calls this process *awfulizing*.

When these shock words represent emotional intensity, is that intensity a reflection of irrationality, a frustration disturbance, or a commentary that sounds exaggerated but you don't really feel as strongly as the words imply? Some people use shock terms such as *awful* to console someone. However, when you apply more specific descriptive words to define experience and emotions, you'd better posture yourself to deal with the realities you experience.

If you believe that filling out your taxes is *awful, too bothersome,* or a *hassle,* then you raise the risk of a delay and an eleventh-hour rush to fill out the forms. But saying that paying taxes is fun for the majority of taxpayers who complete the long form distorts reality. Looking forward to getting it done, or to a refund, may take some of the hassle out of the process. Words like *awful* can exaggerate and exacerbate a normally unpleasant situation and turn it into a greater hassle.

INDEFINITE REFERENTS

We can get ourselves abstractly upset when we overgeneralize and obfuscate our experiences. Indefinite, externalized, and pronoun referents pander to these procrastination practices.

The indefinite referent *it* can fog self-awareness and problem-solving opportunities. To illustrate: a client told me that her mother was forcing her to marry a man she disliked. She said, "I can't stand it anymore." What couldn't she stand? The mother's persuasive attempts? Actually, we finally determined that "it" referred to her fear of expressing her real feelings to her mother and her tension about standing up for what she wanted. When she translated the "it," she managed the problem.

When you tell yourself something like "I can't stand *it*," what is the "it" that you cannot stand? Is "it" the tension, situation, difficulty in controlling an outcome, or something else?

Overgeneralized external referents can also fog judgment in other ways such as obscuring the path to Do It Now! Suppose you believe that *nothing* seems to go right, so why bother trying? What is the "nothing"? What are the exceptions to the "nothing" rule? Does this mean that if you have a variety of significant and costly complications, choosing a particular operation is wrong because the word *nothing* is vague? Sometimes the evidence points to quitting as a viable choice. However, blanket statements can cause self-defeating judgments. That is why oversimplifications, such as "nothing is going right," bear closer review.

Indefinite pronouns such as *everybody, nobody, they,* and *them* pose similar referencing problems comparable to the referents *it* and *nothing.* An idea, such as "they don't like me," can create a misleading picture. Getting specific with names, dates, and situations boosts your chances for definite referencing.

Making your self-statements descriptive requires an additional effort. Fortunately, few situations require such efforts. Otherwise we'd face another mental procrastination pattern where we put off gathering all possible details—even for largely relevant issues. When we cause ourselves significant emotional troubles by procrastinating, developing a realistic, descriptive, cognitive map of the territory we travel can save us time, stress, and duplicated efforts.

This situational exploration process takes nothing from the richness of our emotions, the expansiveness of our insights, the value of our intuitions, or the worth of our sense of character. Instead, we seek to take away the overly generalized, indefinite mental barriers to these human processes, reduce our list of related procrastination problems, and get on with our lives.

DICHOTOMOUS THINKING

When we fall into the traditional black-white, good-bad, true-false, valuable-worthless, all-or-nothing way of generalizing, we narrow our perspective. Many people in this absolutistic mind-set prime themselves to procrastinate on a whole activity because they generalize from a part.

The *all or nothing* outlook incorporates allness and verbal vagueness forms of thinking that influence the way we process information. Thinking about an unpleasant upcoming activity with a deadline, we may catalog the task as bad, frustrating, painful, unfair, or a waste of time. Avoidance may seem good. Tomorrow may seem better.

It's human nature to engage in categorical thinking. It's simple and quick. We don't have to extend our thinking when dichotomies govern our perceptions and perspective. The danger in this form of thinking lies in rendering negative conclusions that may bear little relationship to what is going on in our lives.

Samantha readily falls into the dichotomous thinking trap. She makes progress on her projects, then looks at where she has fallen short, and concludes, "I can't do anything right."

She moans about what she doesn't like to do and declares these activities a "waste of time." Later she blasts herself for falling behind. By wallowing in this mental muck, she fritters away more time than she would expend following through.

Samantha can break from the false dichotomous thinking trap by balancing the idea of "degrees of" with a perspective on what she does get done well and on time. She grimly accepts that some aspects of an activity can prove unpleasant and discomforting. However, if this is a priority, then it's a priority. She concludes, "So what if I don't want to do it. The important thing is to get it out of the way."

This solution normally carries more advantages than delaying does. This idea is consistent with the philosopher Immanuel Kant's reasoned dichotomous view that there are things that we would advisedly do and things that we are obliged to do.

FAULTY-THINKING THICKETS

Extremist thinking, allness thinking, and dichotomous thinking have many close relatives that we can find throughout the mental jungle. You will daily meet many of these "ugly animals" that appear in convincing disguises and who are prepared to waylay the unwary. Each has a special way to fog awareness and obscure the path to truth.

Hidden in the mental jungle thickets, we find the ad hominem monkey that gets on your back by telling you to attack personalities. With a sly smile, it tells you to avoid the issue by discrediting the messenger. The snake tells you to forget about facts. Instead, rely on authority for your answers. After all, does the world not look flat when you observe the horizon? The beetle tells you to support your thinking through omissions. If you don't have the facts that something is true, then the opposite must be so. For example, if there is no ultimate solution for overcoming procrastination, then there must be no solution. The panther offers the non sequitur as a strategy for self-ambush. With the non sequitur you can convincingly force one idea to follow another even when the second idea is irrelevant to the first. Here you tell yourself that people will understand when you procrastinate because you are well-meaning. The alligator tells you that if there is a partial truth to the reasons you give to explain your procrastination, the whole must be true. Tomorrow, for instance, is surely a more convenient time to

MENTAL
JUNGLE

deal with today's challenges. Of course, pipes in the weasel, we must not forget *post hoc ergo propter hoc,* the Latin for "since it happened after, that which came before must be the cause." People with autocratic parents, unstable families, or a traumatic childhood experience can say that their current procrastination was caused by these experiences. The weasel winks and says, let's ignore the exceptions to this backward ploy.

What can you do about these and other tempting procrastination supports? You can challenge these forms of faulty thinking and the following section describes how.

CHANGING FAULTY THINKING USING THE ABC METHOD

Suppose you hindered yourself because you stuck to an *allness* fated-to-fail attitude and believed that whatever you undertake would turn out rotten. You don't really fear failure. You accept failure as your reality. Although you are willing to go through the start-up phases of an operation, like a good *behavior procrastinator* you fade out because you figure you will fail. By applying the ABC technique from rational emotive behavior therapy (REBT), you can effectively combat such fated-to-fail attitudes.

Pioneered and developed by Albert Ellis, the ABC technique gives us a structured way to examine the synthesis of the activating events in our lives, our perceptions and beliefs surrounding them, and the outcomes that follow. In this structure, A represents an activating event, B represents the belief about that event, and C represents the emotional and behavioral consequences.

How can you use the ABC system in combating a fated-to-fail attitude? Suppose the activating event (A) is the opportunity to operate a frozen yogurt shop, and the thought of opening the shop is the (B), and (C) represents how you feel.

Suppose you believe (B) you are fated to fail. So you feel anxious and work halfheartedly on your yogurt shop venture. Under these conditions, can you see how you'd be inclined to procrastinate?

You may wonder how Ellis would tell you to deal with this fated-to-fail outlook. In Ellis's system, the emphasis is upon disputing self-defeating beliefs that lead to crippling emotions and dysfunctional actions. He uses a modified Socratic method to achieve this objective.

The first step is to identify the false assumptions and beliefs that create your fated-to-fail feeling. You then learn to dispute the self-defeating ideas (B) that help maintain these unpleasant consequences. In other words, trace down, flesh out, and negate these irrational ideas. Thus, the ABC system becomes the ABCD system where D stands for disputation.

In employing the D phase of the system, you become your own psychologist and ask penetrating questions such as: how can I be absolutely sure I will fail in my yogurt venture? What will halfhearted attempts at succeeding as a yogurt entrepreneur lead to? How can I be totally inadequate as a person even if I tried and the business proved unprofitable?

Suppose you believe you would be a worthless person if you failed to cope effectively in reducing your procrastinating behaviors. Ask yourself: if my best friend acted poorly, would that friend be worthless?

Realistic answers to these sorts of questions help develop a more accurate and objective outlook concerning the fated-to-fail procrastination problem. Conscientiously answering these questions promotes the possibility of your developing an objective outlook and, with the new outlook, a responsible commitment to make the yogurt shop fun and profitable.

You can use the ABC system in other situations in which you procrastinate. According to Ellis, people who experience anxiety catastrophize. *Catastrophizing* is a term he uses to describe a particular form of faulty thinking that evokes anxiety. Very often this catastrophic thinking takes a form similar to: "I'm going to fail and I'll be ruined for life."

Catastrophic thinking catapults distress when you perceive yourself as helplessly inadequate. Thus you anticipate disasters and see yourself as incapable of coping with these monsters that now inhabit your mental jungle. Let's see how we can employ the ABC model to forcefully contend with this form of anxiety.

Your attack on catastrophizing begins with asking and answering questions such as "Where is the evidence that the doom I prophesied will happen?" Second, after assessing the *probability* that it will happen (not the possibility, as practically *anything* is possible), look for proof that you cannot manage even if some of your worst premonitions occurred.

If you have a hard time seeing how you could cope, pretend someone offered you $100,000 to invent five alternative strategies you could employ to resolve your catastrophizing situation. Under the $100,000 challenge (or another highly motivating circumstance), could you identify five alternative coping strategies?

Some of us fall into the extremist thinking trap when we exaggerate the consequences of situations and threaten ourselves by the images we create. To get beyond self-induced catastrophic threats, redefine the threat experience and make it manageable. For example, if you tell yourself, "I would be destroyed if I failed," what does *failure* mean? What does *destroy* mean? Who would destroy you? Would you make life miserable for yourself? How? For what purpose? What alternative views are reasonable?

USING HYPOTHESES TO EXPLORE REALITY

The philosopher Karl Popper tells us that the cognitive processes of thinking, perceiving, or recalling represent hypotheses that experience answers. This view complements the REBT approach.

Hypotheses are theories, or predictive statements, that we commonly associate with scientific ways of thinking. They provide tentative explanations that we can test. They are probability statements. For example, the hypothesis that most people will marry before the age of thirty-five, is a high probability statement. However, the hypothesis may not hold in a specific situation. Some people marry after the age of thirty-five. Others may not marry.

When you view mañana beliefs as hypotheses, this approach makes it plausible to examine other courses of action as having validity, such as *doing it now*. Considering the facts and information available, the question is: what course of action best serves your enlightened self-interests? The answer to this question is a hypothesis. When you test the hypothesis you find out how close your prediction is to hitting the mark.

Some personal hypotheses are no better than random guesses. Others are like negative self-fulfilling prophecies that we make happen. So it is unclear whether verifying a hypothesis is the same as going on an empirical search for truth. It depends on the hypothesis and the personal motivations that support it.

IRRATIONAL SELF-TALK

Irrational self-talk takes many forms, including hypotheses disguised as facts that prompt procrastination. For example, a hypothesis such as "My life is hopeless and I don't have the capacity to change it," if believed, often leads to *depression procrastination*. The mañana belief "Tomorrow is a better day to work" is a sine qua non of procrastination, but one that experience routinely rejects.

An irrational hypothesis, if accepted as fact, can result in someone having noxious physical symptoms and procrastinating. For example, Connie suffered from different types of headaches. She had been to several physicians to help alleviate her pain—sadly, futilely.

When I first met Connie, she presented herself as an exceptionally demanding person. Preoccupied with a need for people to act fairly and politely toward her, she easily found fault practically everywhere she looked.

Connie so distracted herself with her insistence that people act politely that she retaliated by self-righteously putting things off. When her employers did not routinely thank her for doing a good job, she thought, "I used to try hard, but since they don't appreciate what I do, they can suck lemons while they wait for me to get done."

Her demanding attitude created considerable emotional churning. So I pointed this out and showed her how her attitude could contribute to her stress and depression headaches, and to her current job difficulties. Connie first denied that her thinking was faulty, and even if it were, she claimed it could not cause headaches.

To test the hypothesis that her evaluations influenced her feelings and her stress headaches, we tried an experiment. Connie agreed to be aware of her thoughts, feelings, and actions while driving her car in traffic on Madison Avenue in New York City. At the end of her ride, I asked her to write down thoughts she had when she started to feel herself become tense and to note the situation she was in when experiencing such tense feelings.

Connie took the ride and returned to my office. She said she amazed herself when she realized that she did talk to herself using the negative and demanding terms we spoke about. She felt tense because of what she said to herself. Connie excitedly noted that the first time a cab driver swung into the lane directly in front of her, she tensed up and caught herself mentally cursing the cabbie. As she tensed, she felt her neck muscles and eyes strain and the beginning of a headache.

She recalled telling herself that cab drivers should act with courtesy. The more she thought that way, the more tense she felt. When she recognized what she was doing to herself, she had an insight. She began to view the whole episode as silly and changed her ideas about cabbies to a jovial recognition that the cabbie's action was typical of other cabbies' actions: It was the "nature of the New York beast." With the "nature of the beast" idea dominating, she noticed that her tension diminished.

Connie needed no more convincing. She saw the thought/feeling/action connection. She had challenged a hypothesis that she previously held as an inalterable truth. She now had a fresh and useful perspective on her tension and a realistic hope for change.

The experiment paid great dividends. During the next week, she recorded her thoughts, feelings, and actions. She isolated additional thought patterns that contributed to her stress. As a consequence of her conscientious self-observations, and her work to flip these stress situations into something humorous, she had fewer stress headaches. Her nearly constant low-grade depression headache seemed tolerable, then it went away.

Connie's new awareness, combined with a concerned attempt to look at a situation from more than one perspective, had the effect of significantly reducing her tension, headaches, and *job stress procrastination*. Within six months, she felt she had a stronger sense of command over how she interpreted life's events. She loosened up on her *control procrastination* impulses as she realized that gratitude, while pleasing, does not substitute for a paycheck.

USING ATTRIBUTION THEORY TO CLEAR YOUR THOUGHTS

Attribution theory grew out of the work of psychologists Fritz Heider and H. H. Kelly. These men state that people attempt to understand what happens around them by finding a reason (attribution) for the action. For example, if a drunk swore at you, you might feel mildly annoyed or find the incident humorous. You'd attribute the action to his inebriation. However, if a sober acquaintance swore at you, you'd probably be inclined to regard the action from a different vantage point. The expletives uttered by the drunk and by your sober acquaintance may be the same, but the impact would differ depending upon the explanation (attribution) you make about each incident.

Your attributions and beliefs help promote the reality that you perceive. Your judgments have validity based on your attribution perceptions. However, when you repeat the same sad procrastination patterns, you might suspect that certain attributions are in error. If, for example, you believe you procrastinate because you are a lazy person, you'd feel inclined to continue to procrastinate because you'd believe it is in your nature to procrastinate. On the other hand, if you saw your procrastination as the result of faulty thinking and poor work habits, then you might strive to change.

An important step in this process of change is to be objective in your self-explanation (self-attribution). By thinking scientifically you then couch your explanations as hypotheses and try to reject the hypotheses. This is called *disconfirmation.*

Why not try to prove a hypothesis rather than reject it? That approach raises the risk of bias. For example, people who procrastinate spend too much of their time trying to prove that tomorrow is better, so why not delay until then. But where does that get them?

The disconfirmation process reduces bias and is a more advanced way of thinking. If you can't reject the hypothesis, you provisionally accept it until it is disconfirmed by facts and replaced by a higher probability statement. For example, you hypothesize that all oranges taste the same. To test your hypothesis, you eat unripe and overripe oranges. You taste ripe oranges from different areas of the world. You disconfirm the hypothesis and also conclude that you found equivalence between the taste of oranges of equal ripeness.

As a general strategy to develop your disconfirmation skills, the next time you get into a procrastination mode of thinking, examine your attributions. Tape-record the situation, your thinking about the situation, how you feel, and what you do. Then for the next half hour busy yourself with some alternative activity such as reading a newspaper. At the end of that time, play back the tape recording of your statement. Listen carefully for mañana, the contingency mañana, catch-22, and backward ploys. Watch for vague referents and abstractions. Separate the facts from the inferences and fictions. (If you don't have a tape recorder, a word processed or scripted statement of your thoughts will do.) Now list the false procrastination attributions. When you have accomplished this, you have set the stage to disconfirm your procrastination mode of thinking.

To get beyond the joys of self-revelation, translate what you learned from this exercise into a fact-action plan with the following format. Fact: I have delayed two hours in returning my employer's phone call. Action: I will now return the phone call. (Note in the fact-action sequence the absence of evaluative terminology and false attributions.)

REVERSING THE LABEL

Campbell's soup is different from the label, and if you think otherwise, try eating the label. This statement may sound silly, but it is no more foolish than other statements in which we mistake the label for the real object.

Labels such as "It is *hard*," when affixed to certain types of work and experiences, can emotionally bias the situation. For example, maybe you put off making out your check to pay the monthly rent because doing it seems hard or will consume time. Actually, the task is *easy* and can be done relatively quickly. Not mailing the check is harder and more time-consuming because you still have the task to complete later, and the landlord may bother you for being late. Such an added burden adds difficulty to the task. Thus what appears harder is often easier, and what appears time-consuming is often efficient.

Alfred Korzybski and George Kelly have both said that when people assume a label, they tend to act like the label. So if a person labels himself emotionally disturbed, will he tend to act emotionally disturbed? Perhaps. However, this is a hypothesis. We may find that this person bends over backward to appear "normal."

Labels, as a form of allness thinking, may include partial truths and *sometimes statements*. By spelling out the process the label describes, you'll have a better handle on the meaning of the label.

Concrete or operational terms define labels, but labels don't define people. However, if you find support for the operations defined by a negative label, such as procrastinator, then look to change the process that leads to the label.

The "is" (or "am") of identity occurs in statements like "I am lazy," "He is a rat," or "I am a hopeless mess." Like most other verbal generalizations, this labeling is faulty. The word *is* reflects a character generalization that makes it difficult to see beyond the compartment that the person *is* only one way.

When you translate the "is" of identity to a concrete action, you've taken some fuzz out of your thinking. For example, instead of telling yourself something like "He is a rat," expand the issue somewhat like this: "I don't like Ralph telling Bill that I am crooked." This clarifying expansion raises your level of thinking. Once you translate the issue into a description, you can better determine the validity of the statement.

Various schools of psychotherapy talk about risk taking. The idea of *risk taking* can mean doing something risky to overcome a problem. Another way to say the same thing involves substituting the notion *opening opportunities* for the phrase *risk taking.* Would you prefer to take a risk or create an opportunity for yourself?

You can define jumping into the seventy-two-degree lake waters for a swim as a cold and unpleasant experience or as a cool and refreshing thrill. How you honestly label this experience determines how you anticipate the experience and whether you will approach or avoid the experience.

Valueless as a label does not represent the value of a person but can represent a consensual view of a set of that person's actions. Unless made operational, the *valueless* label is vague, abstract, and objectively meaningless.

If you practice flipping labels (reversing them), you can train yourself to think more flexibly. Try flipping labels, using the following terms as a start:

> ➤ Out of control, weak, and incapable
> ➤ Thoughtless
> ➤ Clinging
> ➤ Carefree
> ➤ Worthwhile
> ➤ Sensitive

Is it possible that you could only be one of the above labels or its reverse?

DEFENSIVENESS

Getting beyond irrational and other faulty thinking is not a drag strip event. You'll find many barriers on the road. For example, defenses block the development of rational thinking in three ways, and each supports *mental procrastination.*

You can block awareness of your procrastination problem by externalizing blame. That is, you can claim that your procrastination is due to the unrealistic scheduling demands of society.

You can block awareness by turning inward and struggling to gain control of yourself to avoid discomfort and promote perfection. When you harp on yourself and insist that you must maintain control, you've already lost it.

The third tactic is *indifference* (neutralizing). You take your procrastination problem as insignificant. You deny having a procrastination problem, when you most certainly do!

Out from the Defensiveness Trap

As a part of your self-help Do It Now! plans, determine if your procrastination actions meet none, few, some, many, or all of an externalizer, internalizer, or neutralizer profile. Do you see yourself in some combination of the three?

If you behave like an externalizer, you often center your thoughts upon exempting yourself from responsibility by blaming others or circumstances. Naturally this attitude puts you at a great disadvantage because you would have to change external forces to end your procrastination. Since it is unlikely that external conditions will change, the battle goes on.

As the battle to gain external control proceeds, the internal battle relentlessly continues. In an internalizer mind-set, you expend your energies in "thinking the problem out" instead of taking action. Your mind meanders around the topic of why you can't overcome your problem. You blame yourself because you know what you *"should do"* and observe that you are not doing it. You see yourself as out of control and feel helpless. So you procrastinate.

When you adopt a neutralizer attitude, you see your procrastination problem as inconsequential. Therefore, you do not attempt to overcome it. In other words, by a simple declaration you exempt yourself from responsibility. Although this form of faulty thinking often provides a temporary sense of well-being, it can crumble at any time, leaving you with a pile of incomplete things to do.

Examine your thoughts and actions for cues that suggest you may be using external, internal, or neutralizing defenses to support procrastination practices. Specifically, watch for circumstances in which you blame others ("They deserve the blame for my troubles"), blame yourself ("I can't do anything correctly; what a jerk I am"), or act indifferently to important matters. Rather than blame or neutralize, concentrate on what you can legitimately do to stop procrastinating.

POSTSCRIPT

You have to do more than just knowing how to exercise if you want to gain the health, concentration, and endurance benefits of this activity. The same is largely true for thinking straight. You probably won't make much progress without practice.

One of the many ways you can maintain your clear-thinking skills is by maintaining a Do It Now! perspective through repeatedly rejecting the irrational logic behind procrastination.

Procrastination has a seductive logical circularity that keeps us on a merry-go-round. Within this channel of circularity, we believe tomorrow is better because things will get done then, and because things will get done tomorrow, tomorrow is better. When you step out of the circle, you are likely to find that what you tell yourself doesn't make sense when measured against results.

You can strengthen your clear-thinking skills and reduce procrastination by taking an empirical look at the results of procrastination. For example, the tomorrow solution does little more than reinforce a procrastination habit. We rarely keep our tomorrow promises. Look at the results of your tomorrow predictions, and you may find it difficult knowingly to pursue the tomorrow solution.

If you practice identifying mental contradictions then you add "muscle" to your clear-thinking skills. For example, many who procrastinate say that they want to get their work done and believe that getting the work done should prove easy. Yet when they don't get their work done, is it because they don't want to (although they say they do), or is it because getting it done is not so easy? At least one of these premises is clearly false. Perhaps both.

Getting in Touch
with Your Feelings

In This Chapter

➤ Intellect and feelings
➤ Contacting feelings
➤ Feeling experiences

Feelings, feelings—what is life without feelings? Our emotions are powerful motivators, so it is very important to understand how we feel, why we feel as we do, and what thinking goes on behind the feeling. However, when you postpone dealing with your feelings, you prime yourself to under- or overreact to emotionally evocative situations. Moreover, you emotionally procrastinate when you avoid, stifle, block, or routinely distort the meaning of your feelings. This avoidance process is especially pernicious as this form of developmental procrastination often places severe restrictions on the quality of your life.

Emotions, like a river, sweep us to different places. We cannot stop the rapids, the currents, the depths, and the shallowness. On this river, the firmness of our thoughts, reason—even unreason—serve as the tiller. Lose the tiller and we are more likely to cascade in procrastination directions.

Our basic feelings (shame, fear, joy, attachment) are hardwired into our nature. They seem to overcome us when we experience a situation that triggers them. For example, try not to be sad at the loss of a close friend. When a loss comes, emotions pour forth, then the river of emotions crests and floods. When the shock passes, our river of feelings slowly recedes to its banks.

We have a wide range of social-verbal cognitive emotions that reflect our social structures, language, beliefs, or attitudes. Satisfaction, indignation, silliness, eagerness, or suspicions all suggest different cognitive and emotional sensations. These cognitive emotions number in the hundreds and include contentment, happiness, hate, concern, love, excitement, peacefulness, boredom, jealousy, care, or trust. Some of these emotions, such as compassion and empathy, propel our social interests. We have *cognitive emotions* such as anxiety and I-anger that erupt from faulty evaluations that can impair the quality of both our inner world and social relationships. The feelings of I-anger, frustration, fear, insecurity, indifference, or depression can make procrastinating seem appealing.

We sometimes mix our feelings: love and hate, anger and joy. Some mixed negative feeling states seem more complicated. Lassitude reflects a state of weariness and lethargy from mental strain.

On the river of emotions, pure objectivity is rare. Subjectivity comes into practically every human situation and decision. Even the choice to let a computer run numbers and draw a conclusion is a subjective decision. This is especially true in our inner world of emotions. For example, our efforts to be fair and objective are, nevertheless, biased by our subjective values and emotional drives. Thus, we can be only more or less objective in our outlook.

INTELLECT AND FEELINGS

People sometimes fear certain feelings or fear a loss of emotional control and therefore try to insulate themselves from all feelings. We play mind games, for example, when we seek to create logic-tight cases to support our subjective preambles. Religions are renowned for intellectually justifying a set of fundamental beliefs and for developing arguments to counter challenges—all in the name of spiritual purity. In bureaucracies, overly intellectualized language often reflects a pseudo-compassion that substitutes for progress.

Some people act as though their intellect dominates their emotional life, which causes them to appear out of touch with their feelings. Looking intense, protectively smiling, projecting stiffness, portraying a false frivolity, they obscure their feelings by mental diversions that form a barrier between themselves and the world. When asked to describe their feelings, they describe situations.

At the other extreme we find people literally driven by their emotions who experience themselves as reeling out of emotional control as if on some rudderless sailboat foundering in high winds. These are emotionally reactive folk who focus upon their feelings and not on their thinking. They can get mushy, weepy, hysterical, or melancholic about practically any sensitized situation. They appear emotionally labile.

Most people ride the river between these extremes. However, for those who routinely overemphasize either feelings or intellect, the net effect is a restriction of the range of our feeling and creative ideas. People routinely have trouble getting developmental things done when residing at either extreme.

Denying or giving vent to emotions occurs on both sides of the river of feelings. Nevertheless, you can't legitimately say a feeling is wrong. You might correctly challenge the logic, opinions, or beliefs that underlie your cognitive emotions. Understanding feelings and their messages is, by far, the safest place on the river.

PROCRASTINATION AND SENSITIVITY

Practice procrastination and you risk feeling closed off to your positive abilities and feelings. Paradoxically, however, the more you feel closed to experience, the more sensitized you may feel.

This last statement requires explanation. People who involve themselves in mental, emotional, and behavioral entanglements often do so because they fear their own "soft sensitivities," or their feelings. They fear showing love and tenderness, expressing annoyance, showing vulnerability, expressing concern or self-doubts, or admitting what they really want. Often covering these sensitivities with a facade of toughness, they fear being overwhelmed or controlled if they expose their sensitive feelings.

The toughness is really weakness, and this presumed toughness reflects a form of maladjusted sensitivity: sensitivity to a self-image, sensitivity to painful emotions, sensitivity to loss of control, sensitivity to being taken advantage of. This is the *procrastination paradox*: the harder you run from exposing genuine strengths (soft sensitivities), the more susceptible and emotional you feel, and the more likely you'll put things off in those sensitive areas. For example, those who live in fear of loss, fear to live.

ROGERS'S APPROACH TO FEELINGS

Psychologist Carl Rogers pioneered the development of client-centered psychotherapy. This positive-constructive counseling system emphasizes that people have within themselves the capacity to understand their feelings and experiences and to help themselves change. According to Rogers, people do better when they have the opportunity to explore their inner world of emotions in a warm, accepting, empathic atmosphere. Rogers's ideas about the importance of empathy have proven effective in therapeutic settings. The outside world, however, is often quite a different place from an accepting emotional incubation chamber.

Empathy, when self-applied, involves understanding your situation, feelings, and motivations. This feeling sensitivity forms a platform for exploring thinking-feeling patterns that evoke procrastination. With such knowledge come opportunities for adjustments, refinements, or radical changes in your emotional bearings toward the Do It Now! plan of getting reasonable things done in a reasonable way within a reasonable time.

Empathy doesn't come from a wish. Carl Rogers talks about the importance of *openness to experience,* and this prelude to empathy challenges us to increase our awareness and acceptance of our personal feelings and attitudes. This enlightened awareness enables us to put ourselves in the shoes of a fellow traveler. Enlightened empathy leads to higher levels of understanding and tolerance but not at the expense of "having to" accept what you legitimately believe is flatly wrong.

With such acceptance comes greater opportunity for changing misconceptions and problem habits, such as procrastination. Defensiveness, on the other hand, increases the probabilities of falling into the same old procrastination traps.

Building toward an openness to experience moves you from the incentives for procrastinating to the incentives for exploring your world through action. This openness includes recognizing and accepting self-doubts, discomfort dodging attitudes, diversions, the happiness contingencies, and other mental jungle entanglements. This idea of acceptance is the opposite of complacency. Here you understand that without follow-through, hopes lie fallow. Acceptance speeds change.

CONTACTING FEELINGS

Most of our interpersonal interactions are highly subjective and can complicate communications when we remove ourselves from the picture. On this part of the river of emotions, using direct questions such as "Why didn't you return my phone call?" carry a subjective undercurrent. The listener could interpret the tone and message as blaming. Depending on their perspectives, listeners also can read the message as reflecting interest and care. For this reason, direct expressions such as the above are sometimes muddled, subject to a broad spectrum of interpretations, and promote misunderstandings.

You don't have much control over other people's muddled messages. You can increase your self-understanding and promote positive communications with others by using feeling words to describe your inner reactions accurately. In such passages, you put yourself into the message.

The following list compares the messages from direct expressions and feeling-word expressions that show the difference between reflecting content and reflecting feelings.

Direct Expressions	*Feeling-Word Expressions*
1. Don't throw your shirt on the floor again. (Annoyance)	I felt annoyed when I found your shirt on the floor.
2. You didn't call me back. Why? (Disappointment)	I felt really disappointed when you did not return my phone call.

Feeling-word expressions include clear referents to your feelings and, thus, add emotional clarity to your message. The listener does not have to interpret what you mean.

When you prefer to make clear, unambiguous, interpersonal communications, the feeling-word expression is a reasonable style for clearly expressing your feelings and thoughts. However, when conveying factual information, such as in scientific or objective reports, you can send out the wrong message through feeling-word expressions. Your audience may be distracted by what you *felt* when their interest is in what you *found*.

FEELING EXPERIENCES

Putting yourself into your experiences (expressions) is an extension of the feeling-word expression. This method can heighten your awareness of your feelings.

Like the feeling-word exercise, putting yourself into your experiences can make your communications accurate and vivid. However, this means of communicating has limitations. In group settings, you may find people often waiting to jump into a discussion with their own ideas. Fleshing out your experience can prove inappropriate in a setting where more pithy expressions are often prized, and so you might wisely use fewer words. But in one-on-one communications, you have greater latitude. In your writings or personal talks, you normally have the greatest latitude to put yourself and your experiences into a feelings expression.

The following illustrates a neutral descriptive style and a feeling experiences style:

Situation: Going to the zoo to see a panda.

Neutral description: I went to the zoo to see a panda. After I saw the panda, I walked around the grounds and looked at the other animals.

Putting yourself into your experience: I felt eager to see the zoo's new panda. So I decided to visit this great beast. I felt an excited anticipation on my way to the zoo. I felt so absorbed watching its funny antics that I watched the panda for at least an hour before moving on to see the other animals.

Putting yourself into your experience (a pithy passage): I felt excited seeing the zoo's new panda.

Putting yourself into your experience is a way to talk to yourself if you wish to explore another of the emotional river's tributaries, and to expand the meaning of special experiences. You can practice putting yourself into your emotional experiences in writing (as in the extended passage above). You can pick a solitary place and talk to yourself about what you have just experienced. Saying to a friend what you experienced in a brief vignette is a way of sharing your feelings. Using word processing and graphics tools, you can simulate an atmosphere on paper that colors the words you experience.

Incidentally, your feelings need not be powerful before you express them. Sometimes expressing a "low-grade" feeling can make the feeling come alive with meaning. Nor must you make putting yourself into your experiences your only style of communicating. If you did, its effectiveness, like that of any overused tool, would soon wear down. However, periodic practice with this method can help you become more sensitive to your own soft sensitivities.

PERLS'S PILLOW TALK

Fritz Perls's Gestalt therapy methods help in identifying misunderstood feelings that bind to procrastination thoughts and activities. Perls's popular pillow talk technique often proves effective in evoking these *emotive cognitions.*

Lynn's case shows my version of the pillow talk procedure. You might adopt it when you reach points of emotional confusion such as when your emotional river changes to white-water rapids and developing new piloting skills has appeal and value.

Lynn's sleep had been interrupted for seven consecutive nights because of a recurring and frightening dream of a "missing thing." She spoke about her problem during group therapy. When neither I nor the group seemed able to help her clarify what was really bothering her, I tried the pillow talk approach.

Lynn's job was to talk to a pillow from the frame of reference of the "missing thing." She could allow herself to say whatever came to mind without censoring herself. She began by saying, "I am the missing thing and I will visit you every night. I will keep you awake and you cannot control me. I will haunt your nights."

Since the word *control* was a key word, I asked Lynn to speak to the pillow as if she were a mental entity called Control. She began by saying to the pillow, "I am Control. You are afraid of me because you can't channel me. I am too elusive for you to manage. I am out of your grasp, but I still command you."

Since the key idea in this sequence was fear (the word *afraid),* Lynn played Fear in the next pillow talk episode: "I am Fear, and you are too inadequate to deal with me. I am too powerful for weak little you to control. Your missing thing is the strength to deal with me. I am all-powerful."

In a brief discussion that followed, Lynn admitted that she felt very inadequate and had many self-doubts. She thought something was wrong or missing within her that rendered her ineffective in dealing with life.

As a last step in this pillow talk sequence, we decided that the pillow would now represent Fear. Using Albert Ellis's ABC technique, Lynn would represent herself and challenge her fear. In her monologue with Fear, I encouraged her to present her strengths and challenge the dual claim that she was inadequate and without the ability to cope.

She actively engaged in this debate, and as the exchange progressed she began to sound firmer and more confident. Nearing the end of the pillow talk, she asserted that she felt a gain in her potential to control her unwanted thoughts of fear and inadequacy.

The next week Lynn reported to the group that her "bad dream" occurred no more. Furthermore, she gave examples of taking action. She finished writing a long-put-off résumé. She followed through on a long-promised dinner party for some of her friends. She asked her upstairs neighbor out for a date (a secret wish she had for many months).

The pillow talk episode helped Lynn to help herself get in touch with her inner fears and inadequacy feelings; the episode gave her an opportunity to express her strengths. She untwisted the lies she had been telling herself about how frightened and inadequate she was. Unblocked, she began to take solid steps toward change and began to do what she had been putting off.

To test the hypothesis that you can weaken procrastination through pillow talk, carry on pillow talk conversations with yourself. Pretend you are Procrastination talking to yourself. Using a pillow, spend five minutes being Procrastination and talk to yourself. Reverse the roles. For the following five minutes, challenge what Procrastination had to say to you.

At the end of this exercise, jot down in your procrastination log what you have learned about your feelings and about yourself from this exercise. Plan how you will use this knowledge for your Do It Now! plan.

Procrastination is a cue to your feelings. When you put something off, how do you feel? If you want to change the feeling, what actions can you take now?

POSTSCRIPT

Among the many compartments in our minds, a few bring forth strong emotions. It is as if each has a spring-loaded lever that triggers the opening of a compartment whenever there is a situation to pull on it. An idea, a memory, or a situation will do. Then out floods the contents.

The emotions we seek and the emotions we want to avoid are within the compartments of the mind. Coming from a place of unreality, some compartments flood us with unwelcome thoughts and feelings that can translate into self-defeating actions. Perhaps the procrastination compartment opens repeatedly when we feel a flickering of self-consciousness, question trust, or see our paths blacken into darkness painted by partial truths, self-deceptions, and false memories. In the procrastination compartments of the mind, our doubts, fears, and angers, along with the tensions we seek to avoid become a channel providing the outlet of delaying to another day or time.

Among the thousands of compartments within the mind, some contain clarity, good recollection, and constructive purposes. They flood our mental plain with reason and prompt our finer motivations. The optimistic compartment of hope brightens, balances, proportions, and motivates what we wish to accomplish today. It acts as a tiller to guide us along the river of emotions.

Following Through by Rewarding Yourself

Getting it done is my reward. The eighteenth-century diplomat, inventor, and writer Benjamin Franklin thus described a self-application of cognitive and behavioral methods in the autobiography that he wrote between 1771 and 1790. Franklin described how he achieved good results by regulating his actions and monitoring his progress, and how his readers could do the same. This marked him as America's first psychology self-help book author.

Since both behavioral and cognitive conditions can trigger procrastination, we shall look at both sides of this coin. In the spirit of the Benjamin Franklin tradition, we'll make a Do It Now! self-regulation program. Then I'll describe advanced techniques to support the plan and a graphing strategy to track the results.

SELF-REGULATION STRATEGIES

A Do It Now! self-regulation program starts with a problem analysis of the harbingers, mental mechanisms, and outcomes of procrastination. After doing this, we'll set behavioral goals and create strategies for change that include rewards and penalties. We'll look at how to generalize this knowledge.

PROBLEM ANALYSIS

If you had an investment that dropped from $60 per share to $25 per share in one day, you'd have just experienced an antecedent event that could stimulate you to act quickly to avoid a greater loss.

Antecedents are the events that precede a reaction. In procrastinating, the antecedent is the "task." In response to the task, you may report feeling too tired to start, feel resistive, or sidetrack into another activity.

Covert Processes

Since procrastination entails a series of ongoing decisions, we need to look at the chain of cognitive cues that sustains procrastination. This *covert* process keeps procrastination perking.

Let's look at one of many possible covert processes that feeds into *decisional procrastination*. We'll take procrastinating on writing a report as an example:

1. The first decision is to tackle a priority activity that may have some unappealing features.
2. The next decision involves when to start. At this point, you decide to start at another time or on another day. This decision often leads to delay.
3. Then you begin to feel the pressure of falling behind schedule. As your tension rises, you decide to start, and you do make some headway.
4. Next you feel "tired" and decide to get back to it at another time—perhaps when you feel more rested.
5. Some of what you do gets misplaced or "stale," and you become frustrated at having to repeat an action.
6. Time is running out and so you begrudgingly decide to rework what you've done.
7. You start and then delay again.
8. Soon you berate yourself because you've put yourself into a corner with little time left. These self-critical monologues reduce your tolerance for tension and heighten your frustration.
9. You abhor the feeling of frustration and you feel an annoyance build toward the frustrating activity.
10. Finally, you decide to get it done and make a frenzied dash for completion. You finish.
11. You promise yourself that you'll reform.
12. Then at the next unpleasant task, you follow the same threadbare procrastination decisions and promissory wishes.

13. You decide that you can't get your act together.
14. You procrastinate repeatedly, and this stop-go process causes you to think that you are a hopeless loser.
15. You feel defensive and work all the harder to cover up this pattern from yourselves and others. This stage is like putting a towel over a dog mess in your living room.

Procrastination is not static. The various phases are intermittent and occur at different times. You may have hours, days, or weeks between phases. Although you can break the procrastination cycle at any of its phases, problems arise. Illusions within this cycle obscure opportunities to break out. The appealing mañana decision often keeps the pattern flowing. Moreover, since time lapses often occur between procrastination phases, we sometimes forget parts of the pattern of delay that have passed. Sometimes we don't anticipate what is coming up next.

Consequences

Procrastination takes many forms and has many potential consequences. These consequences fall into different groupings such as cognitive, emotional, behavioral, or social. They range from a mild inner annoyance to significant life crises. You flunk out of college, lose a job, stress your relationships, risk your health, or depress yourself.

Cognitive consequences involve self-criticism, self-doubts, self-doubt "downing," helplessness, condemnations, or defensiveness. Emotional consequences can include worry, hostility, anxiety, depression, frustration, annoyances, irritation, feeling rushed or pressured, and other unpleasant effects. Behavioral consequences include penalties and loss of reward. Social consequences include loss of status, opportunity, or credibility where significant people don't expect much from you because you don't expect much from yourself.

Sometimes the process leading to procrastination and the results of procrastination blend into a running consequence. Your college professor assigns a term paper. You put it off, get an incomplete grade, then turn in the paper after the semester ends.

The following procrastination events illustrate the running consequences of the early phases of this procrastination process:

1. negative images of the project
2 anticipating that the assignment will prove onerous
3. feeling a mild writing phobia
4. resentment that the assignment takes time from preferred activities
5. evaluation fears

Consequential cognitive and behavioral events can continue and include:

1. Task tension lingers heavily overhead.
2. You risk a lower grade.
3. You practice procrastination by indulging procrastination whims.
4. You reinforce a work style that can spell future job problems.
5. You experience low frustration-tolerance urges.
6. You experience increased self-doubts.
7. You reinforce a subjective response pattern that runs counter to responsible actions.
8. You practice sloppy work habits that favor inefficiency over effectiveness.

But the results of delays in one procrastination zone, such as finishing a term paper, are normally counterbalanced. You will normally have areas in your life where your efforts do produce rewards and where you do gain opportunity.

SETTING GOALS

The next phase in self-regulation is setting behavioral goals. If you don't have goals, you don't know where you are going.

When you set your behavioral goal make it objective and observable so it is clear whether you've accomplished it or not. Vague goals leave too much to chance.

If you use vague, nonbehavioral language, you will probably be less able to decide when you have met your objective. An example of a vague goal is "to become more effective." You can procrastinate on that goal unless you are clear on what to do to achieve the result. On the other hand, a goal of a January 15 deadline for a newsletter article translates a generic goal "to become more effective" into an achievable outcome. When your goal is specific, you will be better able to decide whether you have succeeded in achieving your goal.

In setting behavioral goals, define what you intend to accomplish in ways that you can measure. Consider these examples: (1) study each day at least three hours, (2) do holiday shopping before November 1, or (3) lose ten pounds in the next ten weeks.

Defining the Steps

In your problem analysis, you listed what precedes and follows procrastination. Then you set your Do It Now! goal. Let's suppose you decide to study three hours or more a day between Monday and Friday. That's the goal, but keep an eraser handy.

Now you set your sights on finding a way to accomplish this goal without procrastinating. You begin by logging what you do each day. You review these data to find available study time between Monday and Friday.

Your *log* shows that you have several hours each morning that you could use for study purposes. You normally use those hours for lounging, reading the newspaper, making phone calls, and watching television. You knew this all along, but the written record emphasizes how you ordinarily use this time.

After your time analysis, you make your behavior goal more specific. You plan to study for college courses Monday through Friday, between the hours of 7:00 A.M. and 11:00 A.M. During those times you decide to take one fifteen-minute break each study day between 9:45 and 10:00 A.M.

Setting a time is not enough. This can simply be another antecedent for procrastination. You could, for example, stare glassy-eyed at the pages of books, or at a CD ROM study program on your computer screen. You could doodle while you ponder the question of why you can't remember everything you read. You wonder if you will ever finish on time. You guess that other people have less trouble studying. You begin to wonder if you're in the right field of study. Meanwhile, your priority study in Far Eastern history takes the back burner.

Enter the performance measures. That is where you assign yourself a defined number of pages to read or write, or plan other activities that increase your on-task focus. In this self-regulation phase you piggyback a performance dimension onto your time goal: to achieve a B average or above. However, the grade is a by-product of your performance time on task.

Managing Complications

In the world of procrastination, complications color the outcome. For example, we often feel *relieved* when we make the procrastination decision and decide that tomorrow is better. But do we also feel strain when we realize we are not going to keep the tomorrow promise? Does the escape value of procrastination influence the outcome?

In choosing a Do It Now! approach to life, we set our sights on getting beyond the twisted motivations and convoluted rewards of procrastination. Instead, we focus on rewarding healthy activities. Setting time dimensions, priorities, and performance objectives supports a self-regulation process.

Suppose you have your assignment structured. You've got the time. You are clear on your priorities. You gather your materials. You know how you are going to use the time. Then you fall into the *behavior procrastination* trap.

Your problem analysis can point to cognitive opportunities for changing different elements of your behavior procrastination cycle. The following approach describes how to respond to the cognitive phase of your procrastination challenge.

1. Reflect on how to dispel the myths that bind the mental links of behavior procrastination to unwanted consequences.
2. Look at each idea in the procrastination process with great skepticism. Aim to break the covert mental links in the cycle of procrastination.
3. Since procrastination is an irrational process, the intellectualizations, excuses, and promises that propel this process are significantly or completely wrong. Your job is to prove this to yourself.
4. Logically challenge irrational ideas that support the procrastination process.
5. Look at the empirical evidence that shows the poverty, defeatism, and poor results that ride with the behavioral procrastination process.
6. Force yourself along an action pathway where you place your emphasis on your Do It Now! plan—even when you don't feel like it.

The next phase of this cognitive-behavioral self-regulation program involves identifying and using rewards and penalties to support your plan.

Identifying Contingent Rewards

External rewards and penalties do shape our behavior. We work for money to purchase primary rewards. We hear someone say "good work" about something we have done, and this can encourage us to do more of the same. We receive a rebuff or reprimand for incorrect behavior. This cues us to change our behavior.

Rewards, or *reinforcements*, are conditions that follow a behavioral, or covert, act. They increase the probability of the recurrence of the activities they follow and exist on a continuum from weak to strong. The stronger the reward the higher the probability of increasing the behavior it follows.

If I scratched my head and a $100 bill fell into my lap, you'd probably witness me scratching my head again. This is because getting $100 bills for scratching my head is rewarding to me. I will continue in this and other activities if I get the reward. The reward serves to increase my head-scratching behavior. However, when the bills stop falling, I'd eventually stop scratching my head.

In deciding appropriate rewards you may wish to use psychologist David Premack's principle, which is that any action that a person engages in frequently (high-probability behaviors) can serve as a reward to increase infrequent behaviors (low-probability behaviors). Such high-probability behaviors are usually readily available, and we can use them soon after a desired action.

To identify such high-probability behaviors, go through the day and think of the things that you enjoy doing. Perhaps such activities include: taking a shower, combing your hair, drinking a cup of coffee or tea, or reading the newspaper.

To use these as extrinsic rewards, you simply make one of these high-probability behaviors contingent upon the completion of specified actions. Thus, for example, if you study from 7:00 to 11:00 A.M., you drink a cup of coffee while reading your newspaper. If, however, you do not successfully complete the chosen step, you do none of the above that morning. Using this contingent reward program, it is essential that you only reward yourself after and not before completing each step.

The rewards should fit the behavior that you have just completed. If the reward is too onerous to obtain, or too easy, the reward may not prove helpful.

Whatever you decide to use as your contingent rewards, making your reward reasonable is most important. Say, for example, that your Do It Now! goal is to spend a half hour to formulate a budget or to return empty bottles to retrieve a deposit. Treating yourself to a trip to China is a bit much.

Point Systems

The best type of extrinsic reward is one that you can give yourself immediately after you successfully complete each designated step in your program. This is not always possible for some rewards, such as purchasing a sweater.

There is a way to give yourself quick rewards. Point systems are secondary reward systems. To use this point system effectively, you give yourself a point after you succeed in completing a step in your Do It Now! program. This method of reinforcement allows you to reward yourself immediately by giving yourself a symbol that visually displays your accomplishment. You can make your points visible on a score sheet, or chalk them up in your mind until you can enter them on your sheet. If you want to get fancy, you can represent points with different colored pegs on a board that you arrange in an upward direction.

You may feel good giving points to yourself. These points are also like cash. You use them to purchase desirable concrete rewards.

Points purchase primary rewards. Since everyone's situation is often different, some things you do are worth more than others. So the point system will be subjective. You might assign a point for polishing shoes you have put off maintaining. You might give yourself five points for every chapter of text you study and outline. Two points may reflect the value of each page of a report you write.

You can set your point program to accumulate points to take advantage of buying bigger rewards for delaying gratification for longer periods. Delaying gratification helps support both frustration tolerance and your Do It Now! programs. It can inspire a vision for bigger future rewards for effective actions.

You can designate the number of points needed for different levels of reward. The more points you accumulate, the stronger the reward. For example, when you earn five points, you can read the comic section of your newspaper. It costs ten points to go to a movie, read a novel, or play a round of golf. Perhaps after you've accumulated one thousand points, you'll take a weekend trip. Thus the value of the point system lies in its flexibility.

Identifying Contingent Penalties

Penalties *decrease* the probability of the activity they follow. They also exist on a continuum. The stronger the penalty, the higher the probability that the penalty will suppress the behavior it followed.

But penalties alone do not necessarily work to suppress an undesired behavior. For instance, if you wanted to teach your child to stop insulting you and you invoked a penalty from time to time when he uttered an insult, you still may not stop his insults. For example, the child may learn, through trial and error, to discriminate. If he insults you while you are busy cooking or talking on the phone, you will not punish him. Thus the child may curb his insults in some instances but not in others. Unless you can deliver an appropriate negative penalty systematically each time the child utters an insult, you may not stop his insults. Consistency is a key in modifying undesirable behavior.

When you use penalties in your self-control program, you agree with yourself that if you don't meet your objectives, you will disadvantage yourself. The types of penalties that you can use in your self-control program include: depriving yourself of something that you very much want, or forcing yourself to do something you dislike, such as writing and mailing a very positive letter of praise to a boisterous rival. Naturally, when you meet your self-regulation commitment, you gain the benefits and avoid the penalty.

Reward and Penalty Limitations

Self-regulation, self-monitoring, reinforcement, and penalty techniques have the inherent problem of enforcement. If you don't systematically enforce them, they are of little value.

There is no magical way to enforce compliance in this area. However, you can raise the odds of making these programs work by making public announcements of what you intend to do and why. You can establish rewards and penalties that are relevant—ones that you will carry out.

STABILIZING CHANGE

The final step in your self-regulation Do It Now! program involves stabilizing your behavioral changes. After you have been successful with your program, maintain the reinforcement until your new Do It Now! patterns are stable.

Self-regulation applies to many life challenges, including eliminating alcohol abuse, writing a novel, learning psychology, improving your relationship with your family, or restoring a painting. Thus you can find many ways to generalize on this approach.

If you believe that this approach to getting things done holds promise for you, keep practicing this strategy. Seek new ways to work the system so that you can make it work for you.

YOUR COGNITIVE-BEHAVIORAL SELF-REGULATION PLAN

Use the following structure to draft your Do It Now! cognitive-behavioral self-regulation plan. This starts with a problem analysis of a procrastination activity. In this first phase, you look at the antecedent events, cognitive and behavior avoidance responses, and their consequences. This flows into the next phase, where you set goals, make and carry out a plan, and generalize the good results.

1. *Antecedent event:* _____
   _____

2. *Cognitive and behavioral* avoidance *responses:* _____
   _____

3. *Consequences of procrastination:* _____
   _____

4. Do It Now! *goal:* _____
   _____

5. Do It Now! *plan with rewards and penalties:* _____
   _____

6. *Program generalization:* _____
   _____

Through this self-regulation enhancement method, you reduce the incidence of procrastination by making Do It Now! actions more probable and rewardable.

ADVANCED TECHNIQUES

The following features rewards and penalties systems, contingency contracting, and special alternation techniques to support your cognitive-behavioral self-regulation program.

Procrastination Reduction Techniques

You can gain a reward by doing something to avoid losing a privilege. For example, if you procrastinate on a particular task you lose a benefit, such as driving your automobile to work. Instead you'll rely on public transportation. If the public transportation idea is onerous enough, you meet your objective on schedule to avoid evoking the penalty. This gives you an extra incentive to Do It Now!

You can use this procrastination behavior reduction approach in other ways. Let's suppose that your favorite classic movie, *King Kong*, is going to be on television. You are eager to watch this movie, so if you *do not* have a report you've put off completed and printed before the movie, you won't watch *King Kong*. You know you can escape or avoid this consequence by doing the report, and that gives you an extra incentive to Do It Now!

You also can do something unpleasant to yourself if you fail to live up to your Do It Now! pledges. Suppose you decide to give up smoking. Doing something such as snapping an elastic band against your arm every time you take a puff on a cigarette is an unpleasant consequence. You avoid smoking to avoid the punishing snap.

Let's suppose that you have been procrastinating on buying your spouse a birthday gift. If you don't buy it on time for the celebration, your spouse will get angry. In the past avoiding this outcome has not been sufficient for you to get the gift on time. So you decide to inflict a worse penalty on yourself—one that you would surely take steps to avoid.

You pick something onerous. You'll wear a smelly fish head around your neck for five hours if you don't have a worthwhile gift purchased before your mate's birthday. If the fish head plan is a bit too radical, you could plan to order food you dislike at a restaurant and slowly eat it. If you choose your consequence well, you'll act to *avoid* the usual negative outcome and the double-whammy penalty.

Taking Away Recurring Negatives

Throughout life we find many unpleasant things that we would normally prefer to avoid. These unpleasant experiences include disapproval, disadvantage, guilt, stress, frustration, or self-doubts. When we procrastinate doing activities that affect other people or interfere with effective functioning, we risk unpleasant happenings.

You can gain a reward when you take action to *end* an unpleasant set of conditions, such as ongoing guilt or social penalties. If you feel anxious about stating your opinion, you can feel a rewarding relief by stating your opinion in a way that marks the end of that anxiety. When you replace procrastination with effective actions, you reward yourself when you avoid ongoing unpleasant consequences such as worry.

Let's see how this method of taking away the negatives works with procrastination. Let's suppose that you have let yourself fall behind on a market survey for your company. A preliminary draft of the findings is due in thirty days. You have started to worry. Although you believe you can get an extension, you don't want to recycle the worry. So you pick up your pace to escape the worry.

Reward System—Open-ended

You can use an open-ended reinforcement plan to complete a desired voluntary, discretionary activity in which you don't set a clear deadline. Such challenges include: losing a few pounds, completing the first draft of a book, or learning the basics of a foreign language.

Next you select a suitable reward that you believe will fit with your efforts. You can pick a trip, observe a live sporting event, read a desired novel—anything that appropriately rewards meeting the goal.

You set no deadline to finish your program. Meeting your goal may take weeks, months, or years. However long it does take, you don't get the designated reward until you meet your target weight and maintain it for three months.

You can't lose the reward unless you don't complete the goal. Therefore, it is just a matter of time until you meet the objective. Thus, if this reward is something that you really value, you'll work all the harder to attain it.

Fading the Reward

Instead of rewarding yourself each time you engage in a Do It Now! behavior, you reward yourself only after several instances when you have attained your goal. After studying from 7:00 to 11:00 A.M. for five days, for example, you give yourself a suitable reward. Then you gradually fade the reward by increasing the number of consecutive days of study. For instance, you might next reward yourself after two consecutive weeks of study as prescribed by your self-regulation goal. Eventually, your new Do It Now! habit can become firmly implanted in your schedule of everyday activities without formal rewards.

Contingency Contracting

People are often more inclined to live up to written contracts than verbal ones. To fortify your Do It Now! behavior program, consider a written *contingency contract*. You can add teeth to this contract when you get a friend to help you in this Do It Now! endeavor.

The contingency contract process can be as simple as stating that either you do the laundry within two days or you will burn a $100 bill. First write out a formal contract statement. Then you and your friend sign the statement. Next, give your friend the $100 bill and the contract.

Naturally, this system is not foolproof. It won't work if the loss of a hundred dollars isn't enough to make much difference.

Special Tactics—Alternation Technique

The alternation technique involves dealing with multiple habits that you want to quit but have consistently put off dealing with. Suppose that you overeat, smoke excessively, and chew gum. You want to quit all three of these habits but not simultaneously. To use the alternation technique, set up a system of eliminating each by "playing" one against the other.

This is how the *alternation technique* works. First you set a goal for how much you want to weigh and a new program that involves eating foods only in defined quantities. Every day that you exceed the quota, you stop smoking and chewing gum for the next twenty-four hours. Continue with that program until you achieve your weight goal and have maintained your new desired weight for three months. Next, develop a program to stop smoking. First decide the maximum number of cigarettes that you will allow yourself to smoke per day. (Let's hope this number will be zero!) For every day that you exceed your quota, you can't chew gum the following day. When you succeed in giving up smoking, begin working on giving up your gum-chewing habit. For your program to give up gum chewing, select another habit you wish to get rid of and "play" that against the gum chewing.

Conscientiously applied, the alternation technique has several advantages. You are weakening the gum-chewing and smoking habits each time you evoke the penalty for having exceeded your food quota.

If you rarely evoke the penalty because you are sticking to your weight-loss program, you have mastered an approach that enables you to eliminate other unwanted habits.

In a variation of the alternation strategy, you might use penalties in combination with rewards to support your progress. You select a behavior that you wish to get rid of. You penalize yourself when you engage in it. You systematically reward an alternative positive behavior. You might, for example, find that you spend too much time watching television and avoiding study. So you set your behavioral goal to eliminate television watching and to increase studying between the hours of 7:00 and 11:00 A.M. Then you go on to set up sequential steps that lead to a reduction in television watching and lead to a concomitant increase in studying. You penalize yourself each time you watch television between 7:00 and 11:00 A.M. You reward yourself each time you make one of your sequential steps.

GRAPHING PROGRESS

When you have a numerical way to measure your progress, you can transfer these data to a graph. Graphing gives you a visual way of describing your Do It Now! progress. To help you use this method, let's look at the case of a person with a self-development procrastination problem who used this method to organize her battle against procrastination.

Joan is a thirty-two-year-old bookkeeper with a history of feelings of inadequacy and procrastination. Her major self-development problem centered on her interpersonal interactions. Despite her desire to have friends, her fear of rejection was so great that she usually avoided people. Furthermore, when she dated (rarely) she would select men to whom she was not attracted. Indeed, if any man she dated showed an interest in her, she would stop dating him. She seemed to be living by Groucho Marx's comment that he wouldn't belong to any club that would have him as a member: she wasn't interested in men who were interested in her. She felt too inadequate to try to relate to men she found attractive.

In addition to her problem with men, Joan was petrified to go to lunch with her coworkers, afraid of joining a bridge club, and so on. She thought she was too inept to bang a nail into the wall, flooded herself with invectives, felt humiliated by her flaws, panicked over feeling tense, became tense and impatient if hassled or inconvenienced, and so forth. Although these problems were hardly fatal, they resulted in much misery and suffering.

To help Joan overcome procrastinating, we worked to develop an action plan following this sequence:

1. We first obtained a blank sheet and divided it into three major columns: "Basic Challenge," "Problem Manifestation," and "Action Plan for Change."
2. Under "Basic Challenge," we identified three problems Joan most strongly wanted to minimize: poor self-concept, rejection fears, and intolerance for tension.
3. In the second column, we identified how these problems were manifested in her daily life.
4. In the third column, we developed action-plan strategies to attack the procrastination problems and their manifestations.
5. We developed a separate chart so that Joan could record her progress.
6. We assigned numerical weighting to each activity, based on difficulty level. In the following progress chart you'll see these numbers in the parentheses after each activity. The numbers represent multiples. Thus, each time Joan accomplished a specific change activity, she'd multiply that accomplishment by the assigned number. Assigning a higher weighting to the more challenging activities gave her an additional incentive to try.
7. Each time Joan completed an action-plan activity, she recorded the activity and the appropriate number of points in a notebook she carried with her at all times.
8. At the end of each week, she tallied up the total number of points for each action-plan activity and recorded them on a cumulative graph. She would add each new weekly point count to the point counts of the previous weeks; put a dot on the chart equal to the total number of points (vertical axis) over the week she was summarizing (horizontal axis); and connect the dots from week to week.

The following problem analysis, progress chart, and progress graph illustrate this procedure.

Defeating Developmental Procrastination
Problem Analysis and Plan

Basic Challenge	Problem Manifestation	Action Plan for Change

Poor self-concept	Self-doubts
	Self-"downing"
		Focus on positive attributes.
		Identify and challenge
		    negative self-statements.
		Doubt self-doubts.
		Probe why acceptance
		    presents new challenges.

Problem Analysis and Plan (*continued*)

Basic Challenge	Problem Manifestation	Action Plan for Change
Rejection fears	Avoid social events	Invite acquaintance or colleague to lunch or movies.
	Avoid available attractive dates	Initiate conversations with potential attractive dates.
	Settle rather than select	Express felt opinions. Act friendly and available.
Intolerance for tension	Discomfort avoidance	Eliminate avoidance excuses. Accept discomfort as first phase of getting acquainted. Identify and challenge discomfort dodging thinking. Avoid obsessive prejudgments by taking initiatives.

Defeating Developmental Procrastination
Progress Chart

	Sept. 5	Sept. 12	Sept. 19	Sept. 26	Oct. 2
Self-acceptance development					
Focus on positive attributes. (2)	6	18	14	22	28
Identify and challenge negative self-statements. (3)	9	30	33	27	24
Doubt self-doubts. (3)	0	3	15	18	27
Probe why acceptance presents new challenges. (5)	0	0	5	15	20
Overcoming rejection fears					
Invite acquaintance or colleague to lunch or movies. (5)	0	0	5	0	15
Initiate conversations with potential attractive dates. (5)	0	0	0	10	25
Express felt opinions. (5)	5	0	5	15	30
Act friendly and available. (5)	0	0	0	5	20
Tolerance building					
Eliminate avoidance excuses. (2)	2	2	4	6	20
Accept discomfort as first phase of getting acquainted. (3)	0	0	5	15	25
Identify and challenge discomfort dodging thinking. (5)	5	20	30	25	10
Avoid obsessive prejudgments by taking initiative. (5)	0	0	5	15	30
Total	27	73	121	173	274
Cumulative totals		100	221	394	668

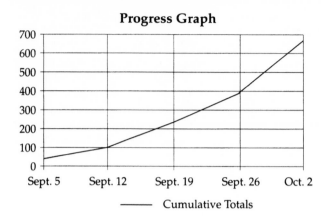

Progress Graph

——— Cumulative Totals

In graphing progress, you may treat daily projects differently from yearly ones. You may assign different bonus points to finishing different activities, such as filing taxes on time. In this way, you can get an ongoing, visual progress measure.

You can carry this exercise one step further. Use moving average computer calculations and computer-generated graphs to compare your actual output against expected output. You can create this moving average using hours on task or by phases of project completion.

Exceeding standards can feel rewarding. However, in the spirit of separating your performance from your worth, the exercise measures *output*, not *global worth*.

Your measure of your worth should not be the worth that society grants you. That archaic belief partially comes from the seventeenth-century social-worth views of the English philosopher Thomas Hobbes. According to his philosophy, society assigns you dignity and worth based upon your value to society. However, who within society does the valuing?

You have every right to follow this social-worth definition, but you risk a contingency worth problem. You also can follow twentieth-century thinking and rate your performance without rating your *self*.

POSTSCRIPT

As a problem habit, procrastination is regenerative and challenging. When you tackle one major priority at a time, and obtain the inherent rewards of your success, you give yourself added incentive to break the habit. However, this process can involve inconvenience and discomfort. When you start an exercise program, for example, you may have to face a number of discomforts—including appearing out of shape at a gym, feeling sweaty and tired, and experiencing achy muscles—before you get to the benefits. Through a Do It Now! self-regulation program, you look beyond the immediate discomforts to the long-term benefits, and then you go for the benefits. Ideally, healthy intrinsic rewards eventually prevail over temporary "intrinsic" procrastination *frustration avoidance* benefits.

Beyond a certain level of development, intrinsic rewards often take on greater importance than the external kind. Indeed, intrinsic motivation relates positively to a Do It Now! plan and negatively to procrastination. For example, the *New York Times* chided the Wright brothers for their ideas of flying before Kitty Hawk. But Wilbur and Orville Wright believed in themselves. In 1903, they flew the first power-driven airplane. Does anyone remember their skeptics and critics?

Planning to End Procrastination

Structure is the target. Without a sense of purpose there is no plan. However, planning can help establish a sense of direction and purpose when there was none before.

In this chapter I will describe three structured planning strategies you can employ to deal with procrastination. They are *action planning, charting,* and *action-pattern analysis.* You can use each tool to free your time to get things done.

ACTION PLANNING

Without visions and plans, you most likely rely on wishes and hopes that the fates will kindly rule your destiny. By waiting for opportunity to knock, you place yourself in a passive role and take whatever happens. Without planning ways to accomplish what you set out to do, your energies will naturally get dispersed. By planning ahead, you increase your chances of selecting rather than settling for the remnants.

Benjamin Franklin recognized the importance of planning when he said, "I have always thought that one man of tolerable abilities may work great changes, and accomplish great affairs among mankind, if he first forms a good plan, and, cutting off all amusements or other employments that would divert his attention, make the execution of that same plan his sole study and business."

You neither have to be a seasoned expert in action planning to create a workable design nor dedicate your life to only one plan. The following provides a basic structure for many plans and ways of operating in the world.

> ➤ Label your goals.
> ➤ List criteria that you believe make the attainment of your goals worthwhile.
> ➤ Define the intermediate objectives or steps leading to the attainment of your goals.
> ➤ Identify the procedures that will help you to move toward the attainment of your goals.

You can adapt this orderly planning structure to practically any major area in your life where you procrastinate. This includes locating a new home, selecting a new job, or rising to the head position in a corporation. Jim's case can enable you to visualize this type of planning process.

Jim's company was permanently shutting down, so he needed to find a new job. But Jim procrastinated on getting a new job. He had two reasons for procrastinating: indecisiveness concerning the type of work that he wanted to do, and indecisiveness regarding what he might enjoy doing. His preliminary goal was to identify what he *could do* and what he would *like to do.*

He thought about the working conditions that he liked best. This proved to be the most difficult, yet most fruitful, phase. In thinking the problem through, he determined that his work would have to provide him with opportunities for: (1) identifying problems hampering productivity; (2) designing solutions for such problems; (3) implementing actions following his planned solutions; (4) exposure to a wide variety of problems within his specialty area; (5) advancement and recognition.

This phase proved most fruitful because it clarified what he wanted from his work. This information made it easier for him to narrow his job search and to compare various jobs with his criteria for satisfaction. After examining his preferred work functions (the activities he most enjoyed), Jim decided to confine his search to the industrial area for a management job. With this goal defined, he moved to step two.

Next he defined the mechanics of his search. He specified and organized these steps as follows:

1. Prepare résumé to support goal.
2. Craft a general cover letter that could be molded to fit a specific job opportunity.

3. Develop interviewing skills to boost changes for making favorable and effective presentation.
4. Identify job opportunities through networking, library research, newspaper advertisements, Internet job banks, and other sources.
5. Make contact and arrange for an interview.
6. Make an effective presentation.
7. Negotiate a contract and close the deal.
8. Work hard and exceed expectations.

He planned for and designed strategies to carry out each of the eight procedures to achieve the goal. For example, in developing his résumé, he obtained samples of well-written, proven résumés. He read two books on résumé writing. He drafted a model résumé and received expert feedback. At the same time, he read and reviewed books on interviewing, created model questions and answers, and tested his answers with objective friends. Simultaneously, he started networking, examining Internet job sites, reviewing company annual reports, and kept up the momentum on multiple job-search fronts. He did expand upon each of the issues he outlined under his procedures and applied his management interests and skills in developing and coordinating each area.

Jim's approach confirmed his interest in planning and implementing. As he proceeded, he threw himself into his plan and enjoyed the work. He felt challenged. As a reward, he found the type of job that met his criteria. Thereafter Jim made another important discovery. When you work hard at what you enjoy, the work is easy.

You, too, can make and carry out a plan to get what you want. Making a written plan will probably serve you best. The written plan reduces the chances that you will forget important details. Although this plan can be spelled out in sentences, my own preference is for an outline format. The outline is easier to revise, and the steps stand out. But you can judge for yourself. The following table, "Action Planning," is the outline for selecting a new job that Jim developed.

CHARTING CHANGE

When you put off dealing with procrastination, you risk creating emotional stress. When you continue to experience stress, you will often put off personal development goals because your energies become dissipated by unresolved problems.

You can get beyond this personal bottleneck by using the *charting your problem* strategy. It is an effective tool that has helped many who previously put off dealing with emotional worries and troubles.

Action Planning
Securing a New Job

Goal	Criteria for Job Satisfaction	Procedures to Achieve Goal
To obtain a satisfying management position	1. Identifying problems	1. Prepare résumé to support goal
	2. Designing solutions	2. Craft general cover letter
	3. Implementing problem-solving actions	3. Develop interviewing skills
	4. Meeting diverse challenges	4. Identify opportunities with promising companies
	5. Creating opportunities for advancement	5. Initiate contact
		6. Make effective presentation
		7. Negotiate contract and close the deal
		8. Work hard to exceed expectations

Using a charting technique, you can map your problems by defining them in solvable terms followed by action solutions. A simple charting procedure involves three major activities:

➤ Problem diagnosis
➤ Defining advantages of change
➤ Action planning

In the "problem diagnosis" step, you identify what motivates your procrastination problem. Your goal is to be both honest and specific with yourself in labeling what you believe underlies the pattern. To achieve this result, introspect or discuss your problem with someone who is not only objective but who also can help you pin down the origins of your procrastination.

In this diagnostic endeavor, your purpose is to identify how you are currently perpetuating procrastination. (Avoid delving into your past for childhood causes at this point. The next section describes a method for recognizing patterns stemming from this period.)

The second step involves identifying the clear advantages of changing your procrastination pattern. You do this to give yourself a positive incentive for change.

The third step involves developing specific action plans targeted toward reducing your procrastination problem by increasing your Do It Now! skills. You make these plans concrete by specifying what you will do to overcome the problem (*how-to* phase). By conscientiously following this procedure, the clarity you obtain can help motivate the changes you make. To illustrate this process, let's look at Bonny's challenge: getting to places on time.

Bonny was chronically late for work and for appointments. She also delayed sending out reports and answering correspondence. After her boss told her to "straighten up or leave," she decided that she preferred to stay.

She charted her problem using this structure: diagnosis, advantages of change, and action plans. The following shows this structure:

Charting Your Problem
Lateness

Diagnosis of Factors Contributing to Personal Ineffectiveness and Lateness	Advantages of Change
1. Anger	1. Relief from unnecessary tension
2. Rebellion	2. Avoid unnecessary hassles
3. Helplessness (basis of items 1 and 2)	3. Improve quality of interpersonal interactions
4. Fear of:	4. Better scheduling of time
a. People	5. Increased time for creative and productive pursuits
b. Change	6. Avoid getting fired from job
c. Expressing anger	
5. Habit	
6. Need for control	
7. Need for comfort	
8. Self-doubt	

Action Plans

Anger and Rebellion	Fear	Discomfort	Self-Doubt
1. Recognize basis of resentment	1. Admit fear	1. Allow yourself to experience uncomfortable feelings	1. Identify strengths
a. Unfulfilled expectations	2. Identify erroneous assumptions	2. Accept tension as part of living	2. Express strengths in action
b. Failure to be victorious, etc.	3. Cope with anxious anticipations	3. Acknowledge feeling as signal for antiprocrastination action	3. Recognize that action involves risk *and* . . .
2. Recognize underlying feeling of helplessness	4. Allow self to engage in problem-solving activities	4. Identify and fight against comfort-seeking tendencies	4. There is no guarantee that action outcome will be successful, *but* . . .
3. Engage in purposeful action			
a. Be honest in self-expression			

Action Plans (*continued*)

Anger and Rebellion	Fear	Discomfort	Self-Doubt
b. Encourage others to express themselves			5. Purposeful activities promote personal growth *and . . .* 6. The development of better coping skills, *and . . .* 7. Habit breaking

Following this charting structure and action plan, Bonny significantly improved her on-time performance and kept her job.

ACTION-PATTERN ANALYSIS

Most people are interested in learning the historical causes of their procrastination. If you wish to embark on a psychological expedition, an *action-pattern analysis* can help. In an action-pattern analysis you look for patterns and trends in your procrastination activities:

> ➤ Focus on one procrastination problem that's hobbled your style for years, and list examples in chronological order.
> ➤ Find the common critical features of each of these episodes.
> ➤ Where possible, identify your excuses, addictivities, and motivations that were part of these episodes.
> ➤ Consider alternate Do It Now! actions to change the pattern.
> ➤ Apply this knowledge to change your habit of procrastinating.

Let's suppose you are a graduate student currently procrastinating about writing a report. You can use this method of action-pattern analysis to gain insights and make changes.

First you reflect, identify, and list examples where you've procrastinated on writing assignments. In tracking this pattern, you recall that while in both college and high school you had a similar problem—putting off writing term papers until the last possible moment.

In comparing examples, your analysis points to two common elements in the pattern: (1) You think you are a poor writer and that your efforts are futile and will lead to failure, (2) You usually write in bed propped up by a pillow and quickly fall asleep. It doesn't matter whether you use your laptop computer or a pencil and paper. The result is the same.

To cross-check yourself, you expand upon the issue for each of the two findings. The evidence for item one derives from the fact that a B– was your best English grade. You received criticisms from different professors that your writing is fuzzy. Your writing includes numerous grammatical and spelling errors. For point two, the evidence supports that you still do most of your writing in bed when you work at home.

To obtain a fair and honest appraisal of your writing history, you also look for evidence to disconfirm your two preliminary findings. Contrary to your first conclusion, you also received praise for your writing of personal letters, essays on topics of interest, and descriptions of your own ideas and opinions. Furthermore, when you write letters, interesting essays, or use your ideas and opinions, you sit at your desk.

By contrasting your procrastination writing pattern against positive examples of your writing, you gain a more concrete perspective on your writing. This perspective points to choices.

Using the information you developed from this analysis, you build these data into your action plan to write your report in a personal style, highlighting your interests, ideas, and opinions. To assure that you won't succumb to sleeping cues by writing in bed, you write the report while sitting at your desk. The result? You get the writing assignment done on schedule.

POSTSCRIPT

People who manage effectively do seven things: (1) They analyze their current and anticipated situations. (2) They make goals according to what they want to accomplish. (3) They follow positive values to guide their actions. (4) They plan a course of action taking into account the consequences and potential responses to their problem-solving initiatives. (5) They organize their personal and material resources to support the plan. In this logistics phase, they make sure they can properly back their anticipated efforts. (6) They put the plan into action. (7) Throughout this application phase they gauge reactions, look at results, and make adjustments. In this evaluation phase, they exercise cognitive flexibility, judgment, and modify their goals and plans.

This structure normally has greater potential in helping you achieve major developmental projects compared with single-issue maintenance functions, such as shopping for groceries. However, when hamstrung with a maintenance, social, learning, competitive, or other procrastination practice, this seven-step management process merits consideration.

Get Yourself Organized and Follow Through

People who are behaviorally and mentally organized normally experience a sense of well-being and control over their lives. In prehistoric times, our ancestors foraged for food and used caves and huts for shelter. They didn't have to concern themselves with such matters as answering mail, creating business plans, negotiating with bankers for loans, studying for tests, having periodic medical examinations, keeping their floors swept, meeting production deadlines, keeping fit, filing paperwork, making luncheon dates, or getting their television sets repaired.

Knowing hygiene and the values of orderliness, keeping up-to-date in our careers, using powerful cognitive self-help change strategies—all of these can provide potential advantages. But this adds up to more to do. Total simplification of life in this modern world is a dream.

What happens when the levels of complexity you daily face have increased and the way you organized your life no longer works well? What happens when you have more to do than you put aside the time to accomplish?

Computer innovations, such as the development of electronic spreadsheets, data bases, and word processing, have revolutionized our ability to produce, calculate, and track information. Electronic mail (E-mail) makes our communications quick and convenient. Because you can run these and other programs in tandem, you can multitask. That's a big advantage.

Electronic opportunities streamline our work efforts and exist in the public domain. As these media for productivity improve, the standards for performance also increase. As before, progress still requires a clear mind, knowledge and experience, visualizing possibilities, and a good personal proprietary control system to help you keep organized.

Electronic productivity tools do require *time on task* until they are mastered. Some people claim that they don't want to waste their time learning such methods and say that their current mechanical systems are better. Perhaps. Old-fashioned pencil and paper can continue to be efficient, providing we don't lose the message.

It's clearly quicker to jot something down than to boot a computer, load a program, type a statement, name the file, save the file, print the file, exit the program, and properly exit the computer. On the other hand, if you have repetitive procedures that you do by hand, you can automate them to your great advantage. For example, if you have fifty people you can reach simultaneously with an E-mail message, why produce fifty separate messages when one will do?

SCHEMES FOR ORGANIZING

With approximately forty million Americans now working out of their homes, many face not only the normal obligatory social requirements, but also new challenges related to their home office operation. They are similar to students with unstructured time, and how well they organize their efforts often determines their general effectiveness. As poor study skills contribute to the complexity of *academic procrastination*, poor time management, low frustration tolerance, low self-efficacy, and weak organizing skills contribute to *home office procrastination*.

How do you remain productive without feeling either swamped by too many details or going to the other extreme by gliding along procrastination pathways? How do you pace yourself to balance social interests with work interests when distractions abound? How do you challenge yourself to advance beyond what you currently do when you can still get by with your current system? The answer is simple: organization, self-regulation, persistence, curiosity, a sense of challenge, and personal dignity are important ingredients for improvement and progress in this fascinating new "home office" world.

People who effectively manage their priorities at home and at work, their relationships, and their lives normally do a better job of organizing their resources than those who feel disorganized and have trouble deciding what to do next. Effective people have known this secret for centuries.

Organizations that have endured have sound proprietary organizing systems, which are systematic ways to maintain their records and conduct their affairs. Corporations spend fortunes to develop their internal control systems and prize such systems for being among their most valued proprietary possessions. They spend billions on computerized control systems and in training and hiring people to use and maintain these systems. That's a strong message. The closeness of the word *organization* to the word *organize* also tells the secret.

WHAT IS THE INCENTIVE?

The benefits of using an effective organizational system are extensive. You process details quicker with less effort. That is the incentive.

Improving your organizational abilities can have a constructive double effect. You'll be able to deal effectively with what needs doing. You'll be building up confidence in yourself as a person who can confront and then organize problems of many types.

Specifically, developing and using an effective organizing system has four solid advantages: (1) You can complete personal maintenance and administrative functions in an efficient, orderly fashion. (2) You can diminish anxiety over misplaced materials. (3) You can avoid living and/or working in a cluttered, disarrayed environment. (4) You can use time freed from needless replication of effort and tedious activities for organizing and channeling your efforts toward goals of self-development and fulfillment. However, developing an effective personal organizing system is no mean feat! If it were that simple, practically no one, except the *behavioral procrastinators,* would ever procrastinate.

HOW TO GET ORGANIZED

Developing and continuing to develop your best organizing system involves a four-step process: (1) identifying "organizing" objectives; (2) determining how you can direct your efforts to increase efficiency and effectiveness in meeting organizing objectives; (3) developing the system; (4) revising and updating the system.

Developing this organizing system can be not only a thoughtful but also a creative endeavor, one in which you can ultimately take a sense of pride. Good organization can result in rewards that go beyond creative satisfaction.

Effective organizing is an art more than a sterile constricting series of procedures, where the outcome is rarely perfect. Even very effective and efficient executives use 60 percent of their work time efficiently and effectively.

Is the effort worth the time? If your organizing system saves you just fifteen minutes per day from rummaging for misplaced items or ruminating over what to start, you will gain the equivalent of almost twelve eight-hour workdays each year! As a practical matter, you can't put all this time spent searching together into twelve consecutive days. But since such searches are normally stressful, the frustration you avoid is probably going to be worth more than the time that you also save.

In modern society, many of us are time starved—we run out of time to do the things we want to do. At the same time, we waste much time. It's a strange paradox. However, by building—and continuing to build—functional organizing systems, you may gain as much as the equivalent of a year or two of time—probably much more—during your life. You can use this freed time for following more creative pursuits, improved productivity, and pleasure. You can also receive an extra dividend in the form of less stress.

To use your time more efficiently, consider the following organizing approaches:

➤ Identify your priorities and work on them instead of other, less important projects.
➤ Develop your skills to estimate the time and effort it will take to complete a project. This estimating skill can help you use your time to maximum advantage.
➤ Continually review your priorities and time estimations and modify them as new circumstances warrant.
➤ Set time aside when you can work undisturbed on your priorities. However, expect interruptions and reshuffle priorities as demands change.
➤ Maintain adequate and up-to-date records.
➤ Establish a workable electronic, mechanical, or combined filing system and use it.
➤ Tackle new work at the first possible moment. If you do it when you think of it or at the first possible opportunity, you'll have one less hassle later.
➤ Manage unexpected events later, if you can't manage them when they occur.
➤ Try to get some of tomorrow's work completed today.
➤ Maintain a reasonable and consistent Do It Now! pace. This avoids *efficiency binge burnout*: brief flurries of activities followed by long periods of inaction, and dread over repeating a burst of catch-up activities.

The four-step organizing process, and these ten hints, merely represent the outline of a good organizing system. Some of the next twenty organizational hints can fit into your organizational system to increase your personal efficiency:

➤ When the mail arrives, immediately rid yourself of obvious junk mail (unless you like to read junk mail).

➤ Set aside a time each day or each week for completing correspondence.

➤ Monitor your progress daily to keep yourself well directed or on target with your plans.

➤ Make use of mechanical organizers such as "in" and "out" boxes, card files, and schedule books.

➤ When a short phone call can substitute for a letter, use the phone.

➤ Delegate responsibility whenever possible.

➤ When working on especially important projects with a tight deadline, find a place where you are not likely to be found or disturbed.

➤ Organize books in your library alphabetically or by subject matter so you can find the ones you want quickly.

➤ Plan vacations well in advance. You are likely to get your preferred accommodations and can avoid starting your vacation with any uncomfortable last-minute stress.

➤ Set specific times aside to do predictable, recurring chores.

➤ Pick a priority task a day as your designated task. If you complete it, consider your day a success.

➤ Keep important phone numbers where you have easy access to them, and keep your phone list updated.

➤ Try to keep one week ahead on at least one priority project.

➤ Avoid overscheduling yourself. It often takes too much time to come up with explanations to justify the results of this overload while you attempt to juggle your responsibilities.

➤ Routinely throw out old clothing and articles for which you have little use. It's amazing how crowded closets, basements, garages, and storage areas get with outdated and unnecessary items. You could, of course, get rid of something that you wish you kept. However, some items are clearly disposable: broken rakes, last year's magazines, pieces of miscellaneous junk. True, some may become valuable antiques someday. But the chances are that most clutter is not worth saving.

➤ Keep only items you regularly use readily available.

➤ Take along reading materials on buses, trains, and airplanes. Having a laptop computer on such trips can be productive.

➤ Arrange for a friendly grocer to take phone orders and deliver groceries.

➤ Order gifts and other retail items by catalog or from the *electronic malls.*

➤ If you operate out of your own home office, multitask mechanical activities and make a game of it. For example, you can start printing a mail list. Then after you get your printer grinding, fax a report, file materials, discard trash, work on preparing your next meal, talk on the telephone. The game is to see how many mechanical tasks you can finish in parallel. This can leave you with more time for the efforts that require uninterrupted, single-minded concentration.

This list naturally consists of *timesaving strategies* that you can use singly or in combination. Some suggestions may not be applicable in your case, but others will. You also can add to this list of timesaving strategies as a part of developing your personal proprietary control system.

The purpose of developing a timesaving system is to give you more hassle-free time for doing what you want to do. If the timesaving process becomes a hassle that detracts from your major efforts, you've fallen into the addictivity trap of substituting secondary activities for primary ones.

How about follow-through? Once you have devised your plan, you can use many strategies to get yourself started and maintain your momentum. Let's consider some helpful aids for following through.

PRACTICAL STRATEGIES FOR FOLLOWING THROUGH

You can use virtually thousands of methods to help yourself follow through on setting up your organizational system. We'll look at the five-minute plan, bits-and-pieces approach, the set-go method, reminder systems, the cross-out sheet, throwing off the time hogs, multitasking, and the catch-up plan.

The Five-Minute Plan

When you consider starting a project, it is sometimes difficult to move from this contemplation phase into action. Your reluctance may be because you view the whole project as burdensome and overwhelming. To answer this challenge, I invented the *five-minute plan.*

To use the five-minute plan, you commit yourself to begin working on the task for only five minutes. You start, and at the end of this time you decide if you will continue for the next five minutes. At the end of that five-minute interval you again decide if you will continue. You work the five-minute system until you decide to stop or the activity is done.

You can pick a different time. Indeed, you may prefer an interval of ten minutes in order not to interrupt yourself so frequently. One caution: if you choose times longer than fifteen minutes, you may be reluctant to start. Nevertheless, experiment with this method until you find an interval ideally suited to your temperament and your specific challenges. The principles underlying this strategy are:

➤ Beginning a task is easier if you initially commit yourself only to a short work interval.
➤ Once you have initiated an action, it often gains momentum.
➤ You may feel a positive momentum to continue with the task because each step brings you closer to completion.

If you want to add a little fun to the five-minute plan, use an imagery technique. For example, pretend that you are running from a thousand hungry wolves. But you have a magic formula for atomizing the pack. Since this special pack of wolves feeds off procrastination, they disappear when the five-minute action first replaces procrastination.

Bits-and-Pieces Approach

Have you ever allowed tasks to pile up to the point where you thought they would smother you? You look around and see that you have dishes piled up and newspapers are scattered everywhere. You can't see where the dust leaves off and the furniture starts. When viewing this frightening sight, you feel overwhelmed and are confused about where to begin.

When you arrive at this state of confusion and can't decide upon your priorities, it doesn't matter where you start. Just start. If you have a backlog of maintenance procrastination activities, try the *bits-and-pieces* technique. Tackle the larger task by breaking it into small parts and deal with it in bits and pieces until you finish.

The bits-and-pieces technique involves selecting a put-off activity. Start with one bit and follow that by finishing another. Writing an overdue report, for example, includes gathering information, starting a computer, gathering paper and pen, or preparing your tape recorder for a transcript. Outlining or free-associating on your preferred medium can help you start the formal report.

Using the bits-and-pieces approach requires you neither to set a deadline nor to dedicate a set time to the project. Instead, you work on the selected task(s) as long as you are able. Then you resume the project, if only for a few minutes, at your next available opportunity. Using this method, chances are you will not complete the huge mound of work in one magnificent expenditure of energy, but you will begin to see progress.

The Set-Go Method

The *set-go* technique can be an effective aid in overcoming procrastination, especially for *behavioral procrastinators*.

Many people do a fine job in their preliminary organizing, like getting out paper and pencil to write a letter, buying detergent to wash the dishes, or gathering basic research to write a report. Once they assemble these materials, however, they turn their attention to other matters and consequently fall behind on the work that was once so carefully organized.

Part of the reason for putting off following through is that just having *set up* to start the task often provides a feeling of accomplishment. Resting on your laurels is a common procrastination ploy. To get beyond this barrier, you change the pattern.

The challenge is not in the *set* part of the set-go sequence, but in the *go* phase. The following are some ideas to help with the go part:

➤ Imagine yourself setting up your work and then without hesitation beginning and finishing. Keep the image in mind as you *set* then *go* with a task.

➤ Use a paradoxical technique in which you tell yourself that setting up a task is easy but following through is absolutely impossible to do. Then prove yourself wrong. Paradoxical tactics sometimes work because of a tendency many people have to rebel against the commanding statement "You can't do it."

➤ Announce in writing to your family and friends that you are going to overcome your procrastination problem by both setting up and then immediately taking a first step to go. (This tactic sometimes works. Excuses fall hollow on the ears of those who make public commitments then back off.)

➤ After you have set up a task, you can try doing something silly to step away from an inertial pattern of stalling and delaying. For example, tap your index fingers together three times, then start. Tapping your fingers, or some such activity, is an interruption in the regular habit sequence of setting up and putting off. This can become a functional ritual for getting started.

➤ Positive switchover methods can bridge the gap between set and go. You set up as usual. Then you switch over to another activity for, say, five minutes. Then you switch back over to the "go" part of the priority activity. This method can break up the set-delay sequence, create momentum for action, and smooth the transition back to the priority "go" activity.

Reminder Systems

Have you done something like this? You went to the bank to cash a check. Upon returning home you remembered that you needed gas. Then you went to a gas station to fuel up. After that you returned home and remembered you needed to go to the grocery store for bread. Upon returning home again, you remembered you needed to mail a letter and to buy milk. However, this time you forgot where you put your keys.

During any day, you can get bombarded with many distractions that sidetrack you from mailing a letter, making a phone call, and purchasing a needed box of laundry detergent. If you try to make mental notes, you'll probably forget some of these maintenance activities. However, consider this jingle: short-term memory goes quick, fix it in your mind, and it may stick.

Doing the task when you think of doing it is one way to meet the memory challenge. In selected areas, that makes the most sense. However, sometimes this practice wastes time. You may make several trips to the grocery store to pick up separate items because you remember that you need these items at different times. That is why organizing your work under categories can save time. You don't have to go to the same place twice when once will do.

Some people are great list makers, and "to-do" lists set the stage for action. Placing notes in your wallet may also help—every time you make a purchase or receive cash, you will see the reminder. If you conscientiously use such systems, you reduce your chances of a delay due to memory lapses.

Especially if you operate out of a home office, make up a reminder list for multiple errands. Depositing checks, mailing letters, picking up dry cleaning, getting supplies, shopping—all can help reduce duplicated trips. Purchase gifts well ahead of needed occasions during these routine shopping trips and you can save future time.

A reminder system, useful as it may be for normal lapses of memory, can be even more helpful for reminding yourself to deal with a procrastination problem. There are several ways in which you can adapt this system. One very helpful method is to make up reminder cards and place them in strategic positions. The cards list a specific task or tasks that you'd like to complete, such as writing a letter to a friend. Place each card in a prominent position so that you'll be sure to see it. When you finish the activity on the card, file it in a box or other suitable container. This method can help you to maintain a fair perspective on your efficiency. Memories are selective. We may remember what we don't do more than what we do accomplish.

Another reminder technique involves using a symbol to signify a task that you routinely wish to accomplish. For example, suppose you select a green dot to symbolize exercising. You could place a small round piece of masking tape on the center of your watch and color it green. The idea is that whenever you see the dot—and that would probably be frequently—the cue reminds you to exercise daily.

A third method involves writing phrases on a card. One of my favorites is "Doing Gets It Done." One of my clients found a good spot for her Doing Gets It Done card. She made a colorful three-foot-square card and taped it to the ceiling above her bed. It was the first thing she saw upon awakening. When she saw the card, she begin the day by doing something positive to support her Do It Now! program.

Computer-based reminders can also help you track where you are with your different projects. Some schedules sound an alarm when you need to remind yourself to go for an appointment. This electronic alarm clock frees your mind of a tedious detail, providing you are on the computer at the time the alarm sounds.

Using a message board for attaching notes to remind yourself of important dates and appointments reduces the risk you'll forget. Clearly visible message boards are good prompts to support future appointments and deadlines.

The Cross-Out Sheet

If you have a daily schedule filled with busywork and administrative tasks, you may put off these tasks because they are dull and uninteresting. You may also get distracted and legitimately forget them. The *cross-out-sheet system* helps you to remember and organize these activities.

The cross-out-sheet system starts as a simple "to-do" list method that involves listing activities that are important to complete that day. When you complete an item, you cross it off. Then you immediately move on to the next item and begin to work on it. This rapid shift from one activity to the next is important because it allows you to use the momentum generated by your previous effort. Include break times on the list, as this can help keep up a reasonable momentum.

The cross-out sheet helps structure your daily activities. It also can serve as a reward if you feel a sense of satisfaction as you cross items off the list. This cross-out method can help motivate and drive your Do It Now! interests.

You need not use a cross-out list for daily entries only. You can have a separate list for weekly projects, or one consisting of items representing your long-term goals. With these weekly or long-term lists, cross out each item as you complete it before you move to the next. Crossing out completed items can give you a rewarding sense of pleasure.

The cross-out list is a versatile, easily modified technique. You can, for example, list the items in their order of priority. Or you can use an alternating sequence. You alternate items you are likely to put off with more pleasant activities. If you follow this sequence, you can find added motivation to complete all the items on the combined list.

The cross-out sheet has many other values and purposes. For example, you can use the cross-out sheet to isolate procrastination practices. For example, on your daily cross-out sheet, transfer the items that you didn't finish to the next day's sheet. If the same items keep coming up, that's a signal to take a closer look at those items. Here are a few questions to consider. Are you including low-priority discretionary activities on your list that really don't need to get done until next month, if ever? Do the activities fall into certain categories, such as problem habit, maintenance procrastination, learning procrastination?

What activities do you finish right away? Do they fall into any groupings? What is the incentive to get each done? How can you apply the same incentive to related activities?

Do It Now! techniques such as the five-minute plan, set-go technique, and cross-out-sheet methods have one thing in common. They are start strategies. Once you get started you are more likely to finish.

Throwing Off the Time Hogs

We all have things to do that take much more time than we prefer to spend doing them. Yet when left undone, they cause us more harm than avoiding them did us good.

Time-hog activities have some importance, yet they require considerable time. For example, we could do some carpentry, mechanical, or electrical work, or assemble children's toys. However, if these are not among your primary skills, then traveling the learning curve to reach a high enough skill level may require more time and effort than you choose to expend.

Delegate, or hire others, for *time hogs* such as house painting, repairs, and other tasks where you may lack the time, skills, or interests. Once you have decided this issue, avoid procrastinating about delegating such activities.

The *do-it-yourself trap* is a prime time-hog activity. Here you try to take care of everything and blend the more important things with trivial things and keep busier with the less consequential activities.

Overorganization wastes time and can be a real time hog. Here you organize every detail rather than turn the system into results.

Here are a few tips for managing time-hog practices:

> ➤ Launch a self-analysis to gain insight into what perpetuates the time-hog pattern.
> ➤ Identify your addictivity time-hog practices and decide what purposes they serve. What are your Do It Now! alternatives?
> ➤ Define your priorities and know your deadlines.
> ➤ Rank your priorities from one to five with one equaling the most important.
> ➤ Schedule your work realistically, where you emphasize finishing the activities that matter most. These are your number one projects.
> ➤ Use one day a month for eliminating lower priority details.
> ➤ Abandon trivial tasks.
> ➤ Block busywork escape routes.
> ➤ Learn to delegate.
> ➤ Avoid taking back the activities you delegate.

Shopping can be a time-hog practice. Suppose you go for a few items. When you arrive at the store, you feel tempted to scan the entire store. You give in to the temptation. A fifteen-minute trip extends to several hours. You return home with more than you planned or need. You repeat this pattern when you shop, and you are more likely to shop when you feel tense about doing something else. Because of these excursions, you know the local mall by heart. You wonder why you feel as if you are running out of time.

The solution to the shopping time-hog practice is simple. Block off time at the end of the week for shopping. List what you want and place a reasonable time limit to obtain the items. This limits impulse purchases.

Make plans for activities that limit shopping time. Arrange to meet a friend at the end of that time. Plan to watch a favorite television show that starts at the end of that time limit. Schedule some other activity that is more important than store scanning. When you have something to look forward to doing after the time limit, you are less likely to expend excess time shopping.

Catch Up, Keep Up, Get Ahead

The pileup of tasks from the past becomes a pain in the present. Imagine what it would feel like if you could get rid of this pain and keep up-to-date in the present. Perhaps you could get ahead.

To make this vision real, divide your work into three groupings: catch up, keep up and get ahead. You can create a mechanical or computer file for each.

Catch-up activities are the things left undone that haunt your present. Sure you can probably stretch them out a bit more, but why let them linger, or "season." Like rotting fruit, they will eventually attract attention. To support your efforts to get beyond this pattern of delay, make a cross-out sheet of what to do. Block off time. Plan to work by project. Tackle them in a bits-and-pieces format—anything to whittle down the list. Eventually you want few, and preferably no, activities listed in this file.

Keep-up activities are current. If you get them out of the way, they don't make it into your catch-up category. Use the resources that you possess, in combination with strategies from this book, to prevent them from getting into your catch-up file. This is where your Do It Now! plan to complete reasonable things in a reasonable way within a reasonable time pays dividends.

Get-ahead activities include those that advance your long-term self-interests. Suppose you want to start your own business. Your get-ahead plan can involve marketing research, developing advertising materials, creating a proprietary control system, financing the operation, and testing the viability of your plan. As you free time from catch-up and keep-up activities, more of your time is available for advancement activities.

Through this three-phase personal effectiveness system, you can challenge yourself to place your greatest emphasis on keeping up and getting ahead. With this challenge in full operation, you'll feel fewer threats because you'll have less from the past to threaten you.

POSTSCRIPT

Some of us work better by project while others work better by schedule. Each approach can involve a different set of organizing responsibilities.

Project people usually like to dig into a major challenge. They place most of their efforts into their major preferred projects. The details that fall outside of this effort often lie fallow and can eventually interfere with the project.

People who prefer to operate by schedule normally prefer to follow a set routine. They prefer doing roughly the same activities from day to day. Although normally good at managing the details, they run the risk of failing to challenge themselves.

Rigid time-management plans normally don't work for either group because such structures deprive both project and schedule people of flexibility and opportunity. Instead, we normally do better when we look for ways that allow us to manage our lives more effectively that fit with our personality styles and Do It Now! preferences.

Afterword: Enjoying the Journey

Getting it done really can be more fun. Procrastination is probably like a mulligan stew. It has its own ingredients and the mix changes. While some of your ingredients might be like everybody else's, the specific configuration of your problem is unique. Nevertheless, I trust that at this point you feel realistically optimistic about improving your ability to Do It Now! Realistic optimism is rewarded by changing faulty thinking and getting yourself into action.

This book described a way to explore yourself and to find ways to meet the challenges that you face in getting relevant things done in a reasonable time and in a reasonable way. In the beginning you looked into a chasm filled with procrastination pitfalls. The chasm represented the gap between where you are and where you want to be. You saw many skills and strategies to pit against the procrastination conundrum with its mañana diversions, self-doubts, discomfort dodging ploys, habit-forming qualities, and more. As you repeatedly breach the procrastination barrier, you can grow confident in yourself as a "doer." More important than simple answers to complex questions about procrastination, you now have a constructive change process that you can apply to any situations where the ideas of Do It Now! squarely apply.

It is not enough to be aware of how and why you procrastinate and to be aware of ways of changing. You have to begin to act the way you would like to act if you want to do better.

What happens when you significantly increase your Do It Now! percentage? You'll probably feel greater emotional freedom. With this freedom comes a stronger urge and confidence to follow your curiosities and to test your abilities so as to discover the person you really are. By following your natural inclinations for getting it done, you'll come to enjoy life more because you will have more time to live, learn, and experience pleasure.

Whereas you can make great gains in shrinking a procrastination problem, you can never completely, totally, eliminate all procrastination for all time. Some procrastination is normal. It is only when the problem is pervasive, habitual, or negatively impacts an important zone in your life that you are in trouble. However, by accepting that procrastination is recurrent, you won't expect yourself to be perfect and then tense yourself and needlessly put off something else. Instead, recognize that it is important to maintain your efforts in getting it done to prevent this problem from spreading.

The recognition that you are progressing in your Do It Now! campaign, and that this is a lifetime process, helps you to rid yourself of the myth that a one-time campaign to stop procrastinating will climax in one final magnificent victory. You accept that you'll have to maintain your Do It Now! plan to avoid the procrastination habit. Moreover, when you work at being better organized and prompt, you are less likely to feel guilty because you believe you are letting yourself or others down because of your delays. You'll have more time to get it done.

By getting it done you will be less centered on your problems and therefore more objective in your outlook. When you are more objective, you will tend to act in your best interests. Consequently, you are less likely to be a victim of your own procrastination.

As a successful doer, you will experience less tension because you will have less to be tense about. When you experience less tension, you will require more than a normal amount of stress to overreact, and so you will overreact less. Thus your judgment will be clearer and better when you are faced with tough decisions. You therefore will be making better decisions.

When you competently contend with the details of living, you will find your style of living to be more relaxed. Your timing and pacing will be better, and you will be more open to your experiences. You'll generally feel more alive and experience life as increasingly more fulfilling once you have freed yourself of the worry, guilt, and depression over what you have put off or are fearful of doing. You'll be less defensive because you will have less to be defensive about. You won't have to excuse or justify your delays with the same regularity as when you procrastinate. Therefore, you will avoid the acute sense of discomfort you typically experience when you try to give excuses for delaying. Your interpersonal relationships will probably improve as a result of your newfound ability to be realistic and honest. That is because you will have little to cover up and so can afford to be authentically yourself.

Without action, passive absorption of information from sources such as this book will get you practically nowhere. Testing the ideas in practice offers opportunities, but no guarantees, for change. However, getting reasonable things done in a reasonable way within a reasonable time mortars the blocks of hope for the future.

The circle of change ends where it begins.

Index

CPSIA information can be obtained at www.ICGtesting.com
Printed in the USA
BVOW01s1253040614

355412BV00001B/54/P